Models of Social Order

Models of Social Order

An Introduction to Sociological Theory

ORRIN E. KLAPP
University of Western Ontario

 MAYFIELD PUBLISHING COMPANY

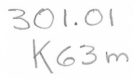

Copyright © 1973 by Orrin E. Klapp
First edition 1973

Library of Congress Catalog Card Number: 72-97842
International Standard Book Numbers: 0-87484-223-9 (cloth)

Manufactured in the United States of America
Mayfield Publishing Company,
285 Hamilton Avenue, Palo Alto, California 94301

This book was set in Electra by Typographic Service Company and
was printed and bound by Kingsport Press. The designer was
Nancy Sears; the editors were Alden C. Paine and Linda Brubaker;
production supervisor was Michelle Hogan.

To Evelyn, Merrie
and Curtis

Contents

Contents

Preface

This book introduces the student to sociological theory by reviewing some of the major models of social order that have appeared in the history of Western social thought since Plato. Examining such roots enables the student to view modern theories with a better sense of where they came from, and to relate them to his own concerns which, after all, are the great human concerns from which the theories arose. Whatever their faults, such ideas are treasures of Western intellectual tradition, and cornerstones of sociological theory. (They alone, of course, do not constitute sociological theory.) Coming from philosophy, even religion and mysticism, they show the range of phenomena that great thinkers have felt necessary to take into account in explaining social order. They therefore satisfy the human need for unity and completeness of explanation, which is a source of their power as theories and ideologies and, at the same time, of their shortcoming as general theory.

I intend this selection of ideas to serve as an introduction to sociological theory for upper-division students, many of whom are not majoring in sociology and few of whom will become professional sociologists. The text is also suitable for sociology majors and for those who plan graduate education in sociology. The book should be helpful to this whole range of students because it presents sociology as rooted in wider human concerns, and conceives it as growing from and helping to shape the mainstream of social thought.

Each of the models reviewed in this book derives order among men from one of the following sources: (1) from *reason*: the conviction that the rational intellect can convert information into wisdom and virtue for individuals and justice for society; (2) from *science*: the hope that the application of scientific method to human affairs will produce a good society; (3) from *transcendental imperatives*: the faith that human order must bring man into conformity with otherworldly demands and goals; (4) from *power*: the view that the real basis of human social order lies in the distribution of power and power-giving information, rather than in reason, justice, or transcendental laws; (5) from *consensus*: the belief that humans voluntarily agree to restrict and coordinate their behaviors; (6) from *market*: the idea that market forms an information system supplying an order beyond what its bargaining and exchanging participants intend; (7) through *class struggle*: the doctrine that the normal working of capitalistic market leads to a conflict of classes which will ultimately be reconciled in a higher order; (8) from *evolution*: the theory that societies, like individual organisms, are evolving through a natural selection process which eliminates less viable social forms; (9) from *progress*: the belief that the changes continually introduced into society by innovative technology and rational thought will lead to a better social order; (10) from *man*: the hope that from man's own nature and needs as a species will come the ability to design and implement that progress which until now has been largely thwarted by existing social systems; (11) from *system theory*: the concept that systems models yet to be formulated will provide the knowledge necessary for man to create the kind of social system that he wants.

Such ideas carry some element of theory needed for understanding the whole of whatever is meant by "social order." To focus on one is reductionism, for sociological theory needs them all. As it happens, most of the great social thinkers, or at least their followers, fail to recognize this danger and try to explain social order within the framework of a single concept. They often attain remarkable insights (as in Freud's work, for instance) but just as often produce caricatures of reality (like

Spencer's "survival of the fittest"). We assume, nevertheless, that each of the great social models has a nugget of truth to contribute to the search for a more comprehensive theory.

The book ends with a look at general systems theory which provides a broader view of how man, using all the sciences and with more than a little luck, may be able to develop an order suitable for himself in the only world he has. By this ending, I have no intention of treating the history of social thought as a kind of grand prolegomenon to what is now called general system theory. This would be presumptuous, to say the least. We have as yet little idea what the better applications of new theory will be. Rather, I trade on the catholicity, the invitation, of the word "general," to mean that theories now known will be synthesized into even more unified theory, whether information theory or something else. I am sure that every thinker reviewed in this book would have applauded that goal.

The reader will note that the sequence of chapters is not strictly chronological, since we begin with the scientific model of positivism, which gives a window through which to view the course of earlier social thought. After positivism, we take up the thought of the early Greeks, where the systematic study of society began. Nevertheless, the book is not a history but a selection of representative thinkers and ideas intended to introduce the student to essential models. Such ideas are often dealt with in courses called "History of Social Thought," or "Development of Sociological Theory." Outside sociology departments, the same essential area might be called social philosophy, political theory, history of civilization, the making of the modern mind, "great ideas," and so on.

The book does not focus on narrowly sociological concerns but on broader philosophical and ideological questions which supply liberalizing and humanizing perspectives, as well as preparing the student for modern sociological theory in later courses, which distinguish science from philosophy, and stake out a domain for sociology separate from that of economics, political science, and other behavioral sciences. The taproots of social theory, of course, admit of no such neat separation and trimming. From the early Greeks to Durkheim, at least, philosophy, political economy, and sociology are intertwined in concepts like the social contract and division of labor. Looking at such older theories, I am concerned that their connection with modern sociology will be visible and that some of the great lessons will come through that have been (rightly) filtered out by strictly sociological theory.

The theme of broader human concern unifying this book might have been "rationality: its promise, success, and failures"—beginning with the Greek idea of putting the wisest man at the head of the government. However, I shall describe the unifying theme as man's thoughtful attempt to account for social order, whether called justice, government, market, or whatever—order being encoded into folkways, art, legislation, philosophy, ideology, and sometimes scientific theory.

Surely our age is faced with conflicts and paradoxes which may require a turnabout from accustomed ways of thinking. What the next step will be new theory must answer. That theory will probably be developed by students now in universities around the world. I hope this book will whet the student's appetite for studying—before deciding—what social systems are real, new, possible, and desirable.

O. E. K.

1

Order in Living Systems

Two things fill the mind with never ceasing awe: the starry heavens above and the moral law within.
—EMMANUEL KANT

Emmanuel Kant was so regular in his habits that people used to set their watches by him, according to a well known story. Plainly this philosopher, whom many regard as Germany's greatest, felt he had discovered in himself something in accord with the farthest reaches of nature: He had a passion for universal order. Had he grasped something fundamental, or was he merely eccentric?

What is social order and where does it come from? Some thinkers see it as divine providence, bestowed by command or revelation. Some see it as natural law, observable in the motions of planets or the structure of molecules. Others feel its source to be reason, conscience, intuition,

1

instinct—ways by which man becomes aware of law in his own inner nature and lives in accordance with it. Yet others see it as mere power. Such efforts to think systematically about the sources of order provide a body of social thought that may be described as orderly thinking about social order.

But we are not content to leave order as the common sense notion of what happens, say, when a deck of cards is arranged, or when father (in one of his symbolic forms) gives a command. The modern point of view which helps to bring together the orders of life, mind, and society is commonly called information theory. By it let us view the unity of the game of life.

The theme of this book, then, is that theories of order are various ways of viewing the various levels of the *communication process*, that life itself is a communication process which all systematic theory—biological, psychological, or social—must reflect. This is the name of the game: Communication, as the encoding and sharing of information, provides the order which overcomes the disorder of the inchoate world, which the Greeks called *chaos*, but which Lao-tse called "the unborn."

Because such an approach may seem unorthodox to those raised on the idea of social science as separate from, even inordinately independent of, biology, we should begin by reviewing the events of the last twenty years that have led to the reconciliation of these two fields.

SEPARATION AND RECONCILIATION OF SOCIOLOGY AND BIOLOGY

For sociology, the nineteenth century was the era of social Darwinism, the theory that suggested that societies were like organisms and that social change could be explained in terms of evolution. Indeed, sociology rode into respectability on the coattails of biology, by borrowing its prestige and assurance. The pioneers of nineteenth century sociology—Bagehot and Spencer in England, Comte in France, Ratzenhofer and Gumplowicz in Germany, and Ward in the United States—thought of themselves as super-biologists. The idea that evolution could be a bulwark against revolution helped make Darwinism popular among conservatives. Instinct also helped explain as inevitable such things as racism, which we now believe can be changed by reform and education.

The cultural sciences of anthropology and sociology had to struggle against this background in the early twentieth century. The work of anthropologists, notably findings about cultural diffusion, lack of proof that societies have evolved, and Kroeber's theory of the superorganic (1917), established the study of culture as a science in its own right, and brought about the divorce of the sciences of culture from biology.

After that point, it became unfashionable in social science to describe human institutions in the same terms as one might use for a colony of bees.

A fairly innocent and happy life for social science then ensued, in which one could almost disregard biological factors like feeble-mindedness or starvation unless they grossly intruded into theory. Economic growth was thought of as independent of biological growth. It was not until the 1960s that it burst through to popular awareness that man, in building culture, was violating the ecological balance of the environment, and hence his own life. But twenty years earlier, what is now called information theory had shown that the separation between the social and biological, even the physical, sciences was artificial and perhaps premature. Three most important discoveries contributing to this breakthrough were: that information is inversely related to entropy (Shannon and Weaver, 1949); that feedback is the essential life-like process (Wiener, 1948); and in molecular biology, that coding and encoding go on at all levels of life. With such discoveries, as we shall see, it became unfeasible for biology, psychology, and sociology to live apart as they had done. Indeed, the environmental crisis forced them to come together in the study of systems: man must either return to his relations with nature, or perish alone.

WINNING AND KEEPING ORDER

The lesson, in brief, is that all life processes are playing the same game and work in the same ways. And what is it all about? Salmon spawning, birds migrating, stags fighting, bees making honey, bears robbing the hives—all these familiar examples show an unending struggle on the part of each species to build and to grow against the disorder caused by the efforts of others to build and grow.

At the human level, what does one see but endless building? Farmers, for example, repair fences, clear land, plow and plant, while other men gather into cities to manufacture and trade. Indeed, civilization consists of peaks of buildings and growth in art, government, religion, and in all aspects of culture.

Yet the struggle is never over, though battles may be won: The barbarian appears at the gates to destroy the citadel, conflict breaks out within the city, erosion eats at the foundations of beliefs—disorder threatens from everywhere.

Nevertheless, the notion of fang-and-claw struggle and waste of life is a gross exaggeration of biologists' view of evolutionary order, for nature establishes delicate balances: The introduction of a fly to a formerly uncontaminated region might bring about a famine or a plague; a variation of three degrees of temperature can be enough to send a man to a doctor. And what is evolution, if not the natural selection of the most beautifully organized members of the species, and where is evolution going but toward higher forms of organization? The ability of living things to balance themselves is called *homeostasis*, discovered by Cannon in 1939, and usually defined as the process by which living systems restore themselves, or maintain steady states within a range of variation, offsetting inputs which would otherwise greatly change or destroy them. We feel a deep, possibly innate need for order, to straighten things out, to solve puzzles, to build and to defend what we have built. And before one criticizes counter-culture youth for disorderliness, one should recall

4

that they were a spearhead of the movement in the 1970s to preserve the environment.

So life is beautifully organized to win and keep order, and to defeat or at least minimize disorder by using information (feedback) from the environment to hold one's own, grow, and adapt. This is the purpose, if such a term may be used, even of cells. A biologist says:

> The finding that all cells have built-in feedback controls that automatically tell them what to do to survive makes cells appear very purposeful, and indeed they are purposeful. Their purpose is to survive, and if they have an independent existence, their built-in purpose is to survive and multiply. Their adaptive stratagems to accomplish these ends are many and marvelous, especially in cases of starvation and lack of water. The usual tactic in single-cell organisms is to go into some kind of spore formation and "hibernate" until conditions are favorable again. Small wonder that early biologists could find *design* in every form of life they studied! (POTTER, 1971:172).

What we have been saying is that life is dedicated to resist *entropy*, the tendency toward disorder, randomness, "shuffledness," or "running down" of things that is described in physics as the Second Law of Thermodynamics. All life is a game against entropy at all levels.

But how is the game played?—By an exchange with the environment and with rival life. A lion tracks his prey, a hunter tracks the lion, by clues, each building up order taken as information from the environment. Man searches for clues (information) throughout the universe, organizing them into knowledge and culture through the use of his brain, an information-processing instrument which would take up 800 square feet of space if housed as a computer. Not only a higher mechanism like the brain, but cells, even organic molecules like enzymes and proteins, take in from the environment information which they use to pattern and duplicate themselves. Indeed, a cell stores a memory or history of its previous "adventures":

5

A gene, if it is a nucleoprotein molecule, is the product of vast chemical adventures, from the formation of atoms and simple molecules in the distant past of its ancestral lineage, to relatively minor shifts in kind or arrangement of atom or radical, the mutations of its macromolecular maturity. The cell is directed in its development, first by the information stored in its genes, later by the structures and substances that have been formed partly under their influence—reduplicating particulates, somatic mutations, adaptive enzymes, and the like. The organism, in turn, develops by virtue of the various cell types that are differentiated early . . . and their later patterning and other modification as tissues and organs. . . . It is hardly surprising, then, that higher level orgs are more individualized than lower level ones, that they . . . carry a richer and more characterizing past (GERARD, 1957:55).

Another biologist calculates that the amount of information contained in one bacterium is 10^3 bits, or a pattern as unlikely as choosing a coin toss "heads" or "tails" one thousand times in a row (Quastler, 1964:4), meaning that living things, even in their molecules, are loaded with information which they have drawn from their environments and ancestors. Such a victory over disorder is what the chemist Schrodinger meant by his famous statement, "Life feeds on negative entropy" (information).

Just as life draws on information in order to live, so it issues information to its environment in order to control it. Wiener says:

The commands through which we exercise our control over our environment are a kind of information which we impart to it. . . . In control and communication we are always fighting nature's tendency to degrade the organized and to destroy the meaningful; the tendency . . . for entropy to increase (1954).

The essential ordering process of life illustrated here is encoding, the building of pattern into what is taken in for metabolism and growth, and into what is put out for message and control. Without encoding, neither life nor society could exist. Encoded information must be recorded on a template, or pattern of some kind, that can be passed from person to person or one kind of structure to another.

> Cells—particularly specialized information processing cells like neurons and cells of endocrine glands—encode by patterning chemical transmitter molecules which, when put out, elicit particular responses from specialized cells that receive them. Organs encode by transmitting from their output neurons in a way which activates the neurons that synapse with them. Human organisms encode into the language of words, tones, or gestures of their associates. Groups encode through the language of their spokesmen, often chairmen, but some, like orchestras, choirs, and ballets, disperse the encoding to all members (J. G. MILLER, 1965:359).

In this sense, encoding is not merely a matter of communication, but the essential ordering process of life, from the protein molecule to the human brain. It is the creation of life out of the inorganic "soup" of minerals. To draw again on Schrodinger's dictum: Life encodes from the entropy of the environment enough information to organize, repeat itself, grow, and evolve. In fact, evolution is another form of encoding: The pool of genes is improved by the selection of better genes that have resulted from the information derived from the struggle for existence. A biologist says:

> We can detect in the progress of evolution a decrease in randomness of all living things. The higher animals are in a sense more different from their environments than are the lower (YOUNG, 1950).

Not surprisingly, some sense of this need for and ability to order is built into the human mind. As Aristotle said, the intellect desires to know. The mind seeks pattern, tracking it like a missile through a sea of disorder. The mind creates probabilities, if only by hunch or magic. Serendipity is a delicious morsel of order found by chance.

Information theory, then, suggests that life's self-organizing ability to encode and to read feedback defeats entropy. Its ability to do this is what makes it alive, more alive than a machine. It is a mortal game to which all organisms are committed. In this game the options are to win, in the sense of holding one's own or better, or to lose.

At the biological level, such winning is called conquest of the environment, survival, or adaptation. At the social level, however, it is a process which is called communication, social adjustment, negotiation, building a culture. Let us distinguish this social level as "communicated order."

COMMUNICATED ORDER

Some kind of communication by signs takes place throughout the living world. Even molecules like enzymes have "signatures" by which they recognize and accept or reject each other, as in the case of allergies and antibodies (Quastler, 1964:30-32). To use a sign, an organism must in some way read the information offered to determine if it is relevant. The higher an organism is on the scale of life, the more information is transmitted, received, and read (encoding and decoding). Organs of the body "talk" to one another through nerves and chemical messengers. And, of course, genetic codes already supply them with much of the information necessary for continuing life in an environment (the blood-stream, for example) which may be homeostatically controlled.

But when living things are detached from one another—floating like a school of fish in the sea—and have to signal to each other through an environment which is foreign, in other words, full of irrelevant and unreadable information, then we are justified in speaking of a *communicated* order, which must be negotiated if they are to have what we call social life. The social problem consists of *finding* one's own kind (those fitted by heredity or learning to give relevant signals), negotiating through signals a readiness to act together in specifically ordered ways, and developing enduring patterns or nets of communication (social systems). By now we have fully arrived in sociology and left biology, not behind, but where it belongs, at the basis of communicated order.

At the level of sociology, the game of life is the game of communicating—forming coalitions, memberships, and shared strategies—and understanding one's relation to them, which may be called social meaning. The collective memory of these meanings, stored in symbols, is called culture.

All theorists recognize a basic distinction between two levels of communication, one of which is shared by all living things, the other of which is nearly monopolized by man; for example, if you spell your dog's name, he won't know you are talking about him, because you have gone to a higher level of encoding which he cannot reach. Pavlov called this the secondary signal system, which conveys "signals of signals." More commonly, it is the distinction between natural signs and the languages of symbols that are arbitrary and man-made. Information theorists put it this way:

> Signs are of two types, natural and man-made. For example, a dark cloud is a natural sign of rain. The word "cloud," however, is a man-made sign of the object, cloud. Smoke is a natural sign of fire but smoke signals are man-made signs of many other things. Messages consist of man-made signs. (ACKOFF, 1957).

> It is the capacity for speech—the ability to produce, absorb, and interpret *symbols*, as opposed to mere signs like the warning cry of an animal—which most clearly marks man off from his humbler brethren. Man is distinguished from the animals also by a much more elaborate image of time and relationship . . . (BOULDING, 1956).

So your dog cannot read the symbols you make of the signs which he knows. And, as children know, we can quickly baffle other humans by inventing codes. The enormously important processes of self-awareness, role-taking and role-playing are also derived from this kind of symbol formation, according to the theory of George H. Mead (1934).

Speaking of order, we are in a position to distinguish three levels

9

at which higher living things, man especially, defeat entropy. At the first level, they leave the imprint of themselves, their habits and intelligence, upon the environment in such a way that it is more ordered to their needs. A cat, for example, turns around to push into shape the place where she will rest. If done with foresight, this would be called building by design. The second level is leaving natural signs and using them for one's own guidance and communication with others, as when deer follow a trail to a waterhole. The third level goes beyond such simple reading of signs to the construction of elaborate systems of symbols, including beliefs which seem at variance with natural signs (a meteor for example, may be interpreted as the arrival of an angel). This process may be called construction of a symbolic order. As we know, to get a person to interpret meteorological phenomena in a certain way requires an elaborate system of encoding which we call higher learning and education. Humans respond, then, to three kinds of reality and seek order at three levels: natural order governed by natural law, natural signs which communicate information about natural order, and symbolic order. The history of social thought shows ways in which men have interpreted these orders.

ORDER IN SOCIETY

According to this scheme, the purpose of life is to minimize entropy and maximize information shared with our fellows at three levels: controlling nature, understanding natural signs, and constructing a symbolic order which will work and win against entropy.

Disorder in any of these arrangements (entropy) is an enemy threatening to destroy our stake in the order we have created, which happens to include us! This sense of entropy as an enemy explains the dualism of good-versus-evil found in most moralities and symbolized, for example, by myths in which a hero rescues the world from a threatening dragon, or the notion of hell as a place for sinners. Moral outrage is felt against the barbarian or the sinner because his pattern violates our own. Few people can tolerate much entropy without a sense of danger or outrage, though scientists are taught to endure it, as is reflected in the phrase "a beautiful theory murdered by a gang of brutal facts."

Here we see that all living things are inherently fated to resist disorder, which takes place in one of two ways: passive resistance (or "holding the fort") or aggressive action, sending out sorties to meet, communicate with, and defeat or convert the stranger.

The *closed system* "holds the fort," opening the gate only selectively. It is the basic *ingrouping process* of gathering together and excluding outsiders which runs as an unending theme through tribal society, ethnic groups, small towns, exclusive neighborhoods and clubs, ruling cliques, bureaucratic inner circles, solidaristic mobs, to say nothing of animal herds and flocks. In-grouping includes establishing territories or hangouts, preferential communication nets, privileges and secrets shared by insiders, and resisting outsiders. Basically it is a tactic of closing ranks against strange elements which represent entropy. Much useful information is rejected as well, but the potential usefulness of this information is traded as a price for the gain in order by closure.

The *open system*, which we are most familiar with as a liberal, democratic society, is dedicated to the proposition that the gain in information from leaving the gate open will, in the long run, be greater than the disorder created by outsiders trooping in. It asserts that transactions of exchange, exploration, and self-revelation (including secrets) — results in higher levels of understanding and cooperation. An open society is therefore willing to tolerate a far higher level of entropy than a closed one. It is not "allergic" to outsiders as are the antibodies of a biological system, but puts its faith in the construction of symbolic order. It believes that secrecy is generally worse for society than the free flow of information to everyone, and that criticism, even hostile views, will do more good if heard, rather than shouted down. By using all available information, the open system is highly adaptive, or morphogenic, able to make and remake itself by information (Buckley, 1967:62).

Enthusiasm for information, however, should not lead us to suppose that an open society can recklessly absorb any amount, any more than a clam can perpetually siphon sludge at the bottom of a bay. All individuals or systems must resist too much entropy at some point. For most organisms, the limits are narrow, since they must select intake according to precise homeostatic needs. Major change is possible only by evolution of the species. Yet even in creatures supposedly governed by instinct, biologists hold that there is a built-in capacity to utilize disorder or variability, for example, the bewildering changes in flight which a moth makes to escape from a predator, or the trial-and-error behavior in many animals, which helps them to survive (Potter, 1971:94-100). At no level does life seek to banish entropy, but to use it. A balance of order and disorder is necessary for life.

Yet, whatever the system, there is always an upper limit of intake —of food, energy, people, problems, information or anything else—beyond which the organism or society cannot survive, that is, the increase in entropy becomes irreversible for *that* system, and personal or social breakdown follows. Unlike biological organisms, a society has two major methods for averting disaster: radical change, symbolically negotiating a new order and set of values (commonly called revolution); and cultural revitalization (Wallace, 1956), perhaps by cultic movements, which pump new energy and meaning into old forms and symbols as, for example, Martin Luther did for scholastic Christianity.

Such a view of the game of life played by open and closed systems gives us a perspective for evaluating liberty as the notion of a totally open society. All players of the game of life must minimize entropy, but the open system does so by opening the gate and trading for a profit in new information. What is liberty but the freedom to seek, by information or other means, better arrangement? No system seeks disorder for its own sake but for a gain in order. To do so, it has to take into account what Guy Fawkes and John Brown as well as Emmanuel Kant have to say. It tries to meet waves of new information not like a stone wall but with the poise of a surf rider.

How much optimism is justified about the tidal waves of new information engulfing society in the name of progress and in the form of problems remains to be seen by looking at the transaction balances of information-overload, entropic communication, social movements, and the processes of ingrouping.

We have tried to show that while biological order is different from symbolic order, they are both playing the same game of minimizing entropy. Though men use signals like flags and television, there is no reason to suppose that they are not negotiating, at another level, what life itself is doing at all levels. This should bring more feeling of the unity of biology and sociology. There is less reason to suppose that something can happen at the cultural level which is independent of what is happening at the biological level. At least it says, what is becoming more evident in an age of ecological crisis, that the social game cannot be played against the rules of biology. Can social arrangements damage and crush life processes? Can culture be against man? (Freud, 1958; Henry, 1964). This is what humanists, existentialists and critics of technology say. Perhaps by thinking of life and social order as together against entropy instead of each other, men can find a better game-plan. And one of the things we may doubt from the study of systems is that any constant or linear policy will work for too long.

MINIMIZING ENTROPY:
OPENING AND CLOSING

Opening and closing is a natural pattern throughout the living world. The sea anemone in a tide pool extending and retracting its green tentacles provides a beautiful illustration of this. Hibernation is a sea-sonal closure after exploring the environment to eat, mate, and rear young. The *Old Testament* says:

> To everything there is a season. . . . A time to get and a time to lose; a time to keep and a time to cast away . . . a time to keep silence, and a time to speak (ECCLESIATES 3:1-7).

The Sabbath is a traditional weekly closure to worldliness. The pupil dilates when the light is dim and contracts when there is too much. Youth generally is a time of risk, while old age is one of saving and stock-taking of gains. The child crawling, reaching, tasting, hungry, crying, then curls up in rest.

Thus what we call aliveness—resilience, adaptability—is not continual intake of food, resources, information, nor any constant policy, but prompt and sensitive alternation of phases of openness and closure. The mind, for example, listens alertly, then turns off to signals like pulling down a window shade. Rest and sleep are not merely slowing down of activity but prolonged closure to food, cold, stress, and noise from outside. The artist retiring to a workshop for solitary creativity or a religious hermit to meditation is another kind of closure after taking in what society has to offer. So it would be a mistake to suppose that transactions go on at a constant level in living systems, open or closed. The natural pattern is alternation; and the more alive a system is, the more alertly it does both.

Similarly, society has tides of openness and closure, peaks of communication and agitation, when fads spread easily and new styles flourish. And then troughs of conservatism and isolationism when the public is mistrustful of foreign affairs, reluctant to undertake new enterprises, when the stock market goes down, ethnic integration slows down, and so on.

The troughs do not reflect, as some suppose, setbacks to growth and progress, but evidence that the opening and closing mechanisms of life are working, that the society has resiliency. Far more alarming than swings from openness to closure would be a deadness of public response. The notion of a totally and perpetually open system is a myth, that only an optimist like the eighteenth century philosopher of perfectibility, Condorcet, could endorse. A perpetually open system that absorbed any and all information without resistance would be dead.

Of what do closing mechanisms consist? We do not need to imagine censors vigilantly controlling the mass media for political purposes. Rather, in a pluralistic society like ours, we see that the ingrouping process is a closing mechanism at many levels, including towns, neighborhoods, ethnic groups, parties, churches, families, cliques, colonies, communes and these collectivities may close ranks to strangers, accentuate their identities, in what theorists of mass communication call the "second step," the cohesion of small groups and vigilance of their gatekeepers over what opinions are introduced. This pulse of ingrouping goes on in every living society, open or closed. Only when it stops is there cause for alarm, for that would mean that the collective struggle against entropy has been lost, that the people of that society are more concerned with abandoning the ship than with manning its pumps. For ingrouping represents the control of too much intake or outflow at that particular time, like tightening capillaries under the skin. A pluralistic open society must do through its ingrouping what open media—held open by laws such as "freedom of the press"—cannot do: sort and control the flow and allow time for rest and assimilation. Further, it must generate effort through ingroups which will pay into the building of broader collective effort and morale in the whole society. The point is that society does not mobilize energy by bypassing ingroups but by enlisting them.

The notion of social opening and closing puts into perspective books like The Greening of America (Reich, 1970), Future Shock (Toffler, 1970), and The Temporary Society (Bennis and Slater, 1968), which describe vast social changes, including great increases of mobility and information, without telling us whether society—either its belief systems or human relations—can absorb the impact. The fate of ingroups will be a deciding factor: Will they be able to transact the changes or will change overwhelm them? How do people exchange information with those close to them in daily life? If input of bad news gets to be too much, the group will protect a member by helping him to shrug or laugh it off. But if he has no ingroup to help him, the entropy may be too much for his exposed nervous system to handle, except by an extreme tactic like hermetic withdrawal or insanity.

We see, then, that ingrouping and the balance of opening and closing are enormously important, for the liberal and the radical must recognize the importance of closure, just as the conservative must admit that of openness.

Plato was the first who saw closure and openness of the ideal society as a funnel of intake guarded by philosophers who screened it and passed it on to the rest as justice. This is not, we feel, a suitable model for a modern society, even if Socrates were the philosopher. But we have much to learn from it about the kind of information a social order needs.

John Stuart Mill represents another extreme of social theory: a veritable anarchy of information under a minimum of law, in which the individual is on his own pursuing whatever happiness he sees fit, under presumably ideal conditions.

In the following pages, we look at many great ideas in the history of social thought, not just to see more clearly the roots of sociology but to gain from the wisdom of early writers for the game of life. We shall unify our study by asking what theory of information and social order their ideas reflect, and how those ideas can be reconciled with the needs of modern society and its sociology. We gain a better view of all social theories, old and new, if we see them as explanations of how man encodes the kind of information that helps him defeat entropy; and how he uses that information to build social systems which he rationalizes by ideologies and perhaps imposes on somebody else.

2

Order in Ideas

ENCODING

The order-making process at the human level is encoding. Culture consists of all the established codes that have been handed down from the past, while communication refers to present use of such codes to signal to achieve coordination with others who know the codes, or to convey new information. Great thinkers are those who have transformed an especially large amount of new experience into codes that others could use. But most of our thought was encoded in the forgotten processes of the collective formation of language.

Although no one really knows how languages began, we can see encoding in daily life, in the artist for example, painting a portrait, or in children making up word games, perhaps an artificial language consisting of words known only to themselves. Any recognized part of experience can be associated with a sign; if I can remember what my experience was by using that sign, I have encoded successfully. If others can tell what I am signaling by a similar encoding experience, we have a successful language and the beginning of a culture, including a body of social thought. Science is our name for a special kind of encoding through observation and generalization according to previously encoded rules of what is acceptable as inference and fact. But collective encoding according to less stringent rules is the very stuff of society. Moreover, once one sees that the environment is organized by symbols, one sees that encoding is the making of the symbolic world. Sociologists are likely to designate as ideology those symbols which represent a world (Mannheim, 1936), or a socially constructed reality (Berger and Luckmann, 1966).

The distinction, however, between rational and non-rational encoding is vitally important. Rational encoding is the more or less conscious abstracting of symbolic forms and the testing of them, for example, by consensus, by consistency with other symbols, or by their effectiveness as means to an end. Non-rational encoding comes from tradition or from interaction with others and occurs without examination or questioning on our part. Most of the social thought with which we shall be concerned in this book comes, of course, under the heading of rational encoding; but non-rational encoding plays a larger part than many have suspected in the most elaborate ideologies, as pointed out by thinkers such as Freud and Pareto.

FORMS OF ENCODING IN SOCIAL THOUGHT

The following sections describe the main forms of social thought, in terms of encoding.

Tradition is collective memory of encoding by ancestors, mostly forgotten, though sometimes represented by culture heroes like Moses, Hammurabi, Prometheus, or Krishna. It is often non-rational and sacred, taking the form of myths like the *Mahabharata* of India, or the *Nibelungenlied*. Individuals have little opportunity to encode new information into such myths, and large obligation to repeat them as handed down. Traditional thought thus consists of ancient decisions and habits, the reasons for which are now forgotten. On the whole, these collective habits just develop, are not deliberately enacted. Sanctified by the past, such habits are highly resistant to criticism, discussion or change (Sumner, 1906). And, since they are accepted non-rationally, without criticism or even awareness, they escape the kind of input from reflection or testing of daily experience that could change them much.

This resistance to change in the rules encoded in folkways is illustrated by the story of a traveler to Katmandu, Nepal, an Oriental land of abundant fields, magnificent pagodas, saffron-robed monks, relaxed people, and happy children. Until 1951, Nepal existed as a feudal society divided into innumerable castes, and cut off from the rest of the world. Life was still regulated from birth to death by immutable religion-based rules. There was little demand for change or knowledge of progress, and no desire to explore the unknown. The visitor observed women doing their chores, carrying everything they needed, including heavy loads of firewood, up narrow paths on steep hills. Why, he asked, didn't the people build a lift of some sort to pull up the loads?

> All that was needed was a rope, a few pulleys, and some sticks. . . . When I asked people about building such a device, the reasons against it were numerous: "Well it would cause great difficulties among the people. Who would tend such a lift? Who could keep it up?" "There is not enough money to buy the pulleys." "Why should they do it? They are quite happy carrying the loads." "What else would the women do? If they don't work they would quarrel." . . . "They are used to carrying, so why change? There is no reason to change." (HOSKEN, 1971).

In such an example, we see the characteristics of the encoding of a static system: strong, sacred collective memory; small intake of new information and small burden of encoding versus remembering. New information is screened largely by gatekeepers such as chiefs or priests, of which we shall see a glorified version in Plato's *Republic*. There is also little public discussion as an active process of forming new ideas, its main function being to reassert and reenforce established codes.

How do such static systems handle the problem of intrusive information and change in their environments? By invoking mythology in some way, perhaps by claiming the intervention of gods or demonic forces. A student of Greek mythology says:

> The most characteristic feature of the *Odyssey* is the way in which its personages ascribe all sorts of mental (as well as physical) events to the intervention of a nameless and indeterminate daemon or "god" or "gods." These vaguely conceived beings can inspire courage at a crisis or take away a man's understanding.... Whenever someone has a particularly brilliant or a particularly foolish idea; when he suddenly recognizes ... the meaning of an omen ... he or someone else will see in it ... intervention by one of these anonymous supernatural beings (DODDS, 1969:10).

So disorder, inexplicableness—the kind of thing that might generate scientific explanation with us, is encoded within the mythology of a traditional society.

Art encodes into esthetic form intensely pleasing or moving experiences which are prized because of their power to evoke similar experiences in others. Aristotle called the emotional intensity evoked through such experiences, especially the dramatic presentation of tragedy, *catharsis*, a satisfying purging of feelings. Such satisfaction comes to us from the pattern which art reveals to us or reaches during its performance. John Dewey said that art has a kind of "energy" which might now be called its information, or contribution to negative entropy. It is this energy which explains at the same time the power of art to "move and stir" and to "calm and tranquilize." It offers a:

unique transcript of the energy of the things of the world . . . by selecting and ordering the energies in virtue of which things act upon us and interest us. . . . Elimination gets rid of forces that confuse, distract, and deaden. Order, rhythm and balance, simply means that energies significant for experience are acting at their best. . . . Art is ideal (in) the sense just indicated (DEWEY, 1934:184-185).

With such a function, art is one of the primeval ways in which order is encoded. The earliest records of man reveal that long before the invention of ideology and theory he was making highly meaningful esthetic forms, not only in myths and legends, but in dramas, rituals, festivals, dances, masks and costumes, drawings, designs on pots, textiles, and tomb walls, burial offerings, monuments to victories and heroes, fetishes, idols, votive offerings, and even in early forms of comedy such as clowning and joking.

Artistic encoding is both rational and non-rational. Freud was the first to point out how much of the unconscious goes into artistic expression, as distinguished from the planning and rationalizing work of the intellect. An artist is not usually aware of *all* his feelings, still less of the social aspect of his work, such as the norms he may be making or changing by his utterance. Art, both fine and popular, is a vast outpouring of expressions that help to formulate social norms, even in such forms as soap and horse operas, popular music, jokes, graffiti, songs, jingles, and social types as models of style. The folk artist spoke for his collectivity; but so does the individual creative artist today, if an audience, by responding to his work, allows him to speak for them.

Legislation is the rational, systematic, and deliberate formulation of new rules for social behavior by a person or group authorized to do so, in response to information about new conditions, with thought also given to formal sanctions to make the rules effective.

Philosophy is a kind of rational encoding in which personal experience is drawn upon to form an independent view of the world as distinguished from that automatically supplied by tradition. It is independent, speculative, daring, critical, often highly logical and systematic. It is generally conceded to have started in the sixth century B.C. with the Greek Thales, who explained phenomena such as eclipses and the nature of water in non-traditional ways. Throughout its history, philosophy has consisted of two main parts: a theory as to the nature of the world, and an ethical or political doctrine as to the best way to live (Russell, 1945:3; 834).

Theology might be called a cousin of philosophy, rational thinking about matters of faith and religious intuition or revelation. It often shows surprising independence and daring, as, for example, the existentialism of Kierkegaard or Tillich, and the creative theory-building and logical rigor of St. Augustine and St. Thomas Aquinas.

Ideology is a social phenomenon in which ideas encoded by one man as philosophy or theology are accepted by millions as doctrine, as an explanation of the nature of things or justification of the order of society. Ideology may be very complex as a system (for example, Marxism or Thomism), but is necessarily simplified from the ideas of the original thinker as it is transformed into popular doctrine. The defining characteristic of ideology is that it is transmitted to individuals, not created by personal effort as in philosophy. Thus, though it provides a way of seeing the world, it is not a direct personal encoding from individual experience of the world. Though perhaps attributable to a philosopher, it comes to the individual as a hand-me-down of traditional encoding, much the way myth comes to a primitive thinker.

Finally, *scientific theory* aims at a rational explanation of things encoded from empirical observation and framed as hypotheses to be extended to the environment in another kind of encoding called testing. It is the method of testing, more than anything else, which separates scientific theory from other forms of social thought.

In this book we shall be much concerned with both scientific theory and ideology. Scientific theory consists of generalizations by a collectivity called scientists who aim at formulating hypotheses for empirical testing, whereas ideology consists of generalizations arising from everyday experience of a social class or an entire society. The function of ideology is to make the social world intelligible, if not true in a scientific sense, for that class or society. Both science and ideology may be highly rational and both are "socially constructed reality" (Berger and Luckmann, 1966). But the prime characteristic of ideology, as pointed out by Karl Marx (1846), and by Karl Mannheim (1936), is that it is strategic, that is, the social (usually economic or political) interest of a collectivity determines what is selected to be believed and promulgated as a world view. Marx was the most explicit, stating flatly that ideologies are instruments of class domination. Among beliefs which strategically serve collective interests Mannheim (1936) distinguished ideology, which defends and rationalizes the existing social order, from Utopia, which may serve a revolutionary collectivity because it contains:

> the unrealized and the unfulfilled tendencies which represent the needs of each age. These intellectual elements then become the explosive material for bursting the limits of the existing order (MANNHEIM, 1936:179).

Of course, nothing prevents scientists as a collectivity from using their findings as a set of beliefs to establish themselves in power, or to advocate a revolutionary political change in society. On the whole, however, they do not do so, partly because their code of objectivity (Weber, 1919) expressly forbids it.

All forms of encoding—traditional thought, art, legislation, philosophy, theology, ideology, and scientific theory—help to build a symbolic world for modern man by providing forms into which he can encode his daily experience and make sense out of his life and society. The remaining chapters will discuss some great models by which humans have supposed they understood the grounds for the existing order or which they believed they could use to improve social order.

PRAGMATIC MODELING

Somehow, information from the environment is encoded within the nervous system as patterns, thought models which represent an order in the environment or within ourselves and can be used to guide conduct. Such models range from fantasy to heuristic planning and can be used in various ways. A child sailing a boat, an artist painting a picture, a utopian thinker visualizing things as he would like them to be, a planner designing a city, an archaeologist reconstructing the past, a writer plotting a story, an inventor testing a machine, or a scientist constructing theories and simulating natural conditions in a laboratory —all are examples of the making of models, a kind of encoding which helps to guide us toward goals by providing cognitive maps and frames of reference for worlds present, past, future, and imaginary.

Models are stored in memory and tradition by further encoding them into signs and symbols. Encoded and stored, they can be recalled, referred to, and built into grammatical and logical syntaxes by subjective processes (such as thinking, perceiving, remembering, imagining, dreaming, meditating, or abstracting) and then communicated to others by overt signals.

Models provide social order in the forms of social thought we have called tradition, art, legislation, philosophy, theology, ideology, and scientific theory. Models also provide every social situation with a cognitive map of acceptable behavior. Linton called such models

> ideal patterns upon which every society depends for the specialized training of its members. . . . As systems of ideas they become a part of the culture of the group and are transmitted from generation to generation by conscious instruction as well as imitation. . . . Although the ideal patterns are carried in the minds of individuals and can find overt expression only through the medium of individuals, the fact that they are shared by many members of the

society gives them a super-individual character. They persist, while those who share them come and go. . . . The sum total of the ideal patterns which control the reciprocal behavior between individuals and between the individual and society constitute the social system under which the particular society lives (1936:99-105).

Social roles carry models of expected performance and the kinds of people (social types) likely to play them (Klapp, 1962, 1972b, 1972c). By sharing such ideal patterns, people are able to find their way about the social structure and understand one another when referring to their own society. Such truths may be called consensual or social, as distinguished from natural truth about the material world.

Natural or social models, however seemingly true, have an inherent element of analogy, metaphor, or fiction. That is, models [what Vaihinger (1925) called "as if"] are not the same as reality, but are constructions of the human imagination. All models are in some sense fictions. This is conspicuous in those scientific models which Max Weber called ideal types (like the "economic man") which simplify and exaggerate reality in order for man to understand it better.

Such considerations help us to understand the pragmatic nature of modeling, that is, a model is only as good or as true as its uses prove it to be. Since most models work fairly well sometimes for somebody, most have some share of truth and are more or less useful for various data-bases. But none, at least among the models of nature, can claim to enshrine absolute truth. This applies no less to ideologies than to scientific hypotheses abandoned after one laboratory test. Indeed, it may be a characteristic of ideology that believers cannot be pragmatic but must claim absolute truth for their model. As Arthur Schlesinger, Jr. says:

What is wrong with faith in ideology? The trouble is this. An ideology is not a picture of actuality; it is a model derived from actuality, a model designed to isolate certain salient features of actuality which the model builder, the ideologist, regards as of crucial importance. An ideology, in other words, is an abstraction from reality. There is nothing wrong with abstractions or models per se. In truth, we could not conduct discourses without them. There is nothing wrong with them—so long, that is, as people remember they are only models. The ideological fallacy is to forget that ideology is an abstraction from reality and to regard it as reality itself. . . . Free men know many truths, but they doubt whether any mortal man knows the Truth (1962).

It is rather important to note this before taking up theories which may be in one context scientific and in another ideological, such as the one described in the next chapter, which proposes to install science as the sole source of natural and social models.

3

Order
from
Science

That victory over disorder which we call civilization consists of patterns which have been encoded into symbolic forms variously called laws, styles, ideas, techniques, roles, and institutions. For the Western world at least, the most outstanding of these are reason, science and technology.

The twentieth century has a social order of unparalleled efficiency, created largely by science. (Does one need to mention that most of the people alive today wouldn't be here without science?) But it has apparently failed to answer certain vital questions which mankind must ask, especially those questions whose answers would increase wisdom, such as "What is good?", or Tolstoy's question, "Why am I here, and what shall I do?" We have only to realize that in recent years scientific laboratories have been picketed, even bombed, by well-meaning persons in seemingly Luddite rebellion against machinery hurting man, to be aware of such disappointment.

To understand how this could be, we can best begin, not by entering the political arena, where ideas are rarely clarified by smoke, but by looking cooly at a doctrine called positivism, which epitomizes much of the problem.

I first became aware of positivism as a university student, attending a lecture by a Marxist. Before he began, he looked around the room rather belligerently and asked, "Is there a logical positivist in the crowd?" No one answered him, and after a silence he began. I was sorry not to find out what would have happened if a logical positivist had identified himself. But it aroused my interest and I became curious to find out more about the viewpoint which so worried him. I became aware, too, of the dramatic clash and excitement of ideas—aware that the intellectual world was not a mere boneyard of fusty scholarship. I later found distinguished modern names associated with positivism and its offshoots, such as Rudolph Carnap, Alfred J. Ayer, Bertrand Russell, B. F. Skinner, John Watson, William F. Ogburn, George Lundberg— going back to Auguste Comte, Herbert Spencer, ultimately to Francis Bacon.

One can tell if a person is a positivist, not by his familiarity with such thinkers, but by his attitude toward the larger questions of life and his approach to practical problems. One question might be sufficient to tell who is, and who is not, a positivist: In this time of uncertainty, if you had at this moment to turn to any one source for a reliable answer to a major problem requiring facts for its solution, what would it be?

Take, for example, child-rearing: When, if ever, should punishment be used and, if so, what kinds? For your answer you may choose between a psychology book written by a young unmarried professor, reporting not his own experience but the experiments of *others*, the latest findings of psychology, biology, and sociology. Or you may seek advice from a grandmother, who has raised ten children of her own, has much experience in child care, and is full of traditional wisdom, including stories, though formally she is only a high school graduate. If you have decided preference for the psychologist, because of the method by which the findings he reports have been reached, over the wisdom of the grandmother, for all her experience, you are probably a positivist.

But let us make the test harder. The issue is now a large question concerning society, drug control, for example. How can harmful drug use be reduced in a way that will be best for society? You may turn to one of the following kinds of authority for your answer: a wise philosopher, such as Confucius, Socrates, Plato, or Aristotle; an inspired religious prophet, such as Mohammed or Moses; or a scientist armed with a computer into which have been fed the latest relevant data on such things as crime rates, treatment statistics, and laboratory findings about the effects of drugs. If you confidently choose the scientist over the wise thinker or religious prophet, you are almost surely a positivist even though you have never heard of the label until now. It is plain that such a preference puts the hypotheses of science tested by data ahead of the deepest philosophical reasoning and the brightest illuminations of the intuitive mind. A positivist would ask: How can the wisest person answer questions about the effects of various kinds of legislation, or the point at which punishing drug users increases crime by criminalizing people? Not only experimental data but systems analysis are needed to determine the optimum results—one wouldn't want to reduce the number of addicts at the price of freedom, for instance. No amount of inspired thinking can answer such questions, says the positivist, but science can. And if science does not have the answers, there is nowhere better to turn.

Where did this ultrascientific approach to social problems, sometimes called scientism, come from? The label "positivism" and most of the credit for popularizing the view goes to Auguste Comte, a French philosopher (1798-1857), who is often called the father of sociology, because he coined that word, too, while he was thinking about the application of science to society.

THE BRIGHT FUTURE

Disrespect for all that tradition could teach did not begin with Comte, but with the rationalism of the Greek philosophers. For countless millennia, folkways had seemed to reflect the nature of things. Only recently (archaeologically speaking) did man begin to think that he could make his own society by applying reason to social behavior: Reason was the key to virtue in men and justice in the state. Plato and Aristotle observed constitutions, and the former designed the first Utopia. Enthusiasm to remake society by reason, after some setbacks, grew into lyric optimism in the eighteenth century, especially in France at the time of the Revolution. The Philosophes, like Condorcet, proclaimed the dawn of a new era of equality, happiness, and human perfection, if only men were free to apply reason sweepingly enough. Despite this faith the French Revolution culminated in the Reign of Terror. Clearly, the rationalistic revolutionists had not answered a basic question: Who is to decide what is reasonable?

This new method by which to sort out from equally reasonable things those which in fact are true had been known at least since the time of Francis Bacon (1561-1626). It was a new method of reasoning from observations which he called *induction*: generalizing from specific cases rather than deduction from principles.

> We must first of all have a muster or presentation before the understanding of all known instances which agree in the same nature, though in substances the most unlike. And such collection must be made in the manner of a history, without premature speculation.

By such careful observation and avoidance of speculation, truth will replace "idols" (false beliefs) which no amount of reasoning without observation can dispel. "My logic aims to ... dissect nature ... this science flows not merely from the nature of the mind, but also from the nature of things" (1620). In his *New Atlantis* (1627), Bacon painted a thrilling picture of the good society that inductive science would make. This extraordinary land was a scientific paradise, in which experiments and observations were performed and every inventor of anything of value had a statue erected to him. The marvels equalled those of the twentieth century:

> We imitate ... [the] flight of birds; we have some degrees of flying in the air. We have ships and boats for going under water ... we have diverse curious clocks ... and some perpetual motions. We imitate also motions of living creatures by images of men, beasts, birds, fishes, and serpents ... (1627).

Although Bacon first truly saw the wonders of the scientific method applied to society, it was Auguste Comte who got credit for the classic formulation, plagiarizing most of it from the French philosopher Saint-Simon (Zeitlin, 1968:56-61). Positivism appeared like a star on the horizon of rationalism.

Comte's Positive Philosophy

The two basic tenets of positivism, as Comte explained them, are that man can design a social order and an ethics by his own reason, which will be better than what tradition supplies (this was the basic assumption of rationalism), and that science with its empirical method is the sovereign guide to what is reasonable—all other guides should be cast aside if they conflict with science. This second assumption, as we have seen, is the cutting edge which separates positivists from non-positivists sooner or later.

Such confidence in a superior method leads to an attack on the past which is much more drastic than that of those whose faith is in reason merely. Embedded by positivism in the modern mind is the idea that progress is a liberation from the "dead hand" of the past, the bad judgment of forgotten ancestors. The American sociologist, W. G. Sumner, in his great work *Folkways* (1906), urged that the folkways be critically studied, though at the same time pointing out how hard it would be to bring about reforms. For this he earned the title of conservative, though I would rather call him, in this regard, a realistic positivist. We must sweep away the so-called wisdom of the ancestors, says the positivist, the sooner the better, because we have science, a new and powerful tool in the search for truth.

Comte felt that theological thought was the first obstacle to science, therefore the first that must go. The mind of man, he said, progresses through three stages:

> the Theological, the Metaphysical, and the Positive or Scientific. Thus man began by considering phenomena of every kind as due to the direct and continuous influence of supernatural agents; he next regarded them as products of different abstract forces, residing in the bodies, ... He ends by viewing them as subjected to a certain number of natural and invariable relations observed ... (WAGNER, 1947:360).

The effect of observation was to shift the explanation for natural phenomena, gradually reducing the number of supernatural agents from many gods to one, from one God to metaphysical causes, and finally from metaphysical causes to scientifically observable regularities:

> Positive Philosophy—laying aside all search after causes, as being inaccessible to the human mind—is exclusively occupied in discovering laws, that is to say, the constant relations of similitude and succession which subsist between facts. ... Seeing that for at least two centuries past, those Theological and Metaphysical methods which presided over our earliest intellectual efforts have become entirely sterile; seeing that the most extensive and important discoveries ... have since this epoch, entirely resulted from the employment of the Positive Method, this fact alone clearly proves that to the latter must henceforward belong the exclusive direction of human thought ... (WAGNER, 1947:361).

Such a new order will come solely by the observation and recording of regularities, preferably by statistics, without metaphysical deduction (as

Bacon also urged). The Scottish philosopher, David Hume (1711-1776), echoing this spirit, gives the feeling of the housecleaning needed in philosophy, saying with some contempt:

> When we run over libraries, persuaded of these principles, what havoc must we make? If we take in our hand any volume; of divinity or school metaphysics, for instance; let us ask, Does it contain any abstract reasoning concerning quantity or number? No. Does it contain any experimental reasoning concerning matter of fact and existence? No. Commit it then to the flames: for it can contain nothing but sophistry and illusion (1748).

Hume owes his position as one of the fathers of positivism to such rigorous empiricism, denying truth to anything which cannot be observed.

Such a stripping away of what cannot be observed leads to a naturalistic rather than a religious or moral view of the world, as Table 1 shows.

Table 1 COMPARISON OF THE RELIGIOUS AND
SCIENTIFIC WORLDVIEWS

Religious View	*Scientific View*
The world is ultimately governed by spiritual forces.	The world is wholly governed by blind physical forces, such as gravitation, the laws of motion, the laws of chemical combination, etc.
The world has a purpose.	The world has no purpose. It is entirely senseless and meaningless.
The world is a moral order.	The world is not a moral order. The universe is "indifferent to" values of any kind. (STACE, 1952:159)

33

As sociologists following Max Weber put it, science, at least the positivistic attitude, has "disenchanted" the world. But at what great gain! is the immediate retort of the positivist.

As Comte pointed out, only science is progressive and cumulative; philosophy and religion stand still, or even get in the way of science. He sketched the development of science, from its origin in mathematics and astronomy, through physics, then biology, finally the social sciences, of which the last to develop was "social physics," or sociology. Why was sociology the last science to become "positive"? Because, said Comte, it is the most complex and rests upon the others, just as biology rests upon the inorganic sciences and mathematics. To understand society, the highest organism in nature, the sociologist must understand all else in the world as well.

There is, however, a reward for coming last, and for bearing the burden of so much knowledge: Sociology is the highest, the most inclusive, science. Arranging the sciences in a hierarchy, Comte reached a conclusion highly pleasing to sociologists: The place of sociology was at the keystone of the arch, not only the most complex but the guiding science for all social change—the science of progress, no less! Other views of the time were similar: to Herbert Spencer, sociology was the science of the superorganic; to Lester F. Ward, who might be called the American Comte, the force guiding the progress of human society was social *telesis*, foresight and intelligence, by which human society, as a great organism, could improve itself in a way impossible in the blind struggle for existence of lower animals. Sociology, of course, was in charge. Moral and religious systems have failed to produce progress; when science is put in charge, when the school takes the place of the church and the scientific lecture supersedes the sermon, then the progressive wheels of society will be set in motion (Ward, 1883).

Such views give us a clearer understanding of the grounds for scientific optimism, the belief that we may have enthusiasm for the future of man if only science is put in charge, and the sooner the better. Such enthusiasm for science put sociology (in the minds of sociologists,

34

at least) in the position of Queen of the Sciences, a rank which in an earlier era St. Thomas Aquinas had assigned to theology. Now sociology would serve as a new guide to a new and earthier kind of salvation.

The Program of Positivism

While the program of positivism was not as alarming as that of Marx and other revolutionaries, it was almost as radical, for it demanded that all the precious heritage of folkways and conventional wisdom— the kinds of things that parents like to tell their children—must go unless they could stand up to the laboratory test. This traditional wisdom included the entire body of moral teaching based on ancient laws and taboos rather than observed consequences, though Comte allowed that positivism would not neglect the moral feelings but give them a new basis: It would "bring moral precepts to the test of rigorous demonstration, and . . . secure them . . . by showing that they rest upon the laws of our individual and social nature." But woe betide the teaching that could not meet such a test. We can imagine, for example, the difficulties of proving that crime does not pay in the face of sociological findings about white collar criminality.

Not only was morality to be scrutinized, but religious institutions were to be revised in a way that would hardly be acceptable to them. Comte was raised a Catholic, and he had a plan for that church: Teach no more dogma, let spiritual truths be subject to empirical test; raise Caesar and Charlemagne to the same rank as St. Paul; eliminate most of the saints and martyrs and substitute great men of history in whatever field they might excel, so long as benefit to man could be shown. Needless to say, this religion could not be Catholicism, but would have to be a new religion of positivism. The idea caught on. President Eliot of Harvard University gave a discourse in 1909 on "The Religion of the Future:"

The new religion will foster powerfully a virtue which is comparatively new in the world—the love of truth and the passion for
seeking it. And the truth will progressively make men free...
when dwellers in a slum suffer the familiar evils caused by over-
crowding, impure food and cheerless labor, the modern true believers contend against the sources of such misery by providing
public baths, playgrounds, wider and cleaner streets, better dwell-
ings and more effective schools—that is, they attack the sources of
physical and moral evil.

But the bite of positivism was not directed mainly at the church;
it was in the schools that the real battle was to be fought. Education
and inquiry were to be entirely free and directed to testing all the
theories about government, about property, and the claims of socialism
versus capitalism. Comte rejected the "metaphysical doctrine of the
Sovereignty of the people" out of hand, as he also did the claims of the
corrupt aristocracy, saying that good government would have to come
from the "new philosophers," wherever they might arise, though the
working class could be expected to support them because of their "sense
of the real" and "preference for the useful." Such new philosophers
would ultimately come from the schools, trained in the latest methods
of science; but not from the schools as then instituted in France "where
the system of Academies has narrowed the mind, withered the feelings,
and enervated the character." The central reform would have to be in
education, both moral and intellectual. After that, political questions
could be decided, such as who should rule and what revolutionary
changes should be made.

In the meantime, until the spirit of positivism should develop,
Comte felt that the main measures should be moral rather than political.
For this, he earned the reputation in some quarters of being a conserva-
tive.

Of immediate political action, and of the revolutionary remedies
of communism especially, he took a dim view, not because he was against
socialism—he approved of the goals and conceded that property was

social—but because he considered the political methods destructive and unscientific. "Positivism, on the contrary, substitutes for such agencies an influence which is sure and peaceful, although it be gradual and indirect; the influence of a more enlightened morality . . . organized by competent minds, and diffused freely amongst the people (Wagner, 1947:378). The emphasis was on organic growth rather than political revolution. "Positivism looks upon insurrection as a dangerous remedy that should be reserved for extreme cases; but it would never scruple to sanction and even to encourage it when it was really indispensable."

This issue of evolution versus revolution became a focal conflict of the nineteenth century between positivists and Marxists (Zeitlin, 1968:83-84). The battle was especially bitter, since both parties preempted the term scientific. Turning its guns on Marxism, one can imagine what questions positivism might ask: What are these "laws" of history? Why is class conflict inevitable? Why should synthesis follow antithesis? What is the data-base on which these generalizations are made?

But neither Comte nor his socialist adversaries could disentangle the scientific aspects of their thought from ideological aspects, which imply a ready-made view of the world that defines its own facts (as we have discussed in Chapter II). Marxists thought they could avoid ideology by unmasking ruling class interests as opposed to those of the proletariat. Positivists thought they could avoid ideology by brushing away the cobwebs of metaphysics and theology through education. As the following century was to prove, neither succeeded in the housecleaning. Yet, judging by the development of social science in countries dominated by positivism on the one hand and Marxism on the other, one would have to conclude, I think, that Comte had a better claim to be an advocate of scientific method than his political opponents. His quarrel was with ideology—Thomism, Marxism, Natural Rights, whatever the "metaphysical doctrine" might be called. Though he did not see the ideology in his own position (he called "progress" a law), he insisted, not on the rightness of his political views, but on the conditions optimal for science: freedom of inquiry and orderly social change by the experimental method. In this he proved a better spokesman of science—armchair philosopher and conservative though he was—than his more violent adversaries on the left.

MODERN POSITIVISM

Positivism is still a potent doctrine today, though it is now more commonly called *scientism*. It may be recognized by four main characteristics: (1) a doctrinaire application to man of "objective" methods, such as tests, scales, statistics; and strong preference for naturalistic, mechanistic or mathematical models instead of humanistic studies; (2) value-neutrality, insisting on the difference in truth-value between statements of preference and fact; (3) a plea that more science—and science only—can save us; and (4) a pronounced preference for pragmatism over absolutism.

George H. Lundberg is one of the best known speakers for modern positivism. His book *Can Science Save Us?* (1961) deplores the blundering trial-and-error methods of politics up to this time. Ideas without scientific knowledge of how to realize or apply them are "pure sophistry." The real problem is not in the "hearts of men" but in a failure of men to use their brains in a particular way, "namely, the methods of science." In the predicament of the world today, "the social sciences alone can save."

> A leader, however admirable in ability and intentions, attempting to administer centrally a large society today is somewhat in the position of a pilot trying to fly the modern stratoliner without an instrument board or charts. Which is to say, it cannot be a very smooth flight. If he succeeds at all, it will be at the expense of

much wreckage of men and materials. It comes down, then, to this: Shall we put our faith in science or in something else?

If we do not use the methods of science, leaders will continue to make the same mistakes they have always made. Through the discovery of anesthetics and vaccines, a few devoted scientists have solved the problems of pain and contagion. Other researchers may resolve the social problems of today, if we will but take the "only medicine which can help us." The results of science will not come in a sudden revelation, but if we give our undivided faith to it, "we shall possess a faith more worthy of allegiance than many we have vainly followed in the past."

Freud, though some of his methods would not please Lundberg, had a remarkably similar position about giving up wishful illusions like religion and putting our trust in rational science, whatever the result:

Science is no illusion. But it would be an illusion to suppose that we could get anywhere else what it cannot give up. (1949:98)

A biochemist, Sir Francis Crick, co-discoverer of the spiral stairway pattern of DNA, states the case even more strongly:

Personally, . . . I think it regrettable that there is so much religious teaching. . . . The old, or literary culture, which was based originally on Christian values, is clearly dying, whereas the new culture, the scientific one, based on scientific values, is still in an early stage . . . although growing with great rapidity. . . . For this reason I believe that all university students should be taught a subject that might be called "The Map of Science." . . . When we do have fuller knowledge our whole picture is bound to change radically. Much that is now culturally acceptable will then seem to be nonsense. . . . Tomorrow's science is going to knock their culture right out from under them (1966).

The case for "objective" methods applied to man is succinctly made by Lundberg. So long as "operational" *definitions* (those which depend on procedures rather than subjective judgments) are used, there is nothing in the human or social realm that cannot be studied in the same way as phenomena of physics. Thoughts, memories, values, meanings, are all real if studied as facts of how people behave and feel, rather than as value-judgments. One can agree, for example, that cannibals think it is good to eat human flesh, without having to decide subjectively whether the practice is right. The test of objective reality is whether observers of varying persuasions can agree that they know:

> through sensory responses of some kind. It is true that both an iron fence and a taboo will keep men from touching an object or going to a certain place. It is also true that the taboo will have this effect only on the behavior of men conditioned to a certain culture, while the fence may have the same effect on all men. Therefore, by men in general, greater objectivity is ascribed properly to the fence. But *to the men conditioned by the given culture*, the taboo has the same degree of objectivity, the test of objectivity in either case being the observed behavior of the men. . . . The fact to keep in mind is that all existence, data, reality, or being is relative to some observer and, of course, to his frame of reference. . . . Things which all or nearly all men respond to in very much the same way, i.e., an iron fence, we call relatively objective, physical, material, tangible, etc. Things to which only relatively few, or only one, respond in the same way without special cultural conditioning are termed subjective, intangible, spiritual, etc. . . . If we develop response technics which permit the checking and corroboration of the responses to things today called intangible, they would then be tangible. . . . data within the domain of science. (1939)

A corollary of such a position in psychology is known today as behaviorism, or operant psychology, which maintains that what goes on inside the "mind" or consciousness of man is a "black box" the contents of which cannot be known scientifically because observers cannot agree; therefore objective inputs and outputs only of behavior are to be studied. Modern positivists in sociology are sometimes known as the "hard data" or "head-counting" crowd (to use a phrase of Saul Alinsky), who insist on statistical methods and have little use for essays and literary wisdom; in their intolerance for old fashioned scholarship, it seems they would bind Aristotle, Homer, and Shakespeare together and throw them off the ship of sociology, if they could; their motto being, as one devotee put it, "If you can't put it into a table, it's literature and to hell with it!"

The aversion to unreliable value judgments led Max Weber to his classic formulation of the position of "value-free" social science. In his essay, "Science As a Vocation" (1919), he says that science has no value presupposition or commitment except that it is worthwhile to try to know nature by scientific methods. It tries to state facts but not to answer questions of value or ultimate meaning. Tolstoy was right when he said, "Science is meaningless because it gives no answer to our question, the only question important for us: 'What shall we do and how shall we live'?" (What, for example, would one think if an astronomer reported that the stars were beautiful, or the moon had romantic significance for him? To say the least, it would be an anomaly, probably ludicrous. He should stick to the facts, his colleagues would say.) So Weber argued, "Politics is out of place in the lecture room," so long as one is speaking *as a scientist*. It is impossible to "plead scientifically" for any value whatever. Let prophets and demagogues advocate democracy, freedom, justice and so on. What, then, can the scientist do for practical life? He can study regularities and means of control, after which he can specify that *if* you choose such and such an end, then, according to scientific experience, you have to use such and such *means* in order to reach your goal practically. But the scientist cannot tell you whether the end justifies the means. He does not play the prophet or leader.

This powerful statement has been almost a credo for social scientists, and has helped many to steer clear of entangling political complications—at the same time earning them criticism for conservatism or aloofness from man's concerns.

The need for value-neutrality in science has been stated even more succinctly by the mathematician Henri Poincaré, who maintains that it is a *logical necessity*, because science, observing only what "is," cannot reach conclusions about something quite different, what "ought to be." Science and ethics are forever separated:

> It is not possible to have a scientific ethic, but it is no more possible to have an immoral science. And the reason is simple; it is, how shall I put it, for purely grammatical reasons.
>
> If the premises of a syllogism are both in the indicative, the conclusion will be equally in the indicative. In order for the conclusion to be put in the imperative it is necessary that at least one of the premises be in the imperative. Now the principles of science, the postulates of geometry, can only be in the indicative; experimental truths are also in this same mode, and at the foundations of the sciences there is not, cannot be, anything else. Moreover the most subtle dialectician can juggle with these principles as he wishes, combine them, pile them up on the other; all that he can derive from them will be in the indicative. He will never obtain a proposition which says: do this, or don't do that; that is to say a proposition which confirms or contradicts values (1913:223-226).

A yet more sweeping position of value-neutrality has been taken by *logical positivism*, a branch of twentieth century philosophy associated with thinkers like Ludwig Wittgenstein, Rudolph Carnap, and Bertrand Russell, though Alfred J. Ayer (1936) was perhaps its most extreme advocate. Logical positivism: (1) dismisses investigation into metaphysical and religious questions such as those of existence or being —i.e., the whole traditional realm of philosophy; (2) separates fact from value statements, and denies truth, even meaning, to the latter, including ethics; and (3) confines itself to the logical analysis of possible meanings of statements that might be tested by science. The astounding conclusion, at least in Ayer's formulation, was that since statements like "I like apples" or "You ought not to steal" are mere emotional preferences (facts about the subject) and not scientific facts about the objects they refer to, all value statements, indeed all ethics and esthetics, are meaningless. Meaningless, that is, about what is, rather than how humans would like things to be.

It is no surprise, then, that another characteristic of positivism is a deep aversion for any form of ideology and its claim of absolute truth, of being *the* view of reality. Avoiding any metaphysical claim so far as possible, positivism takes a pragmatic view of models and their truth. A model, whether atomic structure or the economist's theory of the free market, is not a likeness of reality but a vehicle by which man can think and act. All scientific models are hypotheses to be tested by prediction and observation. A model is true to the extent that it works, that is, predicts results accurately. Anything that does not help to predict may be eliminated, according to the law of parsimony, so that thought is stripped down to only that which gets results. It follows, then, that if two models of the same reality both work (the wave and particle theories of light), they are both to that degree true. So truth is relative. There is no Truth, but only a lot of little truths seeking ever more evidence. Man is forever denied—at least from science—the consolations of philosophy about ultimate being and good.

CRITIQUE OF POSITIVISM

So the effort to make an objective, pragmatic study of men, with conclusions only about what was observable, hailed by Comte as positive science which would bring progress to the world, led in the twentieth century to some uncomfortable conclusions. People felt somehow cheated by "value-free" science; while many humanists felt threatened. The scholarly world separated into what C. P. Snow called the "two cultures," (1963), one exploring the values of human life, the other rigorously pursuing the facts.

One of the most frequent charges against positivism was that of "scientism," that scientific methods were being unduly, and unfairly, extended into human life. William H. Whyte, Jr., for example, found scientism a principal tenet of the organization ethic, where scientific techniques can be extended to create an exact science for control of man. It is all right, in scientistic thought, to probe the secrets of employees by personality tests, for the sake of organizational adjustment (1956: 25-35). Another critic, Floyd W. Matson, depicted "the manipulated society," in which man had become an "alienated machine" under the study of behavioral science, with his image of himself broken by inappropriate models drawn from the natural sciences (1964). Public trust was not helped by the output of think-tanks and computerized predictions like Herman Kahn's cold logic about losses of population in various strategies of atomic war.

Deeper than the fear of manipulation was the concern as to whether democracy itself was possible, or whether the tyranny of a totalitarian state would inevitably result from the positivistic application of scientific control. Salomon took the position that the positivistic theory of progress was little more than a scientific rationalization of totalitarianism (1955). A more familiar picture is Aldous Huxley's dystopia, *Brave New World*, in which babies, raised from glass jars, are sorted genetically, some to be trained into servants obedient to a ruling class. Is this the way it would be if humanity did, indeed, follow Comte's prescription? B. F. Skinner's behavioral Utopia, *Walden Two* (1948), tried to answer this objection by depicting a community in which people are conditioned from birth to make the right ethical choices and manipulated into adjustment by benevolent managers of personal and cultural behavior. Skinner's comment on the need for manipulation in a good society is significant:

> People are manipulated, and they always have been, by their government, their church, their employers, their parents, their culture. Let's control them properly and make a happy world. . . . We experiment with technology, why not with our culture? There must be a better way (1966).

Beyond these apprehensions lies a more serious question: Does the extension of science, with its failure to give values and answers to moral questions, damage and impoverish the human spirit? Science, as has been said, disenchants the world: it introduces exciting new discoveries but takes away much of the wonder and mystery of life. The Nobel prize-winning chemist, Harold C. Urey, says for example:

> Life is not a miracle. It is a natural phenomenon, and can be expected to appear whenever there is a planet whose conditions duplicate those of the earth (1952).

Another biochemist, Dr. Fred Smith, expresses regret that science does not give "answers" that people need for meaningful living:

> As a young student at Birmingham University, and later as a teacher, I was convinced that we should be about the business of intellectual activity.... I was certain that if we could only get enough highly intelligent people together, the problems of the world could be solved, including our personal problems. I thought with my whole heart that this was the right answer.
>
> Yet I knew at the time that the intellectual approach was not sufficient; that it was not producing answers in my own life; and I also knew it was not providing answers in the lives of other people. In reality I was still searching (1965).

A sociologist speaks on behalf of theology against positivism: "Denial of metaphysics" has meant the "triumph of triviality" and a "shrinkage in scope of human experience;" modern man needs, beyond science, "signals of transcendence" to assure him that life is meaningful (Berger, 1968). University students, too, find themselves rebelling against the overemphasis upon facts in education, demanding "relevance," turning to "free universities" and exploring new life styles in a counter-culture. So the larger question is raised, can one live in a society dominated by positivism? Does not positivism, in its contempt for cherished beliefs, and in its zeal for reliable knowledge, throw the baby out with the bath water, reject that which artists, poets, mystics, and philosophers everywhere have been seeking, the good life? For those who had hoped to learn something about the good life from science, the question was, for all its emphasis upon being objective and value-free, must science be a moral imbecile?

A further critique came from the question of the effect of positivism on social action. On the one hand, it was argued that scientism was paralyzing social action, making social scientists morally sterile, causing them to abdicate their responsibility to be human beings as well as scientists. Their objectivity seemed to insulate them from outrage at continuing social problems and to absolve them from the responsibility of engaging in reform action, rather than just investigating it (Goodwin, 1971; Rubinoff, 1968). On the other hand, a problem even more serious than moral paralysis was seen by those critics of positivism who claimed that its extreme skepticism was so corrosive to meaning and belief that it contributed to the social crisis of our time, by undermining rational and encouraging irrational "movements like communism and fascism" (Joad, 1950:152).

The result of such reflections was a rather bitter conclusion among many that science had promised too much (through the impetus of positivism) and failed. The 1970s faced the fact that three centuries after the promise of Bacon many problems seemed to be worsening and the good life plainly had not come for most of mankind. Was it because science had not been given a fair chance, or because it had been tried and found wanting? Or was it because an overenthusiastic interpretation of science had exaggerated its claims and distorted its methods so that it could not produce humanly satisfying results? A social critic took note of what had "happened to the brains business" by the 1970s: The future was being studied as enthusiastically as ever, but the magic results that had been promised had not materialized, while problems were multiplying; there were bitter choices to make, such as between population growth and preserving the environment. Advanced developments like kidney machines were available only to a small minority, for the world-wide stand-

46

ard of well-being had not risen. There was an oversupply of Ph.D.s, and the universities were full of dissatisfied students. Anti-intellectualism was increasing, mainly because "the brilliant future that expertise was supposed to bring" had not materialized, and Americans who had "entrusted the future to experts" had "lost faith in their investment" (Schrag, 1971).

CONCLUSION

This discussion of positivism should result not in disappointment with scientific method, but in a clearer awareness of how its claims can be overemphasized by those who put too much faith in exact, empirical methods versus the sensibilities that are cultivated in the arts and the wisdom that comes from philosophy and the other sources to which man looks for answers to his problem of meaning. Plainly, science, from the very objectivity of its methods, is unlikely to ever supply all of such answers. Nor, apparently, can most men live without them. Thus, while positivism is not a substitute for religion and philosophy, it can supply a clearer distinction between them, and especially between ideology and science, including a clearer appreciation of how ideology can contaminate science. (Can we ever be entirely sure that what we call science is not ideology?) Surely the assumption that the application of science to human affairs automatically results in progress is gratuitous, so long as one does not know the purposes for which control and prediction will be used.

What positivism proposed was to produce a rigorously purified, value-free body of information for society, screened by scientific method rather by censors. Such reliable information would presumably allow any society to adapt most rapidly to whatever problems it had to face.

But missing was the realization, for early positivists at least, that value-free scientific information does not lead to or even support a moral

47

order, and that man cannot base social order on scientific input alone. Plainly, the enormous input of scientific information in the last century has not decreased entropy of particular societies or of the world. The units of organization may be larger, but the disorder of modern times is at least as great as at any time in history. The obvious explanation is that value-free information helps the wicked as much as the good and those who wage war just as much as those who make peace. Indeed, the better the information, the more harm the "wicked" can do. Further, the proportion of value-free information to values seems to have increased in modern times, crowding out value-judgments, as it were. There is little deliberate communication and teaching of values today, beyond what occurs in the accidents of "attitude-transmission," and even these are discounted to the status of mere attitudes. The moral claims of the state, church, and community become mere rhetoric. So, in the midst of enormous overloads of information (Klapp, 1972), we find fewer reliable values to which man can look for guidance.

Will further input of reliable information by science remedy such a situation? In all fairness, one can only answer that despite the century of enthusiasm since Comte, Lundberg was right to this extent: Science has not yet had a fair chance, since no society has wholeheartedly tried to apply scientific method to its problems. Moreover, it is unforeseeable what higher values may come from science.

We are, however, entitled to make one conclusion on present evidence: Knowledge of science has failed to make men good. Judging by men of today, whether ordinary men or savants, it seems plain that however one defines a good man—moral, loving, wise, just—no amount of scientific knowledge that he may acquire will assure that he will be better than he was before. It is just as easy to be selfish, aggressive, cowardly, even foolish, with science as without it. Indeed, with science one can kill in larger numbers and more accurately. In other words, scientific information does not have much to do with virtue. If Socrates or Jesus had had an M.I.T. education and computers, they would not be better men than they were without such things. Nor is there any sign

48

that well-being and happiness have increased for man from more scientific information, as Condorcet believed they would. Prosperity and GNP are not equal to the well-being of men. Scientific knowledge has so far added little or nothing to human character or wisdom.

With such thoughts in mind, we are in a better position to appreciate the philosophy of the ancient Greeks, where all such dreaming about the good life began. We turn to their thought with respect, and with one especially urgent question: What was present in their conception of the rational man that failed to emerge from the scientific method?

 **4**

Order
from
Reason

Something extraordinary must have happened two thousand years ago to produce the golden age of Greece and to explain its persistence as a cultural influence on our civilization. What happened seems to have been little short of a miracle: Imagine, if you will, a North American town of about 100,000 people that harbored such a concentration of genius as Socrates, Plato and Aristotle as schoolmasters; Aeschylus, Sophocles, Euripides, and Aristophanes as playwrights for the summer theater; Pericles as mayor; Phidias as architect of public buildings; perhaps Pythagoras and Euclid as engineers and Thucydides as publisher of the local newspaper. Including these men in the same period stretches historical fact only slightly. That there could be close interaction of such minds was a rare accident leading to the most astounding development of thought in the history of mankind.*

*For background reading on this period, see Edith Hamilton, *The Greek Way* (New York: Norton, 1942) and Alvin W. Gouldner, *The Hellenic World, a Sociological Analysis* (New York: Harper and Row, 1969).

51

To try to describe such a stupendous contribution would be beyond the scope of this book, but some of the most important ideas relevant to social development may at least be listed: (1) constitutional government, that is, government by law, not men; (2) democracy; (3) systematic philosophy (versus the wisdom of thinkers like Confucius and Solomon); (4) logic; (5) the humanistic ideal of the sane, happy, healthy, good, rational man; and (6) tragedy as a dramatic art form. Perhaps the most distinctive of these was the discovery that independent reason could serve as a guide to living, individually as ethics, and socially as politics. The Greeks threw off the shackles of tradition and began to create a life for themselves, governed by what Hamilton calls their "passion for using their minds." For the development of true science, "they took the first indispensable steps:"

> The ancient world was a place of fear. Magical forces ruled it and magic is absolutely terrifying because it is absolutely incalculable. The minds of those who might have been scientists had been held fast-bound in the prison of that terror. Nothing of all the Greeks did is more astonishing than their daring to look it in the face and use their minds about it. They dared nothing less than to throw the light of reason upon dreadful powers taken completely on trust everywhere else, and by the exercise of the intelligence to banish them. Galileo, the humanists of the Renaissance, are glorified for their courage in venturing beyond the limits set. . . . The humanists ventured upon the fearful ocean of free thought under guidance. The Greeks had preceded them there. They chanced that great adventure all alone (HAMILTON, 1942:21-22).

For Socrates, Plato and Aristotle reason was not merely an exercise in thinking but an infallible method for reaching truth, a way of life leading to rule by the wise, and providing their model for the good society. Even tragedy, bloody and heart-rending though the dramas might be, was regarded by Aristotle as leading to greater rationality by purging the passions. Government was seen as a method of living more rationally together. Though the Greeks invented democracy, nothing could be more deceptive than to suppose they especially preferred it; it was not majority rule but a way of thinking—by majorities or minorities—which was their great intellectual and social contribution.

In sociological terms, it was a proposal to order institutions by reason in a way which had never been tried before. The Greeks were the first to propose that all information entering social policy should be sifted through an intellectual testing process that would separate the wheat of truth and good from the chaff of opinion and self-interest. I do not refer merely to the institution of discussion or debate, whether by elders or judges or rabbis or swamis or senators or people as a whole, but to a much more rigorous procedure, discovered and demonstrated by Socrates, that might easily be lacking from democratic processes, and from education.*

This chapter will undertake to explain briefly what the Greeks meant by the life of reason as a way of encoding information into ethics and politics in order to create a social harmony to equal the aesthetic harmony of the Parthenon.

IDEAL OF THE RATIONAL MAN

The Greek way, if it can be described in a phrase, is the life of a rational man. As a doctrine, it is called *rationalism*, faith in the power of reason to free, guide, and save man. As a method, it is *reason*, a distinctive way of thinking which applies standards of logical consistency and balance to all ideas and decisions. The rational man was their ideal, for which the first model was Socrates, who might be called the patron saint of reason.

This is plainly a doctrine of the "head," not the "heart." What is good? Why should anybody be good? Not because the elders say so

*This stress on Socrates' discovery does not, of course, ignore the wisdom attained by other ways of education, for example, Talmudic or Vedantic.

53

or because one's feelings so incline, but because in the light of knowledge it is the most *reasonable* way to act over the long run. Knowledge is virtue, said Socrates. There is a marked analogy between Jesus and Socrates: Both were saintly figures, God-inspired, and both died as martyrs. But the difference is equally clear: The former was the perfect model of love, the latter of reason. Socrates had more than other good men (more perhaps even than Moses, Confucius, Buddha, Mohammed, Gandhi, or St. Francis) of what the Greeks called intellectual virtue.

So contemporary humanists state their support of the ideal of the rational man:

> A man should make up his mind with emphasis as to what he rationally believes, and should never allow contrary irrational beliefs to pass unchallenged or obtain a hold over him, however brief (BERTRAND RUSSELL, *The Conquest of Happiness*, 1943).

> A man with whom one cannot reason is a man to be feared (ALBERT CAMUS).

> You cannot show me that self-sacrifice may not become a vice, that pity does not need, like other passions, to be held within rational bounds. It is still reason, it is still intelligence, that rules (MAX EASTMAN, 1961).

But the essence of the Greek contribution is not the man as model but the method. How does one become a good man? By learning moral rules? By using one's conscience? By associating with good people? Here we must look at Socrates as a teacher, for it was he who discovered the *dialectic*, the rational method for making men good. By inventing and using this he became one of the world's greatest teachers. One of the peculiarities of his method was that he did not teach anything except what emerged from the student's own mind. Do not imagine him with one foot on a doric pedestal giving a lecture. His teaching was a roving encounter with anyone who would talk long enough to have an argument. Do you want to learn from Socrates? First you must say what you think, then agree to answer questions. Here is an example of his method, as described by Plato in his *Republic*.

An argument about the nature of justice is taking place among Socrates and his friends. Thrasymachus, a famous Sophist, appears. After listening awhile, he can stand it no longer and breaks in upon the argument, rebuking the talkers for being fools. Socrates, with typical mock humility, invites Thrasymachus to set them straight:

> Thrasymachus ... don't be hard upon us. Polemarchus and I may have been guilty of a little mistake ... but I can assure you that the error was not intentional.... Why, when we are seeking for justice, a thing more precious than ... gold, do you say that we are weakly yielding to one another and not doing our utmost to get at the truth? Nay, my good friend, we are most willing and anxious to do so, but the fact is that we cannot. And if so, you people who know all things should pity us and not be angry with us.

Thrasymachus, however, is cautious in taking the bait. He asks for money and sets conditions under which he will teach:

> What if I give you an answer about justice other and better ... than any of these? What do you deserve to have done to you?
> Done to me!—as becomes the ignorant, I must learn from the wise—that is what I deserve to have done to me.

Thrasymachus yields but with further misgivings:

> Yes ... and then Socrates will do as he always does—refuse to answer himself, but take and pull to pieces the answer of someone else.
> Why, my good friend, I said, how can anyone answer who knows and says that he knows, just nothing.... The natural thing is, that the speaker should be someone like yourself who professes to know and can tell what he knows. Will you then kindly answer, for the edification of the company and of myself? ...
> Listen, then, he said; I proclaim that justice is nothing else than the interest of the stronger.

The argument is too long to describe in full, but we can give enough to show the method by which Socrates then demolishes stone by stone the position taken by Thrasymachus.

> We are both agreed that justice is interest of some sort, but you go on to say "of the stronger;" about this addition I am not so sure, and must therefore consider further.
>
> Proceed.
>
> I will; and first tell me, do you admit that it is just for subjects to obey their rulers?
>
> I do.
>
> But are the rulers of states absolutely infallible, or are they sometimes liable to err?
>
> To be sure, he replied, they are liable to err.
>
> Then in making their laws they may sometimes make them rightly, and sometimes not?
>
> True.
>
> When they make them rightly, they make them agreeably to their interest; when they are mistaken, contrary to their interest; you admit that?
>
> Yes.
>
> And the laws which they make must be obeyed by their subjects —and that is what you call justice?
>
> Doubtless.
>
> Then justice, according to your argument, is not only obedience to the interest of the stronger but the reverse?
>
> What is that you are saying? he asked.
>
> I am only repeating what you are saying, I believe. But let us consider: Have we not admitted that the rulers may be mistaken about their own interest in what they command, and also that to obey them is justice? Has not that been admitted?
>
> Yes.
>
> Then you must also have acknowledged justice not to be for the interest of the stronger, when the rulers unintentionally command things to be done which are to their own injury (*Republic*, I, Jowett translation).

So appears the first crack in Thrasymachus' position. Later in the argument, we hear Socrates summarizing what Thrasymachus has admitted:

> Then ... no physician, insofar as he is a physician, considers his own good in what he prescribes, but the good of his patient; for the true physician is also a ruler having the human body as a subject, and is not a mere money-maker; that has been admitted?
> Yes.
> And the pilot likewise, in the strict sense of the term, is a ruler of sailors and not a mere sailor.
> That has been admitted.
> And such a pilot and ruler will provide and prescribe for the interest of the sailor who is under him, and not for his own or the ruler's interest?
> He gave a reluctant "Yes."
> Then ... Thrasymachus, there is no one in any rule who, insofar as he is a ruler, considers or enjoins what is for his own interest, but always what is for the interest of his subject or suitable to his art; to that he looks, and that alone he considers in everything which he says and does.
> When we had got to this point in the argument ... everyone saw that the definition of justice had been completely upset. ...

Thrasymachus then becomes angry and begins to insult Socrates. After awhile, he settles down and answers further questions. Finally, Socrates sums up what truth he has gained from the reluctant lips of Thrasymachus:

> We have admitted that justice is the excellence of the soul, and injustice the defect of the soul?
> That has been admitted.
> Then the just soul and the just man will live well, and the unjust man will live ill?
> That is what your argument proves.
> And he who lives well is blessed and happy, and he who lives ill the reverse of happy?

Certainly.

Then the just is happy, and the unjust miserable?

So be it.

But happiness and not misery is profitable.

Of course.

Then, my blessed Thrasymachus, injustice can never be more profitable than justice.

So we see that the great teaching method invented by Socrates, the dialectic, was a way of testing the logical consistency of propositions, in which one does not teach by giving answers but by asking questions. Education is a perpetual cross-examination on what one *thinks* one knows (opinion), till one reaches a view that holds up, on which questioner, answerer and listeners can agree (knowledge). So one's views become sound and one grows wise. Not only are the views sound, but equally important for education, they are one's own because drawn from one's own reasoning.*

So we see that the dialectic was a kind of acid bath for the purification of thought by eliminating dross to get gold. A true dialectician submits himself as well as others to cross-examination. This distinguishes his method from mere logical trickery in order to win, which is called *sophistry*. His goal is not victory but truth. To learn he will take a beating, or give the student one for his own good. Socrates would not even use sophistry to win his own case when his life was at stake during his trial by the Athenian assembly (Plato, *Apology*). The dialectician admits ignorance early and often, knowing that humility is the beginning of knowledge.

Socrates felt it his duty to sting his fellow citizens into self-criticism, finally to wisdom: "I am the gadfly God has attached to this city" (*Apology*). That the Athenians failed to appreciate Socrates' mission is evident from the fact that they finally put him to death. To understand

---

*A startling example is the way Socrates leads an illiterate slave boy to demonstrate the Pythagorean theorem (Plato, *Meno*).

this, one must take into account not only the few of Socrates' students, such as Alcibiades, who did make political trouble but the hundreds he must have humbled in order to make wise.

Plato, Socrates' most famous student, idealized his dead master and the results of his method. It was a way of ascending from one level of knowledge to another, a stairway to Truth that becomes ever stronger and more abstract, until one reaches the realm of absolute ideas, such as perfect beauty and justice. Only dialectic can lead us to these ideas, because we live imprisoned in appearances—the surface of things as represented by the senses. Here we turn to Plato's great metaphor of the cave. The world may be likened to an underground cave, in which men are chained so that they can look only at a wall on which shadows are thrown from the light of a fire. Unable to move their heads, they cannot imagine the light they would see if they went to the entrance of the cave. They think that these murky shadows are all the truth there is to see. But if they could go into the daylight of reason, they would at first be dazzled, but then would see better than ever before. Socrates explains the allegory:

> The prison-house is the visible world, the light of the fire is the sun ... the journey upwards ... the ascent of the soul into the intellectual world.... In the world of knowledge the idea of good appears last of all, and is seen only with an effort; and, when seen, is also inferred to be the universal author of all things beautiful and right, parent of light ... and the immediate source of reason and truth in the intellectual; and ... this is the power upon which he who would act rationally either in public or private life must have his eyes fixed.... Moreover ... you must not wonder that those who attain to this beatific vision are unwilling to descend to human affairs; for their souls are ever hastening into the upper world where they desire to dwell ... (Republic, VII).

This passage has caused many to regard Plato as a mystic, but it should be noted that the stairway is reason, not meditation or intuition.

Plato's most important student, Aristotle, formalized reason as logic, a set of rules for arriving at true statements by means of the syllogism, a triangular structure of thought consisting of two premises leading to a conclusion:

> A syllogism is discourse in which, certain things being stated, something or other than what is stated follows of necessity from their being so.... A perfect syllogism ... needs nothing other than what has been stated to make plain what necessarily follows...(*Prior Analytics*).

For example, all men are mortal; Socrates is a man; therefore Socrates will die. Aristotle distinguished two forms of dialectical reasoning: *deductive* in which certain conclusions are drawn from accepted premises (for example, mathematics); and *inductive*, which infers universal principles from clearly known particulars. So was born logic, the basis of modern philosophy, mathematics, science, and law—all systematic theory.

Now we are in a position to understand what the Greeks meant by a man of intellectual virtue: He was the man who had climbed the rigorous stairway of dialectic, had found the good and the true, and was securely in command of what he knew.

SUMMUM BONUM

Aristotle drew out the implications of Socrates' teachings in his *Ethics*. A man who knows the good naturally will choose it. The more he knows and chooses of the good, the better he is. The obvious pleasures are not the highest, for the good man rules himself by reason to reach higher levels of virtue, such as occupational skill, art, good government, although these may require giving up lesser pleasures. Of prime importance is moderation, finding the golden mean: acting out of courage rather than out of bravado or cowardice, for example. Men should be like archers who aim with their reason not at a variety of targets but at a supreme good which includes all the others in measure. This supreme virtue is not profit, honor, sensual enjoyment, love, or any other particular good, but happiness over the entire span of life. Virtues are merely skills of working for the good. Only the rational man, who aims most carefully and has all the requisite virtues, can hope to hit the supreme target through his whole life:

> We . . . call happy the man who works in the way of perfect virtue, and is furnished with external goods sufficient for acting his part . . . during no ordinary period but such as constitutes a complete life (*Ethics*, I).

Bad fortune does not destroy the happiness of a good man, for he carries the virtue of reason within himself: "no one of the blessed can ever become wretched, because he will never do those things which are hateful and mean. For the man who is truly good and sensible bears all fortunes . . . and always does what is noblest under the circumstances, just as a good general employs to the best advantage the force he has with him; or a good shoemaker makes the handsomest shoe he can out of the leather which has been given to him."

Reason is like a gyroscope, enabling a man to right himself and keep to a course in spite of passions and turbulent circumstances. So long as reason is at the helm, the best course will be set. Human excellence has two forms: intellectual (scientific, theoretical, and practical knowledge), and moral (self-mastery according to knowledge). Together they make wisdom.

We shall understand the Greek formula, knowledge equals virtue equals happiness, if we visualize three rings, containing, respectively, knowledge, goodness, and happiness. When the first two coincide, that is, when the good is known and all knowledge is used for the good, then the third must also. But, where knowledge is used for evil, or the good is unknown or disregarded in folly, then there can be no happiness. That a person could be both wicked and happy or foolish and happy the Greeks would have denied vigorously.

For the Greeks, leisure was necessary to make a good man, because beyond all the skills and habits of self-mastery, there remains the task of acquiring theoretical knowledge called philosophy or contemplation. According to Plato and Aristotle (and surely according to the practice of Socrates) contemplation was the highest activity in which man could indulge, beyond economics, ethics, politics. Since man is the rational animal, said Aristotle, he perfects himself best by reason:

> The life according to reason is best and pleasantest, since reason more than anything else *is* man. This life therefore is also the happiest (*Ethics,* X).

Similar reasoning would have been used by Plato to justify the economically unproductive life of Socrates, who loved philosophy so much he did not even collect a fee for his teaching.

In spite of all that can be adduced in support of leisure as a condition for the life of philosophy, there remains a fundamental North American suspicion of any program of education which puts thinking for its own sake ahead of practical action. Doubtless, some of this comes from the heritage of frontier hard work and a Puritanism which equated idleness with vice. Another source of distrust of the philosopher is the suspicion that he might be a leisured aristocrat, enjoying privileges that the ordinary man could not share.

THE FIRST UTOPIA

What the ideal of the rational man means politically we see most clearly in Plato's crowning work, the *Republic,* the first Utopia, which has influenced thinkers down to the present time, and has given rise to a line of Utopias created by such men as Augustine, More, Rousseau, the Federalists, Marx, Bellamy, Aldous Huxley, and B. F. Skinner, all of whom draw, favorably or unfavorably, from Plato.* His central question is still relevant: If the government is the largest enterprise, requiring the greatest wisdom, then why don't the wise rule? What would happen if they did? Plato could think of no way to bring this about in reality, so he created an imaginary society for men to look at. It was, as he felt, justice written large, where it could be seen as a social whole. Plato felt that justice was not an individual relationship, such as equality of sharing, but a proportion of parts. Like the balance of a cathedral, it was an architectonic conception of justice which could be seen best in a perfectly designed society. Who should run it? Those with the best grasp of the highest concepts of good, philosophers of course.

His Utopia was a small society, indeed a mere town, perhaps 5,000 citizens. It might be called an aristocracy of intellect, for the selection of rulers was by education, not inheritance. The most perfect men and women—wise, brave, temperate and just—were to be selected from those who were most successful in school.

> There must be a selection. Let us note among the guardians those who in their whole life show the greatest eagerness to do what is for the good of their country, and the greatest repugnance to do what is against her interests.... The interest of the state is to be the rule of their lives. We must watch them from their youth upwards, and make them perform actions in which they are most likely to forget or to be deceived, and he who remembers and is not deceived is to be selected, and he who fails in the trial is to be rejected (*Republic*, III).

The guardians were to be subdivided into rulers or soldiers, depending upon whether their strong point was wisdom or merely courage. The rest would be workers and tradesmen. We might imagine an elementary

*See Charles M. Andrews, ed., *Famous Utopias* (New York: Tudor Publishing Co.); also P. Goodman (1947); Boguslaw (1965).

school with teachers selecting the promising pupils and sending them on to appropriate careers. So Plato's *Republic* was intended to separate people into the three classes to which they were best suited. The fairness was not in the equality of education but in the rigor with which selection standards were applied in order to choose the best. It was no easy curriculum: Up to the age of about twenty they were to receive the traditional Greek education, including physical culture and music; for the next ten years came what might be called a liberal arts curriculum of mathematics, logic, grammar, and rhetoric; after that five years of practical experience; then at about age thirty-five, the few who were to become philosophers were called back for fifteen years of intellectual training, until at the ripe age of fifty they were judged fit to rule and join the elite.

To keep the philosophers from favoring their own children, Plato ordained that they should have marriage in common, so that no father would know which children were his. Such children would be raised communally so that they would not know who their parents were. In this way Plato hoped to prevent his Republic from deteriorating into an ordinary class system.

Clearly it was not equal. Was it fair? That was the crucial question? Was it a heaven for the few and a workhouse for the many? Here the answer was not easy. The lower classes had the money and the pleasures of business, property, and normal family life. The guardians lived austerely, like monks or soldiers perpetually on guard duty, with no joy in their own children. It may be asked, what good are power and status if one does not have money, luxury, and children to pass them on to? In contrast to the rollicking good times of the common people in this perfect society, we must imagine the guardians enjoying only service to the state and the study of philosophy. So it is hard to make a case that this was a heaven for the few, unless one believes, as Plato did, that justice and philosophy are heavenly.

With respect to the distribution of power, it was a benevolent despotism, with wise and well-meaning rulers changing laws at will and exercising the power of life or death, deciding who shall marry, selecting children, censoring books, and deceiving the people when it seemed for the good of the state, rather as might a physician keep certain information from a patient. Is this bad? It depends upon how much one trusts his doctor—Plato trusted his guardians very much.

Is there anything in the government of the United States which even approximates the Republic? Its closest approach is the Supreme Court, that group of nine men, appointed for life, immune to criticism, who have absolute power to negate the will of either the President or the Congress when they judge it to be in conflict with the Constitution. While they do not make the highest laws, as did Plato's guardians, they can prevent anyone, except a large majority, from changing them.

To understand why Plato put so much faith in the few rather than the many, we must see that for him justice was the result of a rare wisdom, a lofty sense of harmony in affairs achieved by reason. A simple rule, like equal shares to each, or an eye for an eye, would not require wisdom. Majorities easily make such judgments. But the situation changes if we assume that justice is a complex judgment, and that it very often requires a person to decide against himself or the interests of his friends. We know that not everyone has such qualities; indeed, such justice may be exquisitely rare. The just man, for example, finding a large amount of money on the street, returns it to its owner, as did a janitor in Los Angeles. After the story of his honesty was printed in the newspapers, he was overwhelmed by letters ridiculing his stupidity. Such responses suggest, perhaps, what the majority thinks of a fine sense of justice. How many can be counted on to be just when they do not have to? Plato's view is given by the remarkable story of Gyges, the shepherd, who wandered into a cave and found a gold ring. He was astonished to find that if he turned the ring around on his finger, it made him invisible. With this new-found power, he set off on a career in which he seduced the queen, killed the king, and took over the kingdom (Republic, II). In such a situation, how many could be trusted not to do as Gyges did is Plato's implied question. Who is the most common, Gyges or Socrates? If you say Gyges (with perhaps the popular treatment of the honest janitor in mind), then it is difficult to see how you can put faith in majorities, unless they are hedged with all sorts of safeguards and police powers, which, in turn, raise their own questions of trust. In any case, safeguards could not check the total will of a sovereign people. Plainly, Plato believed that justice is rare, like the skill of the physician or the great artist; he put his trust in the properly selected few.

THE GREEKS AND DEMOCRACY

Paradoxically, then, the Athenians invented democracy but their greatest philosophers after Socrates were less than enthusiastic about it. Plato despised majority opinion and believed that wisdom and justice were possible only for the few. To his mind, democracy was a degenerate form of government which tended to follow oligarchy, or rule by the selfish few whose excesses of demagoguery in turn brought on tyranny (*Republic*, VIII). Aristotle, however, recognized three good forms of government: monarchy, aristocracy, and constitutional government; and three perverse forms: tyranny, oligarchy, and democracy, or rule by popular will (*Politics*, III). Both Plato and Aristotle accepted natural inequality, including slavery, as a fact of life. By contrast, their teacher Socrates was almost a perfect democrat: Without pride himself, he humbled all others before the test of truth. His whole life was devoted to the hope of educating every man to the level where he might be fit to rule. And he accepted the popular vote, even when it meant his own death.

The most severe criticism against Plato was made by Karl Popper (1952), who charged that he was a totalitarian. Unlike Socrates, who was "the champion of the open society and a friend of democracy," Plato, according to Popper, betrayed Socrates by his "grandiose effort to construct the theory of the arrested society" (191-194).

66

Plato recognizes only one ultimate standard, the interest of the state. . . . This is the collectivist, the tribal, the totalitarian theory of morality (107).

But, Popper concedes, Plato was a "sincere" totalitarian:

His ideal was not the maximum exploitation of the working classes by the upper class; it was the stability of the whole (108).

Both Plato and Aristotle rejected the individualistic and equalitarian concept of justice in favor of a "holistic" one, the health of the state. (91). With the *Republic*, Plato

spread doubt and confusion among equalitarians and individualists who, under the influence of his authority, began to ask themselves whether his idea of justice was not truer and better than theirs. . . . Equalitarianism was his arch-enemy, and he was out to destroy it (92-93).

While there is little doubt that Plato despised the masses, we should temper this observation with the reflection that the popular vote condemning his master Socrates was a powerful reason for his bitterness. Also, somewhat offsetting Popper's charge against Plato is the fact that the majority is capable in its collective will, legally or by informal pressure, of exerting a tyranny as bad as that of any dictator, as de Tocqueville noted in his famous study of democracy in America (1840). The treatment of American Negroes in the South is an example. Thus in the face of tyranny of the majority, rule by a wise minority takes on a more attractive light.

To understand Plato's aversion for popular government, one should understand that he lacked the concept of limited or constitutional government, in which all citizens including rulers are restrained by natural and human law as John Locke believed. In such a conception, sovereign authority could never reside in a man, however wise, but only in a law, no matter who invoked it, rich or poor, learned or ignorant.

Plato's contempt for the crowd of Athens was translated 2000 years later into Le Bon's description of the crowd mind (1895); and Ortega's alarm at the masses spilling over Europe with their new claims and governments (1932). To Ortega, the issue was "standards" of civilization versus mass appetites which would bring in (as did democracy in Plato's theory) demagogues (totalitarian leaders) pandering to the debased tastes of an uneducated multitude.

A different effort to sketch the implications of Plato's thought is found in projections of what modern methods of control (technology, neurology, etc.) would lead to in the hands of modern guardians, including the Utopias like those of Bellamy (1926) and Skinner (1948) and dystopias like those of Huxley (1932) and Orwell (1949).

For those who believe, as with Plato and with Locke, that the key to a good society is reason, the crucial question remains: How (far) can rationality be distributed? As we shall see, a vast step separates the Greeks and Locke on this point. According to Locke, justice was distributed equally to all men by natural law; whereas to the Greeks, it was a rare quality perfected only in the wise. According to Locke, since the encoding of virtue (justice) occurred by nature, the state could be a mere umpire in ruling on the claims of citizens. But, according to the Greeks, virtue is not natural; but making men good by reason is a function of education, presumably by the state. Since justice does not result from nature, it must be the product of some fairly complex institution designed to nurture it. So we see the crucial difference between Locke and Plato is whether the average level of rationality in decision (to which the majority are equal) is sufficient to produce a good society. Locke's answer is that natural justice, distributed equally, does not depend on education, age, ability or wisdom. But Plato's is that justice depends on extraordinary wisdom, which must by definition be cultivated in and restricted to an elite. The only way out of this is to suppose that a just society can come from some ordinary ordering process that does not require a high level of personal virtue, for example, divine provi-

68

dence, magic, natural law, or a market mechanism in which bargaining of buyers and sellers or candidates and voters leads to a "fair" outcome. A step further is the romantic notion of Rousseau, that the social order is *inferior* to the general will of equal citizens—which is almost the opposite extreme from that of Le Bon, who feared the crowd mind.

SOME RESULTS OF REASON IN SOCIAL ORDER

In 1887, a German sociologist, Ferdinand Toennies, made what is perhaps the most fundamental and sweeping statement about what it means to introduce reason into social order on a large scale. Known as the theory of *Gesellschaft*, it provides a basis of most later sociological thinking about cities, large-scale organization, bureaucracy, and mass society. The key to Toennies' theory is the distinction between *natural* and *rational will*. Natural will is the feeling that grows from living together in close-knit groups (*Gemeinschaft*), such as loyalty, kinship obligation, respect for elders, love and "we-feeling." Rational will develops from the effort to persuade and argue with people outside of one's own group. In dealing with strangers one cannot appeal to their friendship and loyalty; rather, one must be more objective, using logic directed toward often alien individual interests (what you want, not necessarily what I want). Toennies sees all social interaction as falling in one category or the other, or in some point between the two (as in the "pattern variables" of Parsons, 1951). In situations where *Gemeinschaft* predominates, parties appeal to each other on the basis of consensual claims such as loyalty, friendship, and duty. Where the *Gesellschaft* predominates, they bargain, and ultimately manipulate each other by calculated efforts to get the other to cooperate in order to obtain what each regards as his own interest, mutualized in a contract perhaps. Economic, political, and urban order grows out of these numerous deals among strangers trading outside their *Gemeinschaft* in the larger society. The aggregate term for such deals (including educational, religious and recreational interaction) is *market*: an arena or institution in which values are set by prices people are willing to pay for what others are willing to sell. Political candidates, creeds, works of art—all become market-items, priced, packaged and sold. Even personality has a market (Mills, 1951). Instead of *Gemeinschaft* morality and tradition, public opinion reflected in prices and votes becomes the measure of collective will. Obviously, *Gesellschaft* as the society of rational will is very different from what either Plato or Aristotle visualized. They were *Gemeinschaft*-oriented (paternalistic, concerned with loyalty and the good of members of a small society); but *Gesellschaft* is manipulative, a relationship among strangers, carrying little or no obligation except legality, and permitting exploitation within the limits of what the parties legally agree to. This point is crucial in understanding Plato's guardians, for in a benevolent *Gemeinschaft* they might work; but in *Gesellschaft*, with its lack of obligation and its manipulative orientation, this is very doubtful, and takes us into the thought of Machiavelli (discussed in Chapter VI). Most of the horrors of totalitarianism envisioned by critics of Plato require, in fact, a *Gesellschaft*, however disguised as *Gemeinschaft*. Nor could Plato have been expected to appreciate fully the different kind of rationality that would emerge from the free market of goods and ideas. Nor, for that matter, could Locke, with his belief in natural justice.

Another result of rationality for social order is seen in *bureaucracy*, as the German sociologist Max Weber depicted it (1946), a melancholy caricature of the *Republic*. The "wise men" are officials, legally authorized to direct the functions of the organization. Rules and orders trickle down from the top in Kafkaesque style,* to officials not knowing the full

*Kafka's novel *The Castle* (1954) is an allegory of this situation.

meaning of the directives outside their strictly delimited area of competence and discretion. The average man is in the chains of a machine for which he is trained, whose slots are made to fit him; but the wise man is nowhere to be found.

Yet another view of the results of rationality is found in Freud's *Civilization and Its Discontents* (1958), which argues that man's instincts are frustrated by the restraints of reason, and that Aristotle's perfected self-mastery more often consists of repression and neurosis.

THE GREEK SYSTEMIC MODEL

Our discussion of Greek reason should leave us with an appreciation of the peculiar difficulties that stand in the way of constructing a good social system. The Greeks proposed that social encoding such as laws and institutions take place through Socrates' dialectical process, so that by excluding error and mere opinion, the highest knowledge (wisdom) of the best social order (justice) would be attained. This filtering process was to be carried out by an elite of philosophers already wise and virtuous. But they never explained how to put the wise into command, to prevent the system from falling away from justice and lapsing into tyranny.

Nor did they appreciate the problems of a changing open system. They produced a model of a consistent and stable but closed system, stressing wholeness and balance—the first equilibrium theory. Table 2 summarizes the differences between the Greek ideal system and contemporary society.

Nor did the Greeks really tell us how virtue is taught, still less how a rational order will produce *good* men. The psychology of Freud and the sociology of Max Weber are enough to throw doubt on the moral

Table 2   COMPARISON OF PLATONIC AND CONTEMPORARY
VIEWS OF SOCIETY

Plato's Ideal System	*The System of Today*
Small, closed, tribalistic society.	Emerging humanism, "one world," challenging nationalistic states.
World of "we" surrounded by barbarians (ethnocentrism).	Total eco-system (world) including international society (open sub-systems).
Self-contained system.	Interdependent world system.
Need for defense, boundary maintenance, mutual caution and closure.	Need for communication across boundaries, demilitarization, world security.
Education as consensus: reinforcing cohesiveness within.	Education as dialectic: give and take of different views between outsiders and insiders.
Oral communication system.	Media communication system.
Closed system maintaining equilibrium (homeostasis) by controlling inputs.	Open system, growing by negotiating large inputs of new information from outside, in favorable tradeoff with entropy.*
Conservatism: Group memory more important in wisdom than new input.	Modernism: New input and change a larger part of wisdom than tradition.

*The attack on Socrates itself was a homeostatic response, an ingrouping closing the door against inimical ideas (see Chapter 1). Must one then conclude that Socrates' role was entropic, or that Athenians made a mistake in not appreciating the tradeoff bargain which he offered?

products of rationalization. We still have no scientific or other institutionalized criterion of wisdom, while after the strictures of positivism, there is some doubt that virtue is knowledge at all.

What the Greeks hoped for from reason was a man made wise and good by knowledge. Science, by contrast, has tended to produce specialists who have given up the search for final answers and *summa bona*. Science has a high professional ethic, but there is little reason to suppose that this spreads into general morality and happiness. That is, science has not brought the three rings of knowledge, goodness, and happiness together. Nor have philosophers, those lovers of wisdom for whom the Greeks had such high hopes, fared much better.

As a result of this seeming failure of knowledge to produce good men, some people have begun to argue that it is environments and systems, not the quality of thinking and inner life, that must be improved if man is to become better or have a better life (Skinner, 1971).

So we are left with the question of what a well-planned society, with knowledge-elite armed with expertise and computers, will produce, whether Huxley's *Brave New World* or Skinner's *Walden II*, or something more pleasant. Will intellectuals vindicate themselves, given time, and opportunity?

It must be admitted that Plato's hope for harmony appeals today to a troubled world in which pluralism, mobility, urban sprawl, and planless change have turned into "future shock" (Toffler, 1970) and ecological crisis. The environmental movement today clearly shows the need for a larger systems approach to replace wanton spoiling of resources. The phantom of elitism is not enough to suppress recognition of this need for a systems approach. In other words, alternatives are not simply totalitarianism or laissez-faire—there is much in between. Plato was the first who saw society in holistic system terms—"justice written large." Since the scale is vaster than ever today, perhaps it follows that the need for wisdom or science at the top is also greater than ever.

The point is that the study of systems need not impose a tyranny on man or nature, but aims at a balance optimal for both. In the short run, system design may produce "machines" which are destructive of the environment and man, as the present century proves. But it is already plain that in the long run the study of systems leads to greater respect for the environment and through feedback to greater responsiveness on the part of culture and technology to all human needs.

5

Order from Above

We have described two efforts to create a higher order in human affairs than that which comes from the fiat of leaders or the weight of tradition. With reason, the mind can discover its own laws and reach new truths; with science, man can explore the objective world by inductive and experimental methods. Is there any need for methods other than those of science or reason? Positivists and rationalists would say no. Their faith is expressed in Julian Huxley's famous metaphor likening the universe to a gigantic chess game, in which man moves his pieces of knowledge against an unseen but not unkindly opponent, who permits man to stay in the game so long as he plays by the rules and discovers new ones.

Today, however, few beyond the most sanguine positivists are content to believe that better mandates for man come directly and solely through the language of science. The majority rely on some kind of religion to supply guidance that sheer reason and science cannot give. And there is growing interest in parascience (ESP, telekinesis, etc.)—a spectrum of experience still difficult to define and explore. Another of these dark areas is creativity. By definition, creativity is a solution, a better pattern, which we neither know beforehand nor expect. Creativity proves conclusively to man that there is a source of higher order in his mind which he does not understand and cannot control by reason. No amount of data gathered from the objective world falls into a better pattern except by creativity.

We may call this source of higher order *negative entropy*, a term which can serve skeptics and believers alike, and does not contradict anything which science or higher religions have said. In such terms, religion has always been a way of accounting for negative entropy beyond the ken of man, whether from outside or from within himself.

Throughout history, so many people have been awed by this sense of a higher source of order that they have formed cults to worship it and become more closely attuned with it. The sociology of religion, as in the works of Max Weber and Emile Durkheim, explores the effects on social order of belief in law from above. What happens when men take heaven seriously enough to incorporate it into their worldly order? There is more than one answer to such a question, even within Christian thought. In fact, this chapter will be a story of what sociologists call "accommodation."

OTHERWORLDLINESS, EAST AND WEST

Accommodation is an effort by reason or social arrangements to relieve a tension which comes from incompatible elements in a system. For example, if a large number of head-hunters were suddenly to arrive in Kansas, arrangements would have to be made to reduce possible conflicts between the newcomers and the natives, more constructive than merely fighting and defeating them. Similarly, if there is a belief in a society which does not square with the way people actually live, a tension will arise that some people will try to relieve by new arrangements. For example, ritual might be performed to obtain forgiveness from higher powers for the discrepancy that has been allowed to exist. Doctrines might be advanced explaining why all do not have to live up to the same high standards. Such activities would be called accommodations.

Max Weber was the first to go extensively into the options open to a society suffering from tension from otherworldly conceptions. Not every religion has a "beyond" as a "locus of definite promises." For most early religions, the sacred values were "quite solid goods of this world," such as health, a long life, and wealth. At the opposite extreme are "salvation religions" like Christianity which live in "a permanent state of tension in relation to the world," because they have not only heaven but hell to worry about (Weber, 1946: 277, 328). So Bellah notes that during the first millenium B.C., however, a world-rejecting orientation emerged "all across the Old World." It was

> characterized by an extremely negative evaluation of man and society and the exaltation of another realm of reality as alone true and infinitely valuable. . . . Plato's classic formulation in the *Phaedo* [is] that the body is the tomb or prison of the soul. . . . In Israel . . . the world is profoundly devalued in the face of the transcendent God with whom alone is there any refuge or comfort. In India . . . [is found] perhaps the most radical of all versions of world rejection, culminating in the great image of the Buddha. . . . In China, Taoist ascetics urged . . . withdrawal from human society. . . . For over two thousand years great pulses of world rejection spread over the civilized world. The *Qur'an* compares this present world to vegetation . . . which withers away and becomes as straw. . . . Primitive religions are on the whole oriented to a single cosmos; they know nothing of a wholly different world relative to which the actual world is utterly devoid of value. They are concerned with the maintenance of personal, social and cosmic harmony and with

> attaining specific goods—rain, harvest, children, health. . . . The
> overriding goal of salvation that dominates the world-rejecting re-
> ligions is almost absent in primitive religion (BELLAH, 1970:22-28),

Not all religions with an otherworldly concept are equally uncomfortable in relation to it. To take a familiar example, the Graeco-Roman
gods entertained a fairly easy relation to the world of men. They left
men on a long leash, so to speak. When the gods did intervene in human
affairs, it was often capriciously, and it was even harder to tell right from
wrong when both sides had a divine sponsor. Besides, standards were
lenient: Killing was all right for tribe and honor; love of one's fellow
man was not required; justice, too, was far short of Platonic standards.
Finally, Hades was not a place of hellish punishment but merely of
gloom, where one faced people such as Achilles and Socrates, who had
lived before and whom one might have wronged. The gist of all this is
that the otherworld was definite enough, but it had an indefinite effect
on daily life even if one believed in it literally and acted in accordance.

Not so, as we know, was the otherworldly concept of Christianity.
Drawn from the Hebrew "book," it contained ten stern commandments,
a picture of the fall of man from Eden for disobedience, and a looming
fear of a last judgment. Hell, though vague in the Bible, was vividly
pictured by poets like Dante and Milton and the Devil became a major
character in the human drama: "There was war in heaven. . . . and . . .
that old Serpent, called the Devil . . . was cast out . . . and his angels were
cast out with him" (Revelation 12:7-9). Thus we see a specific scheme
and law for man in this world and the next, with salvation hinging on
right conduct.

The question for a salvation religion then becomes: What are the
ways of coping with an otherworldly risk like this and what kind of social
order best guarantees success with it? Weber sketches some of the main
roads to salvation. One choice is between cultic ritual, such as purification, versus good works of social achievement, as in the "precise book-
keeping" of *karma* or the "life-accounting" of Roman Catholicism.

Orthodox Judaism combines both of these ways (1964:151-156). At opposite extremes are religions which aim to control the world, such as Islam, and those which reject it, such as Buddhism and early Christianity (262-266). For world-rejecting religions two especially important paths are *asceticism*, or denying oneself satisfactions of this world, such as material goods, family ties, even living with one's fellow men; and *mysticism*, a subjective state of union with the divine (1964:166-169). Religious *virtuosi* may go far beyond ordinary men in such matters, perhaps withdrawing to monasteries to work for their salvation (1964:162). Thus, saints or holy men allow us to see otherworldly standards most sharply because they adhere more closely to them, through inspiration or effort. Weber notes a mutual hostility between such *virtuosi* and religious officials (1946:288), and we may recall the trial of Joan of Arc, or the encounter between Jesus and the Grand Inquisitor depicted by Dostoevski in *The Brothers Karamazov*. Weber generalized these struggles into the conflict between charisma and bureaucracy.

Though Christianity and Buddhism both developed a world-denying orientation, there is a striking difference between major Western and Eastern religions in emphasis on the will. Christianity, Judaism, and Mohammedanism, the religions of "The Book" (Michener, 1965), and Graeco-Roman beliefs have in common a stress on will in both God and man. The Eastern religions (Hinduism, Buddhism, Taoism) deny will, either as an important characteristic of man or activity of God, an enormously important difference.

In the West the stress was on will, ego, the person, though curbing will was conceived as virtue or self-mastery. The metaphor is that of a spirited horse bridled, a Promethean or Satanic will asserted against God, or a tragic hero like Brand (Ibsen) asserting his will *through* God. The main part of the self is *conscious* thinking and volition: "I am [the source of] my ideas—*cogito ergo sum*." Improving the intellect through logic, science, planning, etc., is believed to make man stronger.

The Eastern religions are quite different, denying the will, stressing resignation, and teaching that ego, intellect, even the person, is an illusion. The central metaphor is that of a vast river flowing and carrying a boat with a man who is rowing in the fog, thinking he is going someplace, although he cannot see the shore. The main part of the self is *unconscious*: an *atman* to be discovered, similar to unity with Tao, or "the Void," as Buddhism calls it. No amount of logic, science or conscious will helps man discover this true self. Nor is he any stronger by exerting his will.

The Western religions see the source of order, negative entropy, in commands from God, whose will is revealed to people in a Book, after God's initial creation of the world, when He commanded: "Let there be light," and "Multiply and replenish." Man's duty is to bow to God's will, which comes to him in the form of personal revelations or sacred scriptures. Thus the Western religions have encoded an image of will as the source of negative entropy.

On the other hand, the Eastern scriptures record a cosmos without beginning or end, timeless or in unending cycles. There is no act of creation; all is Brahman, Tao, Void. Willing implies duality, a creator and his creation, but reality is One. Lao-tse describes it as follows:

> The Way is like an empty vessel
> That yet may be drawn from
> Without ever needing to be filled.
> It is bottomless: the very progenitor of all
>   things in the world. . . .
> It is like a deep pool that never dries
> I do not know whose child it could be.
> It looks as if it were prior to God.
>
> (WALEY, 1934:IV)

To become aware of such reality man does not receive commands, but listens intuitively, as in meditation, to attain peace, or *satori*, the cessation of willful striving.

In the West, sin is the rebellion of a proud and free human will against the commands of God. Guilt is recognition of one's own wicked will. Punishment in hell will follow sin, but mercy can be earned through penitence or grace. So we see how the emphasis on will could lead to the centrality of sin and forgiveness in the Christian world-view.

In the Eastern religions, there is no sin, only ignorance, failure to attune oneself to the Atman, Tao, Void; failure to resign one's will and find peace—hence suffering. There is no punishment except life itself: a burden of suffering which may have to be endured through many reincarnations, but can be given up at any time by renouncing egoistic will and realizing one's unity with the divine. So, for example, Buddhist compassion does not require forgiveness of sin; it is simply a recognition of common suffering—the basic truth that the mind is the prime source of suffering in all humans. A Buddhist greeting might well be, "Good morning. I'm sorry for you." But he would never call you a sinner.

In Eastern religions there is no drama of the fall of man or of Satan from heaven, as is depicted for the West by Genesis and writers like St. Augustine, Dante, and Milton; nor do Oriental religions embrace the notion of suffering as part of this scheme. D. T. Suzuki, a Zen Buddhist, states the distinction forcibly:

> Whenever I see a crucified figure of Christ, I cannot help thinking of the gap that lies deep between Christianity and Buddhism. This gap is symbolic of the psychological division separating the East from the West. The individual ego asserts itself strongly in the West. In the East, there is no ego. The ego is non-existent and, therefore, there is no ego to be crucified.... The crucifixion ... has a double sense ... in the first sense it symbolizes the destruction of the individual ego, while in the second it stands for the doctrine of vicarious atonement whereby all our sins are atoned for by making Christ die for them.... The crucifixion is the climax of all suffering. Buddhists also speak much about suffering and its climax is the Buddha serenely sitting under the Bodhi

tree. . . . Christ hangs helpless, full of sadness on the vertically erected cross. To the Oriental mind, the sight is almost unbearable. . . . Let us make a geometric comparison between a statue sitting cross-legged in meditation and a crucified one. . . . A sitting figure gives us the notion of solidity, firm conviction and immovability. . . . This is also the symbol of peace, tranquility, and self-assurance. A standing position generally suggests a fighting spirit, either defensive or offensive. It also gives one the feeling of personal self-importance born of individuality and power. . . . Christians would say that crucifixion means crucifying the self or the flesh, since without subduing the self we cannot attain moral perfection. This is where Buddhism differs from Christianity. Buddhism declares that there is from the very beginning no self to crucify. To think that there is the self is the start of all errors and evils. Ignorance is at the root of all things that go wrong. (SUZUKI, 1962:98-103)

Such an emphasis on will in Western thought may help us to understand the great tensions that had to be accommodated in religion, perhaps by legalistic codes of right behavior, or sacramental systems of forgiveness, or "doing good" by social action in the world, or monasticism, or politicization of the church as an arm of God.

We consider now five major solutions, within Christian thought, of the tension between the will of man and the will of God. They are: (1) the otherworldliness of an apolitical sect attempting to live solely according to the will of God; (2) the "pilgrim path" of adjusting to a material world from which one withholds commitment; (3) *hierocracy*, or governing the world according to supernatural standards; (4) individual freedom to interpret divine law according to one's own conscience; and (5) secularization, or renouncing the distinction between worldly and otherworldly standards.

OTHERWORLDLY ACCOMMODATION IN CHRISTIAN THOUGHT

Original Christianity

The world view of original Christianity is described in the New Testament, especially the Sermon on the Mount. The message is clear because it was meant for people who were not learned: Recognize all men, even your enemies, as brothers under God; love them as yourself; forgive all injuries; resist not evil, but turn the other cheek; judge not that ye be not judged, rather, leave judgment to heaven; above all, live for God and for heaven: "lay not up for yourselves treasures upon earth." Like the lilies of the field, "take no thought for the morrow" but "seek ye first the kingdom of God" and "all these things shall be added unto you." "If thou wilt be perfect, go and sell that thou hast, and give to the poor, and thou shalt have treasures in heaven," and "not everyone that saith to me Lord, Lord, shall enter the kingdom of Heaven; but he that does the will of my Father which is in Heaven." In other words, Jesus saw great perils in worldly life, even if one followed the legalistic observances of the Jews (whom he rebuked as pharisees and hypocrites); and even in teaching generosity and love to all men he taught a much sterner doctrine of otherworldliness than the Jews had taught. Though all men are brothers, few are chosen, unless they enter the narrow gate opened by Jesus. The primacy of the life of the spirit over worldly life is unmistakable in the early message of Christianity. As Weber puts it:

> Jesus held in general that what is most decisive for salvation is an absolute indifference to the world and its concerns. The kingdom of heaven, a realm of joy upon earth, utterly without suffering and sin, is at hand . . . (1964:273).

How does one live when the kingdom of heaven is so close that it might come any time, like a thief in the night, to those chosen? By forming commities, becoming careless about secular obligations, and by calling to sinners to renounce the world and be saved, all of which the early Christians did, and which many contemporary evangelistic sects still do. Just as New Yorkers might today, the Romans laughed at the early Christians, then became irritated, and finally persecuted them systematically. What was dangerous about such a doctrine? It seems harmless enough to be chaste, to turn the other cheek, to take no thought for this earth and to live for heaven to come. The commonest explanation of how an otherworldly doctrine could threaten this world is that the Romans misunderstood certain of Jesus' utterances ("I come not to bring peace but a sword"), and supposed that the kingdom he was promising was a political threat comparable to that of Lenin to Czar Nicholas. But sociologists would point out that, despite this misunderstanding, Christianity was a very real threat to the secular structure of the day; especially the dissolving effect of the doctrine of brotherhood on distinctions of class and property. In fact, Christianity denied that these had any value. The new religion dissolved local loyalties to family, tribe, and nation in favor of heavenly brotherhood, which amounted to destroying the dualism between in-group and out-group, including the distinction between Romans and slaves and barbarians, and the "chosen people" versus gentiles. No wonder, then, that so many people were angry at the Christians for dismissing the values on which worldly life was based. The historian Gibbon later pointed out that the very zeal of Christians for salvation led them to harass officials, seeking an opportunity to confess their faith and become martyrs. This very zeal to die for another world created the saintly model of the martyr, which raised believers' morale and helped Christianity to thrive on the very persecutions it endured.

St. Paul carried the otherworldly ideal of Christianity further by developing an extreme doctrine of the sinfulness of the flesh, (a doctrine implied by the fall of Adam, but not so stressed by the Jews). His reasoning is strictly logical. If the kingdom of heaven is all that matters, then it would be better to concentrate on this and not be involved in business and family life. "I speak for your profit ... that ye may attend upon the Lord without distraction." So comes the famous doctrine of virginity: it is "good for man not to touch a woman;" but, if he cannot contain himself, "it is better to marry than to burn."

> The unmarried woman careth for the things of the Lord, that she may be holy both in body and in spirit: but she that is married careth for the things of the world, how she may please her husband (CORINTHIANS I:1).

This is the beginning of the monastic ideal, later to be developed by the Saints, Augustine, Benedict, and Francis. So, by logical extension, Christians began to build ideology.

To understand where this could lead, we might imagine what would happen if St. Paul and some of the original disciples had a power bloc in the United States Congress. What would be the practical implications of otherworldliness, as such pure men tried to rule for the good of a society whose daily life was so different from their standards? What kinds of education and legislation would they favor? Would there be one established church? Censorship? Forced integration in the South? A military draft? Income taxes? Equal distribution of income and welfare? Some form of socialism or communism? Would these saintly men favor a hierocracy (rule by a priestly class), or would they prefer to remain as they were, an apolitical sect, in conflict with but apart from the secular order, as they were at the time of Jesus?

The Pilgrim Path

The next great chapter in the story of Christianity's evolution in the world is St. Augustine's *City of God*, written in 413 A.D., in North Africa just after the fall of Rome to the barbarians. Augustine tried to explain to Christians their position in a disorderly world, especially their obligation to a city like Rome which might harbor them, but whose ways they could neither approve nor follow.

The Christian of this time was in a dilemma between the world in which he believed and the city in which he lived but felt himself to be like a stranger. We might appreciate this, not by putting ourselves back in Augustine's time but by imagining ourselves to be persons of deep otherworldly faith, a Jehovah's Witness or a Salvation Army worker, for example, living in a modern city rife with gambling, prostitution, and drug abuse. In this situation our otherworldly believer feels keenly his duty to be good himself and to save others from sin so that they, too, can reach the Kingdom. What, then, as he wanders among the roulette tables and vendors of illicit merchandise, is he to do as his Christian duty in this city? Should he, for example, become a social worker? Work to build schools and hospitals? Run for mayor and start a reform program?

According to Augustine's reasoning, such a course would be quite illogical for one who believed in heaven. There are two cities in which men are fated to live: the city of earth, where one lives "according to the flesh," or secular state; and the Heavenly City, where one lives according to the spirit. We are born into the former and are "condemned to perpetual torment with the devil." But by the grace of God we are destined to reach the Heavenly City, if we follow the straight and narrow path. The Christian has a duty to both domains at once, but the duty to Heaven is far stronger.

Regarding the earthly city, we must recall that Augustine accepted the doctrine of original sin, as implied by the fall of man from Eden. Man was, therefore, condemned to live on earth, and all the evils of the time—war, crime, slavery—seemed but rightful punishments. What can man hope for in such a world but to endure what punishment he must, and "lead a quiet life in all Godliness and charity"? The best the earthly city can offer him is peace, but it cannot protect him from the inherent evils of secular life. It is a rough world that Augustine describes, for men live under the curse of original and continuing sin:

> In the justest war, the sin upon one side causes it; and if the victory fall to the wicked (as sometimes it may) it is God's decree to humble the conquered, either reforming their sins herein, or punishing them. . . . Sin, therefore, is the mother of servitude, and first cause of man's subjection to man (*City of God*, XIX).

So it behooves the citizen to support the law when it brings peace, and welcome such justice as he can find.

What, then, is the duty of the Christian toward this corrupt civil order? Surely not to support it when it is wicked, nor to hope to basically improve it when it is under sentence of punishment for sin. The answer is found in Augustine's famous definition of the *pilgrim path*. Christians should consider themselves travelers passing through the earthly city, while keeping their eye on their heavenly destination:

> in full expectation of the glories to come, using the occurrences of this world, but as pilgrims, not to abandon their course towards God for mortal respects, but thereby to assist the infirmity of the corruptible flesh, and make it more able to encounter with toil and trouble. . . . The "Heavenly City" . . . lives (while it is here on earth) as if it were in captivity, and having received the promise of redemption . . . willingly obeys such laws of the "temporal city" as order the things pertaining to the sustenance of this mortal life . . . (*City of God*, XIX).

So the Christian, though he respects the laws of the earthly city, is not bound to obey them when they conflict with those of his heavenly destination, any more than the tourist would so feel passing through a country whose ways were not his own. Indeed, the analogy is apt, for the obligation of the Christian to the local community, with all its corruption and disorder, is only that of a disdainful tourist who wishes to avoid trouble and get on with what he has to do. Since he is not expecting to be there long, broad programs of sweeping reform are out of the question. His practical work in the community would be more like that of the Salvation Army or Jehovah's Witnesses than the Red Cross. His mood while doing his Christian duty would be rather like that of a gloomy preacher who hopes to save a few souls but not to do much about the state of the world. Indeed, it would be rather like this handbill passed out by Jehovah's Witnesses:

> IS TIME RUNNING OUT FOR THIS GENERATION? Yes, time is running out for this generation! Not because researchers assure us that there will be global famine by the year 1975, when the population explosion is expected to have produced far more mouths than can be fed. Not because the world's peace-keeping machinery is plagued with flaws that make it incapable of preventing another world war. Not because the current breakdown of morals and respect for law is leading inevitably to an era of greater violence and crime. But because the most dependable timekeeper, Jehovah God, informs us that we are now well over half a century into the "time of the end" of a doomed system of things. ... Read ... what Jesus Christ foretold for this "time of the end." (LUKE 21:7, 10-11, 25-26) And read what the apostle Paul was inspired to say about what we could expect in these "last days."— 2 TIM. 3:1-5, 13.... The semimonthly magazine *Awake!* will aid you to keep awake and survive a doomed generation.

With an attitude at all like this, a person's long-term contribution to the earthly city would be negligible. The relevant activities would be moral preparation, prayer, and preaching to those who would listen. The Christian would do what he could to help his brothers in need, but the attitude toward social work would be rather negative. He would put up with government, law, and taxes as necessary evils, the price of peace, but would withhold obedience that compromised his higher obligation. For example, he would likely refuse military service, or accepting it, leave the bullet out of his gun.

So we see how Augustine proposed to find a compromise between the claims of the heavenly and earthly cities. For those who take the world on Augustinian terms, there are two main options: *monasticism*, for the person who wishes to withdraw and work energetically for the final end without ties to the earthly city; and the *pilgrim's path* for anyone caught up in the toils of daily life in a world he does not approve of but cannot much change, who only hopes to move on as soon as possible. So the famous evangelist, Dwight L. Moody, recommended:

> Christians should live in the world, but not be filled with it. A ship lives in the water; but if the water gets into the ship, she goes to the bottom. So Christians may live in the world, but if the world gets into them, they sink.

The monastic response is recommended by the Trappist monk, Thomas Merton:

> Do everything you can to avoid the amusements and noise and the business of men. Keep as far away as you can from the places where they gather to cheat and insult one another, to exploit one another, or to mock one another with their false gestures of friendship. Do not read their newspapers if you can help it. Be glad if you can keep beyond reach of their radios ... keep your eyes clean and your ears quiet and your mind serene (1949).

Some idea of the preference for such solutions among persons deeply influenced by Augustine is given by the proportions of paths followed by saints: isolation, 9 percent; monasticism, 31 percent; work in the world, 46 percent. (Sorokin, 1950).

So we see that Augustine's thought provided a stepping stone between the complete otherworldliness of a radical sect and an established church which is at home in the world. Augustine's was a middle position, in, but not of, the world, a pilgrim—not really participant, yet not in conflict either. It was, therefore, an accommodation, reducing the tension of sectarian conflict and buffering the Christian, whether by isolation or the pilgrim path, from full involvement in the secular city. This typical movement from a sect status, through *accommodation*, to church status has been analyzed by sociologists like Park (1924), Troeltsch (1931), and Niebuhr (1957). The essential picture is that of a sect in conflict with the existing order, trying to carry on against the "wicked" values and false hopes of happiness of the "world," and finally coming to peace through some kind of accommodation, involving a certain amount of compromise or secularization of otherworldly values.

Hierarchy of Law

Now we turn to an outcome of Christian thought that is quite unexpected from Augustine's delineation of the pilgrim path. Like Plato's Utopia, Augustine's *City of God* depicted a justice that could not be achieved on earth. It was a testimony to the impotence of Christianity to obtain the world it wanted, and its pessimism affects many today. Thomas Aquinas, a Dominican monk of the thirteenth century, made a very different statement. Using Aristotle's logic he created a scholastic structure—a veritable cathedral—of Christian law for the entire world which, far from confessing defeat, claimed dominion over every part of life.

By the thirteenth century, Christianity was far stronger in the world than it had been at the time of St. Augustine. Its problem now was to explain, not why the Church was outside the world, but how it had come to permeate every part of it. We find a spiritual empire, a "Church Universal" of all European nations. The Church had a sacramental monopoly in confession and forgiveness; even kings had to be consecrated by the Pope. Doctrine was dogmatic, with heresy punished by excommunication. It was customary to submit all books to the Church for censorship, as Galileo did, for the clergy were in an enviable position as custodians not only of spiritual truth but all serious thought.

Such institutions expressed the medieval worldview, which was unlike our secularized modern view in at least two ways. First, there was a greater feeling of mystery: Angels intervened in human affairs, and miracles and revelations were in the order of the day, while Satan waged a hidden war with the Church for the possession of men's souls.

A second major difference was a tremendous sense of order, law, and design, not merely as seen in political rules and laws of nature, but in God's will expressed in providence and moral law, to which man was subordinate: Pride was sinful and obedience was virtue.

We can understand such an overwhelming sense of law by quoting a modern Thomist, Monsignor Fulton J. Sheen:

> If our wills are on the side of God, we cannot be discouraged, for the side which we have chosen is always victorious, is never flouted. God is self-preserving, and evil is self-defeating. The reality of things is ever on the side of God. Evil is necessarily unstable, because it runs counter to the nature of things as they were made. All the laws of our human nature nudge us toward our proper destiny of holiness, as of health. If we attend to our bodies properly, obeying the rules of health, we are healthy; if we break these laws, our rebellion brings sickness, and few of us would take proper care of ourselves if the violation of the laws of health did not carry some penalty, as a reminder.
>
> We are free in this and other fields to break the laws God has set down, but we are not free to escape the penalty that breaking His laws entails. To jump from a window does not destroy the law of gravitation; but it may destroy our lives.
>
> Nature is on God's side, always; it will betray our wants, but never His commands. And this is as true in the moral sphere as in the physical.
>
> When men sin, there is no need for God to intervene to see that they are punished: our natures are so made that we cannot oppose Him without being in opposition to ourselves. If we break the law of temperance, a headache follows. God did not send that headache by a special Act; He had already made us in such a way that our evil deeds result in evil effects.... When we reject the moral law, we suffer, not because we intended evil, but simply because we defied a force stronger than ourselves: the reality of things. In sinning, we thus produce an effect which we did not intend, this never happens as the result of our good actions. If I use a pencil to write with, the pencil is unharmed; if I try to open a tin can with it, I break it in two. I have used the pencil in a way contrary to its purpose, and so destroy it.

If I live my life according to its highest purpose—and that is the attainment of Truth and Love—I will perfect it. If I live according to my animal impulses, I frustrate myself as surely as I would frustrate a razor by using it to hew a stone.

Evil is always mutilation of the self. If I live as I ought to live, I become a man; if I live as my whims dictate, I become a beast, and an unhappy beast. This is not a result I ever planned, but it is still unavoidable. The man who wills to over-drink does not intend to ruin his health, but he does just that. The man who over-eats does not count on indigestion, but he gets it. The man who wills to steal has not aimed at prison, yet that is where he lands. . . . Disorder is a stern teacher, and a slow one, but a certain one. The Spanish have a proverb: "He who spits against Heaven spits in his own face" (1950).

We hear an echo of such Thomism in a sermon by an Episcopal priest: "The man who steps out of the tenth story window does not defy the law of gravity but only illustrates it."

The source of this overwhelming sense of law for Christians was St. Thomas Aquinas, who, in his *Summa Theologica*, developed a system of law down to a minute catechism for every kind of action. His central principle was "law makes men good." "The virtue of any subordinate thing consists in its being well subordinated" Aquinas was so thorough that he even argued that a skillful thief was better than a poor thief.

What was the source of all this law? Aquinas distinguished four orders of law to which man is subject: (1) *Eternal* law is God's plan for the universe. Although it is unknowable, its existence can be inferred; (2) *Divine* law guides man to his spiritual end (Augustine's heavenly city). It is known through the revelations of the scriptures, prophets, and saints; (3) *Natural* law is what man perceives in himself as the faculty of reason and what he dimly perceives by reason in nature. (4) *Human* law is devised by man's reason for his convenience, well-being, and earthly peace (the rules of Augustine's earthly city). It should be easy to classify such things as "two plus two equals four," the Ten

Commandments, Darwin's theory of evolution, and the First Amendment to the Constitution, into these categories.

Plainly these laws are in a hierarchy, from the vast plan which man cannot know, to divine, to natural, to human law, the most fallible and least authoritative source of order. It should be plain, also, that there is a hierarchy in the institutions which are custodians of these forms of law: The Church as bearer of the word of God (including theology as "Queen of the Sciences"); science, philosophy and education as discoverers of the laws of nature; and, finally, government and custom. Thomists are at pains to show that there can be no conflict between divine and natural law when all investigations are completed. But with respect to politics, Thomist thought concluded that the proper guardians of society are neither politicians nor Plato's philosophers but properly ordained priests. Thus, Aquinas' logic, if carried to its full implications, justified a *hierocratic*, or theocratic, society. Needless to say, this result was as pleasing to some churchmen as Comte's conclusion about sociologists was to that profession.

The closest approximation today to an actual hierocracy along lines envisioned by Aquinas is the Vatican, a separate sovereign state, with its own boundary, customs inspection, guards, radio system, ruling body of priests (the cardinals), and ambassadors from other countries. Other examples of hierocracy, though farther from Aquinas, would be the Massachusetts Bay Colony; or the early Mormon state of Deseret in Utah.

So we see that in the theology of Aquinas, Christianity had advanced from the position of an accommodating sect to a universal church with authority over secular government.

Even today, some writers see a threat to political freedom in the claims of Thomism (Blanshard, 1951). But according to Jacques Maritain, an eminent Catholic writer, a new state of affairs has come into being which does not require the Church to play a political role:

> The modern age is not a sacral, but a secular age. The order of terrestrial civilization and of temporal society has gained complete

differentiation and full autonomy, which is something normal in itself, required by the Gospel's very distinction between God's and Caesar's domains.... The supreme, immutable principle of the superiority of the Kingdom of God over the earthly kingdoms can apply in other ways than in making the civil government the secular arm of the Church, in asking kings to expel heretics, or in using the rights of the spiritual sword to seize upon temporal affairs for the sake of some spiritual necessity ... these things we can admire in the Middle Ages; they are a dead letter in our age (1951:159, 162-163).

On the contrary, Maritain reassures us:

The Kingdom of God is essentially spiritual, and by the very fact that its own order is not of this world, it in no way threatens the kingdoms and republics of the earth.... Let us remove from the word "superiority" any accidental connotation of domination ... it means a higher place in the scale of values, a higher dignity (153).

Therefore, we may continue to assert the principle of "the superiority of the Church—that is, of the spiritual—over the body politic or the state" (153). But how is this superiority to be expressed, if not by ruling? First, the Church and body politic cannot live in isolation from one another; there must be some influence. Nevertheless, there are freedom and separation of the state from religion and different religions from one another:

The unity of religion is not a prerequisite for political unity, and men subscribing to diverse religious or non-religious creeds have to share in and work for the same political or temporal common good (160).

How, then, is the superiority of the Church expressed in the modern world? First, it is absolutely free in spiritual matters from any interference from politics. Second, the Church no longer regards the state as

94

"the secular arm of the spiritual power." Having renounced such connections, the social power of the Church has shifted to:

> vivifying inspiration.... Moral influence and authority; in other words, to a fashion or "style." ... The superior dignity of the Church is to find its ways of realization in the full exercise of her superior strength of all-pervading inspiration (162).

So there is implied a division of spheres: external actions, which a secular authority can regulate, for example, the requirement of paying taxes; and interior motions of the heart and will—matters of faith regulated by divine law and the Church. In theory at least there should be little conflict in such matters, but when divine law is translated into action, for example regarding military service, conflict between Church and state is possible.

Protestantism

It was not to be expected, with secular forces loose in the world, that a hierocracy could retain sovereign authority, whatever its theory. And there was also the powerful heretical force of sectarianism to be reckoned with. These changes prepared the ground for the Reformation, a movement begun by the Augustinian Martin Luther.

Luther's dissatisfaction with the Church, which began with a disillusioning trip to Rome in 1510, grew to an attack on doctrine and practice which finally led to his excommunication. The central target of Luther's attack was the sacramental monopoly, the idea that the channels of grace were the exclusive prerogatives of the clergy. One radical change he proposed was reducing the number of sacraments from seven to two, retaining the Lord's Supper and baptism, but eliminating confirmation, marriage, ordination, penance, and extreme unction. He argued that only these had been instituted by Christ. More serious was his reduction of the Mass to the Lord's Supper. He rejected what he felt were magical elements, holding that it was not the performance of a rite which was important, but the experience of a presence. Worse (for the status of the Church), he held that priests had no special power in a Mass or any sacrament; indeed, he repudiated the whole idea of ordination as a requirement for performing Christian services. He affirmed instead the "priesthood of all believers," that is, any congregation may commission any member to perform sacraments. Even today, the Lutheran minister, at the beginning of the service, asks the congregation if they will accept him as the called servant of the Word. Thus Luther abolished the necessity of priests, even saints, as intercessors between man and God. He said, in effect, let no man stand between me and God; let every man be his own priest.

Following from this were other reforms, such as the attack on "idolatry," including veneration of saints' relics and figures, even of the Virgin Mary Nor should there be any more veneration of even the highest priest.

> The Pope should not receive the sacrament seated, proffered to him by a kneeling cardinal through a golden reed, but should stand up like any other "stinking sinner." (BAINTON, 1955:119)

Nor need the clergy be so set apart, as in monasticism; they should be permitted to marry (Bainton, 1955:105-120).

By destroying the special intercessory position of the priesthood, Luther threw the whole burden of Christian guidance upon individual interpretation of scripture. He said, in effect, let your conscience be your guide: No one can give you grace, unless you have it directly from God. This is consistent with the fact that Luther was an Augustinian monk: Once he saw that the Church was a worldly power, he repudiated it, affirming again the pure doctrine of spirituality.

If the church is not needed for confession and absolution, how then does a Christian know his spiritual status? In answer, Luther advanced another great principle, that faith, what one believes, not "work," what one does, is all that is necessary for salvation. This is commonly called "justification by faith." The church had taught that going to Mass, doing penance, performing charity and so on, were necessary to earn God's favor in order to expiate original sin. Protestants never argued with this, but reasoned differently: Man is *so* sinful he cannot *deserve* God's favor; further, if you want God only for the good he can do, still worse try to bribe him with acts of penance, you are selfish and sacrilegious. Therefore, salvation is acceptance of God's purpose, whatever it may be, not satisfaction of a human need. Such sheer affirmation of faith, accepting what God chooses to mete out is justification by faith.

John Calvin (1509-1564), a French leader of the Reformation, developed the doctrine of *predestination*, which explained even more plainly why works are of no avail, either within the church or outside it. Though the eternal plan could not be known by man, it was possible to infer whether a man was predestined to be saved or not. In fact, Calvin asserted that one should be willing to be damned for the glory of God. A modern evangelist, Billy Graham, explains it this way:

> There is a certain truth to predestination, for God would not be God if he did not know from the beginning of time who would be the ones to receive His Son. Certainly He knew this. When He sent His Son into the world He knew that the death of His Son would make atonement for people who are known to Him also (1960).

Jesus brought salvation to a few, known only to God; these Calvin called "the elect." Such a belief enabled those who imagined that they were among the elect to feel that, as Weber put it, despite transgressions, their behavior was acceptable to God and flowed "out of an inner relationship based on the mysterious quality of grace" (1964:203). What, then, can the church do in such a situation? Weber described its role in these terms:

> The elect need no church for their own sake. . . . By no means does the church exist for the salvation of souls. . . . The church

exists not only for the blessed but also the condemned, so that, for the greater glory of God, it can suppress sinfulness, which is common to all men and separates all beings irremediably from God: The church is a scourge and not a vehicle of salvation. (1969:330)

Calvin's was a pessimistic doctrine contrasted with that of Aquinas, who believed that all men could strive for good and perfect it in their nature, with the help of the church (Borkenau, 1969:289-291).

As Luther and Calvin illustrate, Protestantism said that divine will had no direct supervision of human affairs through the church. The Protestant sects created the principle of freedom of conscience:

The consistent sect gives rise to an inalienable personal right of the governed as against any power, whether political, hierocratic or patriarchal. Such freedom of conscience may be the oldest Right of Man (WEBER, 1969:321).

It was a "declaration of independence" for secular life, of great significance for the world of business. As we shall see in Chapter 8, it influenced the political and economic declarations of Thomas Jefferson and Adam Smith in 1776.

Some thinkers charge Protestantism with having inflicted a burden of strain, anxiety, and guilt on man by separating him from a church to which to confess, and putting him on his own, yet retaining original sin, as both Luther and Calvin did (Fromm, 1941; Kahler, 1957; Walzer, 1966). In fact, Durkheim used the solidarity of Catholicism versus the individualism of Prostestantism to explain higher suicide rates among the latter (1951). Protestant thought did not, then, accommodate men to religious tension by freeing them from the claims and duties of ecclesiastical authority, but merely transferred tension to the individual "alone with God."

But traditional Protestantism was not the end of the story of accommodation. Another major development was possible within the limits of Christianity's otherworldly orientation, although it was almost the opposite of St. Augustine's position. It is sometimes called "social action" or Christian secular humanism.

The Secular City

Secularism emphasizes the reality of what is observable and possible while de-emphasizing considerations such as spiritual ideals which escape such a test. Secularism holds that the Church and its members should work in and for *this* world, not the next. That is, a so-called spiritual or ultimate standard must be judged alongside a secular one in terms of its fruits in this life. Secular humanistic Christianity sweepingly rejects such concepts as "hell" and "sin" except insofar as they can be observed in actual human situations. Sartre, for example, portrayed hell in his play, "No Exit," by simply showing three people locked in a room together, tormenting each other for all eternity.

It is not possible for Christianity to abandon the fight for good against evil, but there is a stunningly simple way to obliterate the tension between otherworldly standards and this world. It is to assume that what we know of God comes to man through the world and its standards, is immanent rather than transcendental. It is human experience that teaches us that sin is inhumanity, hell is suffering, and salvation is to be achieved by appropriate social action. Such an accommodation does not abandon standards, but reduces them to a scale that it is reasonable to expect people to live up to: All the tensions left are simply those of human claims, against one another, or of a person on himself.

Perhaps the best known example of such a view is found in Harvey Cox's book, *The Secular City* (1966). Cox rejects the antagonism of otherworldly religion to worldliness: "We have the right and duty to become passionate about the things of the earth." He rejects the view of the world as a "horizon...subsumed within another one." Man should turn his attention "away from worlds beyond and toward this world and this time" (Callaghan, 1966:117-119). Cox urges that we accept secularization and the problems of urbanization, not as "sinister curses to be escaped, but epochal opportunities to be embraced." He negates Augustine's pessimism by an "affirmative vision of the urban world as man's responsibility" (1966, xi). He reverses assumptions of St. Paul, Augustine, and for that matter, Luther and Calvin, by saying that Jesus' life does not show rejection of a sinful world, but a "partnership of God and man in history." Plenty of "renunciation and repentance" are required for work in the secular city, but the Kingdom of God is not "somehow beyond or above" history; it is rather "in process of realizing itself" in history (97-98).

In practical application, Cox reverses the assumptions of Augustine, recommending a much larger acceptance of and participation in worldly activities, and removing the tension between the heavenly city and the secular city by converting that tension into secular conflicts and renunciations only. Similarly, he blends Aquinas' distinction between natural, human, and divine law into secularization of all standards. The modern church becomes "God's avante-garde" of social change which can, for example, help to clean up ghettos and change "bank practices, zoning laws, school financing, and tax structures" (108-124). So the church embraces secular tasks, uses political power, rolls its sleeves up, and goes to work in the world, quite contrary to what Augustine implied. Cox argues that God is not outside the world; we meet him everywhere in the secular city for "God manifests himself in and through secular events" (233).

It is no surprise that this book raised a storm of controversy among more conservative churchmen, Catholic, Protestant, and Jewish alike. A few typical objections may be given from *The Secular City Debate* (Callaghan, 1966). Cox "welcomes the organization man as the new Christian" (148). His secular city is only another version of the "easy optimism of the Social Gospel," to which "a generation of critics, including Reinhold Niebuhr, has given the lie" (79). Misgivings are expressed that a pragmatic man who does not recognize the difference between otherworldly mandates and relative secular standards will be a "dangerous man" (98). Rejecting the idea of God immanent in the world means that there are "no values and standards beyond man." When men create their own standards, "everything becomes possible," including "ethical monstrosities" like those of de Sade or Stalin. On the contrary:

> God is beyond the world, not in it—and so is His Kingdom.... Christians are still shrinking from the imperatives of the law and in its stead put their faith in the present (SCHWARZCHILD, in CALLAGHAN, 152-54).

Nor were all the objections academic. Conservatives deplored the political action of priests like Father Berrigan and of the World Council of Churches providing legal defense for prisoners like Huey P. Newton and H. Rap Brown.

Such objections give an idea of the unsolved problems raised by the conception of the "secular city." Will Christianity stop here, or will it continue to change, perhaps returning to options tried before?

CONCLUSION

This chapter has discussed how social order is modeled if a Supreme Being is conceived as providing direction. What are the options for such a society trying, with Aristotle's logic, to resolve the tension of living with otherworldly standards?

Eastern religions stress resignation toward a vast impersonal Reality, which man seeks union with by meditation rather than reasoning or repentance. More important for Western religions is chastening the rebellious will and subordinating it to divine law. The five main forms of

Christian thought reviewed here show various solutions to this problem: (1) The pure sect, illustrated by original Christianity, seeks spiritual rebirth, breaks away from the world, and attempts to live solely in direct communion with divine will. Such a breaking away can also lead to extreme asceticism and to monasticism. (2) Augustine's pilgrim path shows the sect accommodating itself to the world, charting a course through it with minimal involvement. (3) Thomism represents the supreme involvement in the world of institutionalized Christianity, God's arm for the good, recognizing one world, but distinguishing a hierarchy of order, divine, rational, and human, with their appropriate authorities. So long as these authorities respected their subordination, no conflict could occur. (4) The Protestant Reformation shows sects once again breaking away from the world, this time perceived as a corrupt church, while their demand for "freedom of conscience" unwittingly prepared the way for the eighteenth century doctrine of economic and political liberty. Once again, two worlds. (5) Finally, the "secular city" concept was another attempt to unite the two realms by reducing the tension between otherworldly and secular standards: Whatever law God meant for man is seen as being manifested and perceived entirely through human experience.

In such various systemic options, the main effect of "order from above" was either to check the scope and sovereignty of secular authority, or to put priests and holy men themselves into positions of authority, so that information entering the system was filtered to give priority to transcendental signals. With such a conception of order, neither philosophers, as recommended by the Greeks, nor scientists, as recommended by positivism, were fitted to rule except in subordinate spheres of human or natural law. Only in the version recommended by Cox is the tension between worldly and spiritual authority removed, but at the price of man's giving up any hope of receiving direct mandates different in kind from those of the natural and political worlds.

For sociologists, such ways of dealing with "order from above" seem to form a cycle, first formulated by Weber and Park. There is first a breaking away from worldly standards, a movement toward sectarian monasticism or communalism, then a drift toward compromise, a cycle which seems to be repeated wherever ideals come into conflict with the practical world, not only in religion but in art, education, scholarship, even economics and politics. Once again, in the 1970s, "Jesus freaks" were appearing in the streets of the secular city, forming communes in order to live directly with and for God. A "whole earth" movement, embracing vegetarianism and reverence for life, seemed to indicate the growth of a new nature religion. A deep anti-intellectualism, with a romantic and mystical search for ecstatic, occult, or prophetic experiences also flourished. Was the cycle beginning again? And who would be the new Luther?

6

Order from Power

Cynic n. *a blackguard whose faulty vision sees things as they are, not as they ought to be. Hence the custom among the Scythians of plucking out a cynic's eyes to improve his vision.*
—AMBROSE BIERCE

In the teaching of Niccolo Machiavelli (1469-1527) we find a social model so different from the Greek and Christian models of goodness, justice, and concern with otherworldly standards that Machiavelli seems an enemy of faith and justice. His reputation has caused him to be classed with such villains as Iago, Volpone, Don Juan or Caesar Borgia.* Yet the fascination for Machiavelli cannot be experienced

---

*Madame Merle in Henry James' *Portrait of a Lady* is a more contemporary example of a subtle Machiavellian character.

merely as fascination for a picaresque bandit or a tyrant. Rather, people have felt that he discovered a new truth, although not a pleasant one. Francis Bacon thanked him for showing plainly "what men are accustomed to do, not what they ought to do." And political scientists credited him with creating "a more scientific statecraft" by studying the mistakes of the rulers of his day (Butterfield, 1956:16). Successful leaders, including Richelieu, Disraeli, and Bismarck, are said to have been students of Machiavelli. But a contribution to scientific statecraft is hardly enough to explain the fascination of his teaching; there is something more. Machiavelli felt he had a secret to impart to those who were ready to listen. Perhaps we could characterize it by saying it was a ring of Gyges, for which he had provided instructions for how it might be twisted.

MACHIAVELLI'S DOCTRINE

Machiavelli lived in the rough-and-tumble world of Florentine politics, which was thick with conspiracies like those of Lucrezia and Caesar Borgia and their father (sic) Pope Alexander VI. It was a time of political adventurism among Italy's five warlike states with new princes and tyrants everywhere trying to rule by intrigue and the use of mercenary soldiers. In such a world, Machiavelli's position was somewhat less than scholarly: Accused of conspiracy, he was arrested, tortured, finally banished from Florence; he spent the rest of his life trying to get back in good graces. Such a turbulent world might be called an authority vacuum not unlike that in which St. Augustine wrote his *City of God*. Yet Machiavelli's formula for living in such a world was very different.

Of Machiavelli's thirty-nine works, only three are very well known: the *History of Florence*, the *Discourses*, and *The Prince*, of which the latter is unquestionably the book that made his reputation. In an effort to win favor, he dedicated it to Lorenzo de Medici, the reigning prince:

> It is customary for those who wish to gain the favor of a prince to endeavor to do so by offering him gifts of those things which they hold most precious. . . . It is not in my power to offer you a greater gift than that of enabling you to understand in a very short time all those things which I have learnt at the cost of privation and danger in the course of so many years.

This gift was so valuable that the manuscript was circulated and copied surreptitiously far beyond the eyes of him for whom it was intended.

It also caused a much greater stir than the *Discourses*. While both books praised republics, the *Discourses* analyzed the conditions for good constitutional government and lauded religion as an influence in the state. But *The Prince* had a different message, outlining what a new ruler should do to get and keep power, a kind of handy practical guide for despots or usurpers. Some say that together the books represent a balanced statement of Machiavelli's views, but others point to the inconsistency, implying duplicity (Bhattacharjee, 88), even that his "deliberately exaggerated praise of Roman republics" was a sop to prevailing opinion, to offset the daring thesis of *The Prince* (Strauss, 1958:37).

The books are not so different that a common view does not emerge, although more boldly in *The Prince*. The six main components of that view are:

1) The prime goal of government is getting and keeping power. Security is the best condition of successful government. Although justice is not mentioned, tyranny is condemned as a weak form of government because it arouses resentment and corrupts rulers.

2) Besides strength and above all else, a prince needs prudence. This is not justice, but the wise adaptation of measures for maintaining power. It is prudent, for example, to seek victory and no more; to abstain from threats and insults to one's enemies which produce no

advantage in power and may infuriate them to retaliate (*Discourses*, II:XXVI-XXVII). Sheer wickedness may succeed; but it is not glorious, and may generate trouble: However, if one is going to be cruel, it is better to do it all at once and get it over with. In general, it is prudent to avoid those things which will make one hated or despised:

> He will chiefly become hated ... by being rapacious, and usurping the property and women of his subjects, which he must abstain from doing, and whenever one does not attack the property or honor of the generality of men, they will live contented; and one will only have to combat the ambition of a few, who can be easily held in check in many ways (*The Prince*, XIX).

The difference between prudence and morality is clear in his conclusion that it is "more dangerous to threaten a man than to put him to death;" once a man is dead, he "can no longer think of revenge, and those who are alive will soon forget him." In short, Machiavelli wanted a consistent and thoroughgoing policy of increasing power; anything was permissible that served this. Prudence was the best choice of measures.

3) Cunning is preferable to force as a component of power. The prince:

> must imitate the fox and the lion, for the lion cannot protect himself from traps, and the fox cannot defend himself from wolves. One must therefore be a fox to recognize traps, and a lion to frighten wolves. Those that wish to be only lions do not understand this.... Those that have been best able to imitate the fox have succeeded best (*The Prince*, XVIII).

Even for democratic rulers, success in winning popular favor depends "on cunning assisted by fortune" (IX). In short, Machiavelli believes that cunning is the most useful political virtue: When force is rampant, the cunning one waits; when force rests, the cunning one takes over.

4) Goodness does not pay in the world as it is:

> How we live is so far removed from how we ought to live, that he who abandons what is done for what ought to be done, will

rather learn to bring about his own ruin than his preservation. A man who wishes to make a profession of goodness in everything must necessarily come to grief among so many who are not good. Therefore it is necessary for a prince, who wishes to maintain himself, to learn how not to be good, and to use this knowledge and not use it, according to the necessity of the case (*The Prince*, XV).

He concedes that scandalous vices may lose a ruler his state, but points out that such vices may be needed to save the state. Later, noting the sad fate of an honest man, he concludes that "hatred is gained as much by good works as by evil" (XIX). The suggestion that ideals should be used rather than believed is called cynicism, or the doctrine of expediency. In any case, it reveals Machiavelli's view that there is "no correspondence between success and justice" (Strauss, 1958:200); virtue is simply that which succeeds, what Sumner called a "success ethic" (1906). Fixed principles are not to be expected, for "changing conduct with the times" is the only way to constant success (*Discourses*). But, however chameleonlike a prince may be, he keeps posted about popular feeling (*The Prince*, XIX).

5) Human nature is base, and mankind is willful and selfish. Indeed, this baseness is their strength, especially when combined with cleverness. Though the people are conceded to be more honest than certain rulers (*The Prince*, IX), in general men are.

> ungrateful, voluble, dissemblers, anxious to avoid danger, and covetous of gain; as long as you benefit them, they are entirely yours ... [but] the prince who has relied solely on their words, without making other preparations, is ruined.... For love is held by a chain of obligation which, men being selfish, is broken whenever it serves their purpose ... (*The Prince*, XVII).

How easily men may be corrupted is carefully noted in the *Discourses* (XLII). So, though one should not count on it, it is easy to win popular favor when needed (*The Prince*, IX).

In this low view of human nature, Machiavelli has paradoxically agreed with St. Augustine that men are by nature compelled to sin. But he uses that belief to justify his advice for obtaining power: Men are good only when they have to be, and only strong government can force them to be so. Besides, there is no need for bad conscience if those one abuses are bad too, only weaker (Strauss, 1958:192-94).

6) From such a view of human nature, it follows that there is no need to keep good faith and live with integrity; it is better to confuse men by one's astuteness:

> A prudent ruler ought not to keep faith when by so doing it would be against his interest. . . . If men were all good, this precept would not be a good one; but as they are bad, and would not observe their faith with you, so you are not bound to keep faith with them. . . . It is necessary to be . . . a great feigner and dissembler; and men are so simple and so ready to obey present necessities, that one who deceives will always find those who allow themselves to be deceived (*The Prince*, XVIII).

It is desirable to seem merciful, faithful, humane, sincere, and religious, but one must always be ready to change to the opposite when needed.

> A prince must take care that nothing goes out of his mouth which is not full of the above-named five qualities. . . . Everybody sees what you appear to be, few feel what you are, and those few will not dare to oppose themselves to the many. . . . For the vulgar is always taken by appearances and the issue of the event; and the world consists only of the vulgar . . . (*The Prince*, XVIII).

In a similar vein, the *Discourses* recommends strategies of deceit: One can feign liberality when paying out of the public treasury (LI); a climber can use deceit better than force to rise from a lowly position (II:XIII); that it is better to simulate folly when one has not enough strength, and suspect any "manifest error" of an enemy as a stratagem (II:II, XLVIII); it is easier to deceive people in general matters than in particular matters which they know well (I:XLVII); and one should detect and shun flatterers who are playing the same game (*The Prince*, XXIII).

The emphatic lesson is that appearances are what count, that one should operate behind a screen of guile and dissembling to gain reputation (*The Prince*:XXI) and avoid changes which might cause deception to be discovered and reputation ruined (*Discourses*:XLI). Whatever he is himself, the prince should show himself a "lover of merit," give honors and art prizes, and keep the people diverted with festivals and shows (*The Prince*:XXI). Thus Machiavelli outlined a comprehensive art and policy of managing impressions.

In short, Machiavelli's main principles were: that (1) the primary goal of government is power, not justice; (2) strength and prudence are more important than other virtues in a leader; (3) cunning is better than force as a source of strength; (4) goodness does not pay in the world as it is, but badness often does; (5) human nature is base; (6) dissembling is essential to maintain the image that will give maximum power.

Opinions vary as to whether Machiavelli's emphasis is on power rather than virtue, simply on unscrupulousness, or on letting the end justify any means. But apart from the moral aspects, it seems a fairly straightforward formula advocating secrecy and feigning to take advantage of the ignorance of others, an ignorance which one has helped produce. With secrecy, there is no binding force to any agreement or obligation: Machiavelli has twisted the ring of Gyges into a theory of power without any responsibility other than that of maintaining itself.

In developing these ideas, Machiavelli greatly changed the assumptions of earlier and many later, theorists. For him there is no providence, divine law, or otherworldly tension working directly in human affairs, as Aquinas, Augustine, Dante, and Savonarola believed. There are only earthly forces to be considered; God is passive in a world where men's wills are exerted against fortune and the strength or cleverness of others.

Power is the goal of politics, not justice, as Plato and Aristotle believed. The wisdom sought in rulers deteriorates to mere prudence, even craftiness; gone is the noble philosopher. So Machiavelli answered Plato's question: Why is it that unscrupulous people always seem to be in control? Because unscrupulous behavior is the way to power. Ideals, if sincerely practiced, are a route to failure. As someone put it, "saints sit in ivory towers while burly sinners rule the world." Machiavelli was a rationalist but his rationalism was not that of Plato and Aristotle, aiming at a life of reason to produce the good life for good men. Rather, it was a mere calculation of means for ordinary advantages—power, honor, and wealth. Nor, having denied supernatural goals and absolute ideals, did he believe that "natural right" was built into men (as Locke and the Federalists were later to hold self-evident). About all that was left of traditional doctrine was the sinfulness of men, now seen as selfishness and baseness; and a greatly emphasized policy of duplicity, secrecy, and impression-management, as the way of dealing with those from whom sincerity, duty, or natural goodness could not be expected. Plato might have called him merely a sophist who had added systematic deception to the old argument of Thrasymachus, Callicles, and Protagoras that might makes right.

If we discuss Machiavelli's idea of control without consensus in terms of information theory, we find that for him information control is the prime source of power. A leader cannot obtain power by merely shoving matter and energy around, whether by bulldozers or by tanks; he must manipulate information to maximize what he knows and minimize what his opponent knows, by deception, noise, or propaganda. Secrecy is the heart of Machiavellian strategy, since without it maximum differential of information is unlikely to be achieved. He discovered that, in a situation where men are constrained by ignorance or loyalty to ideals and commitments, he who manipulates information most thoroughly without being found out—from the highest levels of government to interpersonal relations—has the greatest and cheapest advantage over others with the minimum expenditure of physical force and resources. So he proposed to turn all forms of information—symbols, creeds, laws, customs, persons—to advantage by using them to constrain and fool others, but never allowing the others to predict when they would be constrained, except when surface conformity was needed to keep credibility. It was the first total propaganda of word, creed and deed. But, like a system for beating the roulette table at Las Vegas, it doesn't work very well if everyone knows it.

What has Machiavelli's insight contributed to modern attitudes? It has led to a coolness about ideals, unless realities are faced; and a certain contempt for moralists (Riesman, 1950; Hofstadter, 1955). A modern Machiavellian would see wheels of self-interest and collusion behind everything, insisting that he himself is not paranoid but simply a realist. He would assume that something is hidden behind every screen, that legality is only a facade for other powers. Reformers like Lincoln Steffens have felt that before progress could be made it was necessary to reveal the Machiavellian strategies of rent-profiteers and corrupt officials. Others feel hopelessly disadvantaged by the same kind of perception.* For example, as Black revolutionary, Eldridge Cleaver, refuses to believe that white programs for welfare are not part of a hidden game:

> We think this is essentially just surface appeasement..., a deceitful approach that will not buy off the masses of black people as they become fully awakened to the fact that these programs are palliatives—though there's no denying that some have already been bought off (1968).

Others seize Machiavellianism as the only practical way to do business, as in a remark attributed to J. P. Morgan, who told his lawyer, "I don't pay you to tell me what I can't do but how to do what I want to do." Another example is James Hoffa, described in *Life* (August 26, 1966)

*Seeing the ascendancy of Machiavellian types, one better understands the despair of the counter-culture: What can a good man do in a world of Machiavellis? Some even lose heart to the extent of dropping out from the ego games of society.

as a man with an "absolute conviction that everyone is a hustler and everything a hustle," who dismisses all calls to conscience as pure rot. Machiavellianism often leads to a kind of Mafia mentality: Let us be true to our friends and dishonest to everyone else.

MODERN POWER THEORISTS

Machiavelli is called the father of power theorists, those thinkers who see the underlying reality of society as essentially a relationship of forces acting as constraints on men. Power theorists believe that social order rests upon power, the only thing that counts—as Theodore Roosevelt said, "speak softly and carry a big stick." Thomas Hobbes was a classic power theorist who held that men were doomed to perpetual war unless restrained by a sovereign power. A power theorist believes that without some kind of external constraints, society would fly apart as would negative ions, and that power is especially needed to stabilize inequality and subordination. Such theorists usually view man pessimistically as disobedient, rebellious, sinful, or disloyal, unless forced to behave otherwise.

Power theorists tend to deny the effectiveness of ideals, principles, and laws as a basis of social order, except as a working agreement for power games. The true reality is conflict of interest, not consensus. What really matters for order is the disposition of power in the form of influence, control, know-how, resources, and prestige. So the first question of a Machiavellian theorist is "Where are the buttons of power?"—that is, where is the carrot and where is the stick? Thinkers of the power school insist on tracing the flow of real influence that sustains a status quo, dismissing ideals and ideology as a mere smoke screen hiding real forces. If people are ruled by beliefs, this is because

114

beliefs are another form of power. Almost any power situation can be legitimized by inculcation of belief; in this sense, might is right.*

In short, a Machiavellian theorist says not only is the deck of social order not complete without the aces of power; but he goes further: all the other cards, however good they look, are deuces.

It is no accident that power theorists tend to be elitists who see little chance for rule by consensus. Gaetano Mosca and Vilfredo Pareto were disciples of Machiavelli. Mosca held in his work, *The Ruling Class* (1884), that there never would be any form of government but a ruling minority, whatever the ideals proclaimed. Pareto was a positivist, who helped develop mathematical system or equilibrium theory, but his chief interest for us here is in two contributions to power theory set forth in his book *The Mind and Society* (1935). One was the famous doctrine of "circulation of elites." Along with Machiavelli, he held that the world of effective leadership is divided into lions and foxes. Lions tend to be conservative, loyal to nation, class, and city;

---

*By contrast, Max Weber, who was not a power theorist in this sense, avoided the reduction of all social effectiveness to power by the concept of *legitimacy*. He defined power as ". . . the probability that one actor within a social relationship will be in a position to carry out his own will despite resistance, regardless of the basis on which this probability rests" (1947:152). The state enjoys a monopoly of legitimate violence (in police and warmaking powers), while dominating classes and leaders use all kinds of power; but "the legitimacy of the power-holder to give commands rests upon rules that are rationally established by enactment, by agreement, or by imposition" (1946:294). That is, voluntary enactment and agreement are part of the basis of legitimacy, and legitimacy is part of the basis of power. So some power comes not from coercion but people's willingness to accept it as authority, or, as we shall describe it in the next chapter, consensus. Weber distinguished three ideal types of legitimacy: charismatic, traditional, and legal, all with a strong mix of voluntary but not necessarily rational recognition or agreement (1946:295-299).

This does not rule out a legitimate power-holder also using illegitimate force, domination, or manipulation. But as Goldhamer and Shils point out, "it is clear that manipulation cannot be legitimate power, since . . . there is no recognition by the subordinated individual that an act of power has been effected." Likewise persons subject to force often "do not recognize the legitimacy of such acts of power" (1939: 171-2). Thus, recognition of legitimacy remains an element of power which cannot be compelled.

but foxes are climbers, for example speculators and demagogues. Foxes do not usually challenge the reigning order by force; rather, they infiltrate, indeed are recruited into it, for their cleverness is needed by those who rule. As a result, there is continual upward circulation of foxes, especially in a democratic society. Were the ruling class not open to these new-comers, it would decay, and social equilibrium would be upset. Circulation, therefore, is at the same time a safety-valve to relieve tensions and a source of strength for the status quo. Should the safety-valve fail and the old elite be overthrown, it would only bring in a new crew of lions and foxes.

The other major contribution of Pareto to power theory was his concept of *residues* and *derivations*. *Residues* are the real motives of men, and include instincts, drives, habits, and sentiments like loyalty and hatred. *Derivations* are ideals, theories, philosophies, and principles by which men represent to themselves and others (Freud would say rationalize) what they are doing, but which have little effect on action. The true causes of human action are residues, which are often at variance with theories. Indeed, the study of ideology is of little value in predicting what men will actually do, since, contrary to Aristotle, he saw interests and passions, not ideas, as the real impetus to action. In other words, it makes sense to say "I feel like thinking," but none to say "I think like feeling." It is enough here to point out that a theory like democratic equality or an abstract principle like justice would carry no weight against Machiavellians astutely manipulating the residues by propaganda.

Robert Michels was another important elitist whose book, *Political Parties* (1949), established the "iron law of oligarchy," the inevitable concentration of power in any large organization into the hands of a few because of the "technical incompetence" of the many to organize for effective action, except in such a way that put the few in charge.

Accompanying the inability of the masses to rule themselves is the incurable oligarchical tendency summarized as "the law that it is an essential characteristic of all human aggregates to constitute cliques and sub-classes," which, "like every other sociological law," is "beyond good and evil." Michels agreed with Plato that "the ideal government would doubtless be that of an aristocracy of persons at once morally good and technically efficient;" but where shall we find such leaders? Democracy is the least of the remaining evils. One may struggle to maintain it, but the prospect is gloomy:

> The democratic currents of history resemble successive waves, they break ever on the same shoal. They are ever renewed. . . . New accusers arise . . . they end by fusing with the old dominant class; whereupon once more they are in their turn attacked by fresh opponents who appeal to the name of democracy. It is probable that this cruel game will continue without end (1949:400-408).

Later, Michels found hope in the charismatic leader as a force to excite the masses to great things. He welcomed the rise of Mussolini in Italy, and was invited by the latter to accept a professorship at the University of Perugia in 1928 (Lipset, 1962).

The philosopher Friedrich Nietzsche (1844-1900) is famous for holding that the "will to power" is the ultimate reality and for glorifying it as a mystical source of right. He is perhaps best known for his thesis that morality is a drug used by the many to weaken the noble few, in other words, that morality is merely a form of power available to the many, but not needed by the strong (1887).

Another major thinker who may be described as a power theorist is Karl Marx (1818-1883), who, though he held up communal Utopianism as a goal, said the means was unmasking the hard economic interests which lie behind "bourgeois ideology," and defeating them by class war and a dictatorship of the proletariat. Marx regarded even morality and education as expressions of economic power. He denied any real harmony or consensus in capitalism, recognizing only the underlying fact of exploitation and class conflict. Lenin went further, emphasizing force as the only way of dealing with the ultimate intransigence of ruling class power, declarations of liberal sentiment to the contrary.

From such insights came analyses of democracy in the spirit of *Realpolitik*. Merriam's *Systematic Politics* (1945) analyzed the propaganda uses of symbols of power; Lasswell's *Politics* (1936) was appropriately subtitled "Who Gets What, When and How?" Thurman Arnold traced the immoral undercover organization of democracy, such as lobbies, political machines, and black markets, as an "invisible government." He held that without such immoral organization, it would be impossible for democracy to proclaim its high ideals and still function practically (1935, 1937). With more than a hint of Machiavellian influence, Edward L. Bernays treated propaganda in democracy as "engineering of consent." (1928). And C. W. Mills searched for "power elites" behind the facade of democracy (1956).

The liberal Bertrand Russell provided a hard-headed analysis of the forms of power—economic, military, "naked," traditional, and priestly—in order to tame it and prevent concentrations of it from interfering with freedom. Though his political values were different, he agreed with Marx and Machiavelli about the underlying realities of power as distinguished from ideals:

> Most talk about principle, self-sacrifice, heroic devotion to a cause, and so on, should be scanned somewhat skeptically.... What goes by these fine names is really something different... (1938:298).

Love of power and glory are the chief human motives and are reflected in social reality:

> The fundamental concept in social science is Power, in the same sense in which Energy is the fundamental concept in physics. Like energy, power has many forms.... Power... must be regarded as continually passing from any one of its forms into any other, and it should be the business of social science to seek the laws of such transformations (1938:12-14).

By the 1970s some sociologists had reached a radical extreme of power theory: Institutions are inherently absurd; there is no real underlying meaning or consensus or normative system which legitimates or holds them up. What is real is a plurality of power games, in which "social order somehow emerges from the chaos and conflict" (Lyman and Scott, 1970:9). What does matter is power and how it is used; "he who has the power can define the game being played as well as win out;" theories and ideologies are attempts to "shore up fractured social relationships and mitigate ... the Hobbesian state of nature." Everyone is a Machiavellian, participating in a more or less risky power game in which coolness and poise are prime virtues (213-220). Since the underlying fact is conflict, and since society is inherently absurd, the only source of meaning is to become aware of this fact and to acquire meaning by "continual rebellion in the face of absurdity" (Goodwin, 1971).

Such theories show the value as well as the risk of Machiavellian insight: It serves to sharpen perception and leads one to refuse to accept face-values, but to look even more deeply for underlying realities, including the real source of power. At very least, Machiavellian theory has sharpened the distinction between false consensus and whatever true consensus there may be.

By contrast, consensus theorists, as we shall see in the next chapter, put more emphasis upon the natural harmony possible among humans. The Greeks, for example, felt that community is naturally prior to the individual. Unlike power theorists, who see the social bond as a force applied from the outside, consensus theorists assume that common interests and innate qualities, such as reason or natural rights or sympathy, supply social cohesiveness and make it fairly easy for people to agree in enduring ways. They believe such social bonds are not merely an illusion, as extreme power theorists would hold, but are a fact prior to power relationship. Indeed, they hold that social power, except for sheer physical force and threat, is ultimately based on consensus. Ideals of brotherhood and justice are not illusions, but a statement of a higher consensus than what we actually have. Such a difference—between something, however large or small, and nothing—

comes to be the issue between sheer power theorists and consensus theorists.

MACHIAVELLIAN SITUATIONS

Such questions may never be settled on the vast scale of macro-systems of national politics and power elites, even of large cities. A closer look comes from scaling down to systems more easily visualized and empirically explored. Many studies, for example, have been made by sociologists of power relations in small communities (Hunter, 1953; Rose, 1967). Gaming simulations of real life situations help. For example, the "prisoner's dilemma" and other bargaining and coalition situations have been mathematically analyzed for optimum strategies and outcomes (Rapoport, 1970).

An interesting analogy is to suppose that life is like a card game, where you are dealt a "hand" and must play cards (power) according to rules (consensus) for stakes (life values and goals). For example, suppose that life is like a contract bridge tournament, a game which you have some liking and skill for. However, now the stakes are high: your career and future earnings depend on where you place. The game is about twenty per cent run, when you are told that over fifty per cent of the players are cheating (you do not know who, except that it is not your partner). Officials may be cheating too. Already, your score is slightly below what you expected. The conditions of this Machiavellian game are that: if caught cheating, a person will be disqualified and lose all points; but, if officials are dishonest, he may be framed for something he did not do, while the guilty are let off.

The question then would be: What, in fact, would happen in such a game if it were simulated; or it might be put to subjects by questionnaire, "What would you do?" Table 3 shows the responses of some university students to such a question:

Table 3 THE WORLD OF MACHIAVELLI:
WHAT KIND OF ORDER DOES IT GENERATE?

What would you do?	Responses (%)*
1 Report the fact of general cheating to officials and request action to detect and stop it.	18
2 Try to trap and deal with cheaters directly:	
a. report to officials after detection	15
b. apply pressures and sanctions directly	13
3 Form coalition with other players you think are honest to try to enforce rules; hope for enough support to make a difference in the game.	24
4 Play harder, but honestly.	19
5 Do whatever necessary to win, by hook or crook.	16
6 Ritual for supernatural help (luck, magic, prayer, etc.).	5
7 Call time out; appeal to players, ask for vote to:	
a. elect new officials	21
b. change rules	10
c. call off the game	11
8 Quit the game and give up its rewards	9
9 Other responses (describe):	
a. New device, rule or source of information to increase fairness	25
b. Set up a new advantage for oneself	1
c. Disrupt game	1

*Respondents were 100 upper division sociology students at California State University, San Diego, Fall 1971 and Spring 1972. Students were instructed to check whatever responses they felt were appropriate; thus, responses total more than 100%.

As you see, in this relaxed, hypothetical "rat race," some (16%) chose to "do whatever necessary to win, by hook or crook." A few chose in despair to quit the game and give up its rewards. Most stayed as conformers, law-enforcers, reformers or ritualists. What the proportions would be in a real-life situation with high pressures and frustration (say a ghetto), we cannot tell from this. But it is reasonable to suppose that more strain would lead to a higher rate of deviation from norms.

According to the theory of Robert K. Merton (1938), an *anomic* situation, one in which there is a gap between the goals of a society and means of attaining them, encourages such deviation as illegal innovation, rebellion, or retreatism, among those who feel disadvantaged. When the game is "rigged" and "hustlers" are the only ones winning, some kind of Machiavellian counter-strategy seems reasonable, or, as a little boy in a cartoon said, looking into his father's eyes: "Dad, tell me the facts of life. How does one beat the system?"

Even the role-playing of daily life may have manipulative aspects. Role-manipulation occurs in what sociologists call a "closed awareness context"; for example, doctors and nurses of a hospital staff may collude to keep a patient from knowing that he is dying (Glaser and Strauss, 1965:29-46). Closed awareness, of course, can be extended to include all the secrecy of Machiavellian strategy, but at the interpersonal level it consists of games by which one party achieves a goal not perceived or agreed to by the other, such as emotional satisfactions (Berne, 1964), or a therapist's manipulation of a patient according to some theory (Rogers, 1961; Wheelis, 1958; Laing, 1967), or when confidence men "cool a mark out" (Goffman, 1952). Divide-and-rule Machiavellian strategies are even used by children against parents (Chapman, 1968: 70-73). Basic to such models is a conflict view of role-playing, which is seen as bargaining between parties with different interests, and the outcome of which is not exactly what either wants but compromise (Goode, 1960) likely to be closer to the goal of the one with the most power.

No one has gone farther than the contemporary sociologist Erving Goffman in analyzing impression-management and power relationships in social role-playing. Role playing is a "kind of information game—a potentially infinite cycle of concealment, discovery, false revelation, and rediscovery." It occurs by means of scene and impression management, in which parties present "fronts" to each other, which are not accepted at face value but strategically interpreted, to achieve a "working consensus." A performance is "all the activity of a given participant . . . which serves to influence in any way any of the other participants." Teams of colleagues work together to stage performances, the background of which the public is excluded from. Where the background or personal reality is different from the front, effort must be made to "sustain the definition of the situation" by managing the discrepancies in order to hide them or gain advantage from them (1959).

Manipulating others by impression management and secrecy is even clearer in strategic interaction, or "calculative, game-like aspects of mutual dealings," of which a prime example is spying operations. Such games are especially intense efforts to manipulate others by impression and secrecy, but, since both parties are sophisticated, are not so one-sided as a "con game." The player calculates "control moves," aimed to "produce expressions that he thinks will improve his situation" whether or not he believes them himself. A "fundamental predicament" of strategic interaction is that credibility (not necessarily trust) is needed by all players; for example, if a bluff, feint, or threat is to work, the opponent must have grounds for believing it. So parties cannot destroy all credibility, though one may build up trust credits until it is "worthwhile to expend" them in betrayal. Goffman also explores various moves for camouflage and misrepresentation: "covering" moves (secrecy), feinting and feigning, "accounts and explanations," "uncovering moves" (to check or reveal an opponent), and "counter-uncovering" moves, for example forestalling suspicion. He also explores the constraints on power: physical superiority, participants' knowledge and technical competence, human nature, and social norms. People can be used as players, pawns, tokens or mere information sources.

Situations are also explored in which communication and credibility deteriorate to the point that one is unable to manipulate the other; for example, if too much is at stake, a point may be reached at which the motive to dissemble and betray is so great that no sign can be trusted. On the other hand, stability of relationship can be achieved without consensus, as, for example, when mutual blackmail ability puts each in a position to undercut the other, so both keep silent. (Goffman, 1969). Life is not a spy-thriller, but Goffman's analysis doubtless is an insight into what happens in daily relations.

When does a situation or relationship become Machiavellian? Such responses are encouraged under the following conditions: (1) when a situation is anomic: the more anomic it is the more realistic it is to be Machiavellian to win or to defend oneself; (2) when cooperation ceases to produce mutual benefit and becomes a zero-sum game in which one person gains only at the expense of the other, thus putting a premium on defeating and manipulating the other; (3) when gullibility, as a weakness of one party, encourages the other to be Machiavellian; (4) when secrecy tends to give one party increased power and decreased responsibility; (5) when a situation is ambiguous, because it is then harder to catch the Machiavellian in a deception or deviation, the opponent is not sure where he stands and so cannot respond effectively; and complex, in-depth strategies can be more easily camouflaged. So, psychologists observing the performance of "high Machs" in simulated con games found that their subjects were most successful when the situation was ambiguous, enjoying "a protective screen of obscurity" in which the other's ignorance could be used for bluffing and other misleading tactics (Christie and Geis, 1970, 110-11); (6) when one is dealing with outsiders or strangers to whom one feels little personal commitment and with whom one shares few values. In such a relationship, it is easier to make the Machiavellian assumption that men cannot be trusted.

Out of such tenuous relationships, how does order arise? It occurs so long as one party (or both) is constrained in some way, so that the other can calculate him; and so long as enough credibility exists for the parties to influence one another by their signals. But the game only gets interesting when one party enjoys an advantage in power and secrecy over the other, when, in other words, one adheres to—so is bound by—what to the other has become a source of freedom. So long as both parties are breaking the rules about evenly, there is little gain in power. But if one breaks the rules which the other is following naively, then great advantage accrues. So, taking advantage of the sincere, the Machiavellian rides on the credit of a system in which others are more committed than he is. Both Machiavellian and non-Machiavellian use consensus, but differently: To the former, it is an instrument for achieving an undisclosed aim; for the latter, consensus is a commitment without a hidden aim or reservation. The Machiavellian cannot operate with full disclosure; the non-Machiavellian can.

The existence of both Machiavellian and non-Machiavellian personality types has been shown by studies in which scales were used to identify the types according to their performance in various situations. "Manipulators" display lack of interpersonal affect, lack of concern for conventional morality, lack of gross psychopathology, and low ideological commitment. Such people are "charming immediately," but "impersonally task involved" in a game. They tend to treat others as objects and are manipulative and exploitative (but not vicious, vindictive or hostile) in encounter and game situations, maintaining eye contact even when caught cheating. Needless to say, they win more often in bargaining and "con" games (Christie and Geis, 1970).

In a similar vein, Guterman (1970) defines Machiavellianism as "an amoral manipulative attitude" toward others combined with a "cynical view of man's motives and . . . character" (1970:3). In a study of hotel employees, he found that highly sympathetic individuals are less likely to be Machiavellian than those who are lacking in sympathy. Those revealing more feelings of intimacy (Gemeinschaft) and solidarity exhibited fewer Machiavellian characteristics, and vice versa. Also, the greater one's rapport with parents and the stricter they were, the less likely one is to be Machiavellian (1970).

From such studies by sociologists and psychologists, we see what Machiavellianism means in relationships and systems. Common sense recognizes the Machiavellian as the "smart operator," "wheeling and dealing," or perhaps as a "good soldier Schweik" dodging amidst the interstices of a power structure (Klapp, 1954 and 1962).

THE MACHIAVELLIAN MODEL OF ORDER

Assuming a secular view of reality, what are the implications of the power model that Machiavelli gave the world? If everybody were Machiavellian, one would expect an unstable system of people exploiting and dominating each other by force or deceit, ready to explode into war at any time. Standards would be based mainly on self interest and would not be held binding when they ran against it. Trust and credibility would be low, with every party trying to outguess, second-guess, and see through every other. The need for whatever secrecy one could get would favor forming cliques and small coalitions with a common interest—as, for example, a black market operation stabilized by mutual blackmail. A stable hierarchy would be unlikely to develop with so many opportunists ready to seize power or to betray each other. A "grand slam" of power, however, might set up a despotic oligarchy that centralized decision-making, ruled by force and secrecy, and closed off discrepant information from outside. With modern technology, such a world could resemble *Brave New World* or *1984*.

But where information is readily available and widely distributed, both from outside and from leakage of the secrets of cliques, oligarchy is unstable, because information gives power to new groups of upstarts who can fabricate new forms of power. Rebellions are likely. With such redistribution of information and the resulting realignment of cliques and coalitions, one should expect a continual struggle to seize advantage in a pluralistic power game.

On the assumption that most people are *not* Machiavellian, which seems closer to the evidence, we would expect that those who disbelieve rules and violate them with secret strategy, would obtain maximum advantage over the others. We can suppose two outcomes. One is that non-Machiavellians would be disillusioned and withdraw from what they experienced as a "rat race," perhaps setting up a non-Machiavellian system elsewhere. There might be a continual drain of non-Machiavellians out of such an open system. The other outcome is that non-Machiavellians would not withdraw but remain to play the game honestly. The Machiavellians, having the advantage of secret strategy, would then rise in power and privilege, perhaps forming cliques with a double standard for friends and foes, infiltrating power positions and displacing non-Machiavellians (as in Pareto's circulation of elites), and ultimately becoming fairly stable oligarchies, monopolizing important decisions and information, and skillfully dominating the non-Machiavellians. So Plato's guardians would be replaced by foxes. Such a situation is not unlike Sutherland's picture of white-collar crime of big corporations (1949:230-33). Non-Machiavellians, however, continue to be useful in a world of Machiavellians: they are trusted, so they can be used as spokesmen and pawns; they perform guardian (police and military) functions loyally and preserve the secrets of oligarchy; above all, they play the game "straight," taking symbols at face value, honorably revealing their intentions, so that they form the profit and power base for Machiavellians to thrive on. In other words, non-Machiavellians are a needed subordinate stratum in a hierarchical Machiavellian system.

But is not Machiavellianism, because it feeds on credibility and trust, a parasitic strategy? Like the mistletoe, does it not finally strangle the oak? Will not the supply of non-Machiavellian idealism dwindle, as more and more become aware of the "rat race," and leave, or become

Machiavellians themselves, in order to survive? Such a rat race might deteriorate to a total loss of credibility toward those in power. But where next could it go? Could honest Brutus turn Cassius and Anthony back into non-Machiavellians? Or would the system merely continue indefinitely at a low level of trust and credibility, unless a grand slam installed another oligarchy to close information channels in order to reduce instability?

It might turn back to the *Gemeinschaft* of small groups (see Chapter 7) in order to create a community of interest and a sincerity of communication, and to close the distance that is necessary in order to manipulate people continually. (Such freedom being one of the advantages of city life, as Simmel observed [1950:404-5, 416].) The big organization or society multiplies the angles, the niches, the complexity of rules and situations, the secrecies, the ignorance of outsiders, that can be worked to give power to those who play the Machiavellian game. This is not, of course, to imply that small groups will not be Machiavellian to one another.

The success of Machiavelli's model hinges on information management and closure. Machiavelli taught the advantage of secrecy as a strategic power gain with loss of responsibility (control by others), possible through the ignorance of others. Equal access to information, on the other hand, puts all persons on an equal footing and is perhaps the best recourse for those who wish to keep the game fair. "Knowledge is power" is the more true as others lack it.

In the long run, because Machiavellianism feeds on trust, it may ultimately increase entropy in the system, whatever its contribution to order in the short run. This increase might become evident not in gross power upsets but in the deterioration of society and its meaning, as shown by such symptoms as identity problems due to lack of reliable feedback (Klapp, 1969), and dropout, mental illness, and suicide rates. Thus, research is needed to show more of the system effects of Machiavellianism—its tolerable levels, possible utilities, and true price.

There may be, however, a brighter side to Machiavelli's model. For those who can see through the game, its strategies, fictions, and ideologies, and who can thereby defeat oppressors and evade rules for humanistic rather than dominating purposes, the model can work for freedom:

> If one views society as a comedy, one will not hesitate to cheat, especially if by cheating one can alleviate a little pain here or make life a little brighter there. One will refuse to take seriously the rules of the game, except insofar as those rules protect real human beings and foster real human values. Sociological Machiavellianism is thus the very opposite of cynical opportunism. It is the way in which freedom can realize itself in social action (BERGER, 1963:162-3).

On the other hand, there is serious doubt among many that Machiavellianism can ever be truly humanistic, because of its low view of man, and its tendency to emphasize power at the expense of morality. There is a basilisk-eyed coolness in the Machiavellian view, which disposes a person to accept too readily the present, even to *justify* things as they are rather than to ask what they ought to be, perhaps because the person feels that nothing exists beyond the physical world, and that nothing can ever take place except by physical power. This idea appeals strongly to those, including many scientists, who would like to see all phenomena described in terms of physical science, and who insist that the only source of human action is an electrical impulse traveling along a nerve. This might seem to imply that information theory in behavioral science must follow the same path. But, as we shall see in Chapter XI, modern system theory, accepting the idea of emergence of higher patterns and properties, does not have to reduce social phenomena to physical levels, nor for that matter, morality to power. If higher patterns can emerge as scientific realities, why not ideals— even divine laws? "Too much sanity may be madness. And maddest of all, to see life as it is and not as it should be" (Miguel de Cervantes).

7

Order from Consensus

... There is such a thing as a fellowship or society between all men in general: the bond or cement that holds this together is reason and discourse, which, by teaching, learning, communicating one with another, etc., easily make men agree together, and unite them all in one natural sort of conjunction and community: nor does anything set us at a greater distance from the nature of beasts; for we oftentimes talk of the courage of them, such as lions and horses; but never a word of their equity, justice, or goodness: and why is this, but because they are destitute of reason and discourse?
—CICERO (Offices, XVI)

The hopes for human agreement have often been disappointed. Perhaps the first recorded disappointment was the Tower of Babel. As we have seen, the Greeks doubted that the majority could justly agree, even in a small city. Positivism left open the question whether progress was a matter of consent or control. Machiavelli and the power theorists have just had their say: Men cannot be trusted; most ideals are shams by which those who believe are ruled by those who don't adhere. Today consent has rather a hollow ring, from Bernays (1928) to the evident role of "image merchants" (Ross, 1959; Boorstin, 1962). The implications seem to be either that men cannot reasonably agree, or if they do, it won't be what they really want but what somebody else wants.

Nevertheless, there are theorists who hold that ability to agree by communication is a distinctive trait of humans, and the kind of order they achieve is largely the result of such agreement. These are consensus theorists. They usually hold that there is a sweet reasonableness or sympathy that enables humans to get together with each other and with more different kinds of beings than can any other species. In no way do they ignore the truth that humans are also the most warlike species. But faith in the power of communication leads some to talk idealistically of a world order.

Further, such theorists hold that communication leads to an ordering of relations which becomes *binding* through consensus. That is, over and above the need for one another, there is the mutual agreement on and acceptance of the rules for interacting. Such common acceptance, or "common will," is the bond that holds society together. It is the basis of any social structure, whether a family, class system, or modern state, by supplying the rules of behavior.

> For democracy to survive, the members of society must enjoy some area of consensus, supported by the informal contacts of daily life, by formal communication networks, and by common ideals (HOMANS, 1950:465).

A political theorist says:

> What we ordinarily describe as democratic "politics" is merely the chaff. It is the surface manifestation, representing superficial conflicts. Prior to politics, beneath it, enveloping it, restricting it,

conditioning it, is the underlying consensus on policy that usually exists ... among a predominant portion of the politically active members. Without such a consensus no democratic system would long survive. With such a consensus the disputes over policy alternatives are nearly always disputes over a set of alternatives that have already been winnowed down to those within the broad area of basic agreement (DAHL, 1956:132-133).

Or in more popular language:

A nation is held together by shared values, shared beliefs, shared attitudes. That is what enables a people to maintain a cohesive society despite the tensions of daily life. That is what enables them to rise above the conflicts that plague any society. That is what gives a nation its tone, its fiber, its integrity, its moral style, its capacity to endure (GARDNER, 1970).

If common norms and ideals are essential to hold society together, then it is obvious that loss of consensus constitutes a danger to social order, perhaps even a disaster (Lippman, 1955; Angell, 1958; Ropke, 1950; Sorokin, 1941). A popular book describes "future shock" as a "crackup of consensus" in which the "core culture" of American life will diversify into innumerable "pockets" of values, leading to "over-choice," cognitive dissonance, and crisis of adaptation and identity (Toffler, 1970:284-322). In the main, consensus-theorists see failure of people to follow common rules of the game as *anomie*, a kind of break-down of social order (Durkheim, 1951; Merton, 1938); whereas Machiavellians are more likely to see it as a normal state of affairs.

Indeed, "realistic" power theorists are likely to regard such talk about consensus as "mystification." Machiavelli's basic insight was that little happens unless you have power, with secrecy giving an ace in the game to one who can withhold information from another. In the face of such an argument, how is one to understand a social order which claims to rest on free exchange of information, mutual good will and trust, and free consent to be bound by agreements, whether or not they are enforced? The power theorist seems obliged to answer that if there is to be cohesiveness, it must be based on a tangible force (motives, beliefs, and biases can be forces); but "free consent" is very suspicious to him. Are not all human actions determined and ultimately constrained from outside? Some power theorists (Marx, Pareto) minimize the effectiveness of ideas on conduct. And even a rationalist like Bertrand Russell sees power as a basic reality.

Suppose, however, we keep Machiavelli out for awhile and try to imagine social order generated freely by men of good will. To explain such a "mystification" of how a free relation could be binding and stable is the problem of consensus theory. We shall explore how such an explanation evolved, from the idea of social contract, to Park's synthesis of consensus, and finally to a model of collective identity based on information theory. The latter asserts that when a communication net functions well, Machiavellians do not manipulate it. In such a case, the people are sincerely committed to the system, and true togetherness, perhaps even justice, is possible. In short, consensus theory seeks to analyze social order not as a series of push-pull relationships but as a voluntary bond.

THE SOCIAL CONTRACT AND NATURAL RIGHTS

We hold these truths to be self-evident; that all men are created equal; that they are endowed by their creator with certain unalienable rights; that among these are life, liberty and the pursuit of happiness; that, to secure these rights, governments are instituted among men, deriving their just powers from the consent of the governed; that, whenever any form of government becomes destructive of these ends, it is the right of the people to alter or to abolish it, and to institute a new government

—*Declaration of Independence.*

As we have seen, the Reformation began a rebellion against "divine right" which did not stop with religious authority but went on to destroy the authority of kings. It opened the way for a new deciding force in the Age of Reason: popular will based on natural right. Once one gives up the notion that governments rule because sacred tradition so prescribes, one must deal with the question of stable order other than by force: What principle can be found with which enough men will agree that they can legitimize an order without the need for force? The obvious answer is to declare that there is a right created by natural law which can be perceived by any man. Men could no more argue with such a right than with the law of gravitation. Suppose, then, a government were constructed that would simply institutionalize such rights in human law. It too would have the authority, not merely of human will but of nature.

This is the basic theory of the United States Constitution, constructed as a bulwark to protect human rights. It has no authority over those rights; rather, what authority the government has comes from them. Suppose, for example, someone with a badge comes to the door of your home and orders you, in the name of the government, to shoot your next door neighbor. It hardly needs to be said that you would challenge this order, saying in effect: "What gives you the right to order me to take this man's life? Where does it say 'in the fine print' that the government has or ever had such authority?" The "fine print," of course, is statutory law under the supreme law of the Constitution. The Constitution itself is the original contract which authorizes and limits all subcontracts (such as statutory law) and political actions. And all this authority comes from some act of consent by the people or their representatives*, legally solemnized as a contract empowering their government to do certain things and nothing more, "nothing more" above all

*The compact signed aboard the Mayflower in 1620 announced that signatories "Solemnly & mutualy in the presence of God, and one of another, covenant & combine our selves togeather into a civill body politick. . .".

135

in the domain of natural rights. This is the familiar doctrine of the limited state, first created by the theory of the social contract.

The idea of the social contract has unique advantages as a legitimizing device for government. It provides a natural and reasonable explanation for getting together to set up an authority over free men. It is believable in terms of the rationalistic ethos of the time. It has derived stability from its roots in the past and has the authority of natural law. Above all, it has a binding force which was especially appealing to the businessmen who drew up the American Constitution. For all that, it is free and changeable, since a contract is revocable and never superior to the purposes for which it was intended. It is thus an ideal device to replace "divine right" in a secular era, and serve as the authority for a social bond among people who are not kin.

Actually, the idea of a social covenant is old: Leviticus tells how Moses bound his people to agreement with God; 300 years before Christ, Epicurus said justice is a "kind of compact not to harm or be harmed" *(Principal Doctrines, XXXIII).* The Magna Carta provided a model of how people could go about bargaining with a king. But the first important shape was given to the idea by Thomas Hobbes (1588-1679), who conceived of the state as a vast "leviathan," born of a covenant (1651). His picture of the state of nature made it easy to see why people would prefer a contract:

> During the time men live without a common Power to keep them all in awe, they are in that condition which is called Warre.... Where every man is Enemy to every man ... wherein men live without other security, than what their own strength, and their own inventions shall furnish them withall. In such condition, there is no place for Industry ..., no Culture of the Earth, no Navigation, nor use of the commodities that may be imported by Sea; no commodious Building; no Instruments ... no Knowledge of the face of the Earth; no account of Time; no Arts; no Letters; no Society and which is worst of all, continual fear, and danger of

violent death; and the life of man, solitary, poor, nasty, brutish, and short (1651).

In such a state of natural war, men possess the right, or liberty, to do what they can to preserve themselves, including appropriating anything they need, even making slaves of others. Aside from this right, Hobbes saw no justice in nature, but conceived men as selfish, greedy, and rapacious (as did Machiavelli), inevitable victims of war in which there could be "no security to any man" (like Augustine's picture of the curse on the earthly city). In such an unendurable condition, any sensible person would be "willing to give up his natural liberty to gain peace," argued Hobbes; so government was formed as a source of power to restrain the rapacity of men in their natural state. Once formed, such a compact was absolutely binding: No person could withdraw because his liberty to do so had already been surrendered and there were no rights outside the compact itself to appeal to. Besides, who would prefer war over a government however bad? Since the state was the source of all law, the rebel was outside the law and had no more rights than a hunted animal. As tutor to Charles II, Hobbes' purpose was not to give men liberty but to strengthen the king's authority. He thought he had found a splendid device for reestablishing monarchy.

How wrong he was only became apparent a century later. The revolutionary implications of his theory were far stronger than the conservative ones. The trouble was that one cannot argue that government is *reasonably* based, without implying that government is man-made, hence *changeable*. All one has to do is change the assumptions, to say that human nature is not so bad as Hobbes claimed and that the contract is not so strong because natural liberty is not given up to government but only "secured" by it. So argued John Locke (1632-1704) and Jean Jacques Rousseau (1712-1778), fathers, respectively, of the American and French Revolutions.

Locke's view was revolutionary because to him the "state of nature" was not nearly so bad as it was to Hobbes. In it man had a kind of justice, consisting of:

> a title to perfect freedom, and an uncontrolled enjoyment of all the rights and privileges of the law of nature equally with any other man. . . . A power not only to preserve his property—that is, his life, liberty, and estate—against the injuries and attempts of other men, but to judge of and punish the breaches of that law in others as he is persuaded the offense deserves, even with death itself (CONCERNING CIVIL GOVERNMENT, VII).

From such natural justice, man moves by contract into:

> political society, where every one of the members hath quitted this natural power, resigned it up into the hands of the community . . . and thus . . . the community comes to be umpire. . . . Those who are united into one body, and have a common established law and judicature to appeal to, with authority to decide controversies between them and punish offenders, are in civil society one with another but those who have no such common appeal . . . are still in the state of nature, each being . . . judge for himself and executioner, which is . . . the perfect state of nature.

So man may have either natural or civil justice. He is not bound, as Hobbes thought, to accept a bad contract simply because there is no other way to get justice. According to Locke, man could always return to the state of nature and try again.

Rousseau's theory was more revolutionary, in fact, almost anarchistic. The following passage describes his concept of man before he had government:

> I see an animal . . . satisfying the calls of hunger under the first oak, and those of thirst at the rivulet; I see him laying himself down to sleep at the foot of the same tree . . . and behold . . . all his wants are completely satisfied. . . . He knows no goods but food, a female, and rest; he fears no evil but pain and hunger. . . . His moderate wants are so easily supplied with what he everywhere

finds ready to his hand, and he stands at such a distance from . . . knowledge requisite to covet more, that he can have neither foresight, nor curiosity . . . (DISCOURSE ON INEQUALITY).

Here we have a picture of a savage who is too simple, if not too noble, to be really unjust. It is in society, argued Rousseau, that man learns to be bad—to be greedy, covet property, take slaves and make war:

As he becomes sociable and a slave to others, he becomes weak, fearful, mean-spirited, and his soft and effeminate way of living at once completes the enervation of his strength and of his courage.

Such a romantic picture of the preferability of nature to society led Voltaire to remark in a letter to Rousseau: "No one has ever been so witty as you are in trying to turn us into brutes; to read your book makes one long to go on all fours" (1755). Such a favorable view of the state of nature combined with an unfavorable one of society made it easy for Rousseau to advocate revolution and the abolition of civil government. Indeed, in his view the people were always sovereign, and whenever they gathered together, the government representing them lost its authority. The "general will" was what counted; the social contract was not only revocable but loose. As you see, Rousseau's position was almost anarchistic.

Yet there were also totalitarian tendencies in his thought, since the general will of the natural man may easily be irrational. The general will is the sovereign expression of collective decision by which law—the social contract—is made. It is plainly not individual will, but more surprising, it is not necessarily the will of all, nor even majority opinion. Rather, it is the true common interest that might be reached after successful deliberation: as Rousseau said, "the general will is always just and always aims at the public good; but it does not follow that the deliberations of the people are always right" (Social Contract, II). By the same reasoning individuals, even a majority, could be forced to obey the "general will" if they come into conflict with it (Social Contract, I).

The ambiguities of the concept were such that one could not be sure *which* will was the "general will" or *who* had it. Suppose men found no interest in common—was there still a general will? And it is but a step further for the state or an elite group to claim as propaganda for power that their will represented the "general will," thus converting Rousseau's doctrine into something quite contrary to what he intended (Jones, 1947:318-326; Brinton, 1953:132-135).

Table 4 summarizes how the conservative contract doctrine of Hobbes became an invitation to revolution with Locke and Rousseau.

Table 4 COMPARISON OF HOBBES, LOCKE, AND ROUSSEAU ON THE SOCIAL CONTRACT IDEA

	Hobbes	*Locke*	*Rousseau*
Man (in nature)	Egoistic (bad)	Self-centered but just	Innocent of morality
Nature	Intolerable (war)	Tolerable (natural justice)	Idyllic
Government	Necessary	Useful	Useful but usually corrupt
Rights	Alienable (only one: self-preservation)	Unalienable (life, liberty, estate)	Unalienable (freedom)
Contract	Irrevocable	Revocable	Loose
Sovereign (authority)	Ruler, state	People	People
Revolution	Treason (war)	Justified if necessary to overcome tyranny	A good idea every once in a while
Strength of government	Strong, despotic (organismic)	Limited (umpire, constitution)	Weak, unstable

It is important to note that what legitimizes either democracy or revolution in contract theory is not majority will *per se* (which is merely another form of power) but the likelihood that it represents natural truth. Both Locke and Rousseau held that, regardless of education and status (even in spite of them), men were equal in their ability to judge natural truth. Locke called this ability "reason" and Thomas Paine called it "common sense." Locke said that any man can recognize and follow the laws of nature because he is a rational being. His liberty

> is grounded on his having reason, which is able to instruct him in that law he is to govern himself by, and make him know how far he is left to the freedom of his own will (1690).

In short, the perception of natural law, not the power of majorities, is what justifies democracy in contract theory. Locke was no less aware of differences of ability among men than was Plato, but he saw the ability to perceive natural justice as equally distributed. So we see that Aquinas was very much alive among the makers of the Constitution in their thoughts about God's nature, except that the church was no longer the supreme arbiter: Luther's conscience had become every man's perception of self-evident natural law. So Locke and Rousseau were more optimistic than Plato about democracy; and perhaps it was Rousseau who inspired Jefferson's dictum that "a little rebellion now and then is a good thing."

In terms of information theory, what we find in the social contract is the notion that men are programmed so that they naturally perceive the justice which Plato thought had to be the result of rigorous education. In Locke's view, every man was equipped to see natural law within himself (his own reason), hence in society. Because all men could perceive justice, they could enter into decisions which Plato felt had to be restricted to the few. The "contract" was the institutionalization in collective memory, as in a constitution or governing charter, of the justice of past decisions. Information flow, as in news and education, had to be free and equal in order for men to apply justice and vocalize popular will in particular issues. The majority could be deceived in particular circumstances by poor information, but not about natural law, the general principles of which every man possesses innately.

So Rousseau and Locke felt man was protected from the mob mind that Plato feared. They argued that because of the existence of natural, rational law, democracy could be just, whether instituted by a contract or by revolution.

So contract theory is applied in America today, by rebels advocating "civil disobedience" on the authority of laws higher than those which are man-made, while conservatives urge "strict construction" of the Constitution to avoid change which might threaten a natural right such as freedom of speech or private property. Neither strict constructionist nor rebel is eager to recognize his kinship with the other through their common acceptance of social contract theory.

The theory of a social contract among men was the first effort to provide an account of how men consented to form societies larger than the kinship group. The basic idea was of a natural encoding of reason, justice, and equality in all men, which could provide a durable agreement that would be more than a mere coalition of self-interest, just or unjust.

Do modern men still believe in such encoding of natural rights, or has it eroded to the extent that they must move on to new legitimizing doctrines? The troublesome question today is, what is "self-evident" about natural rights? Jurists for example have questioned whether belief in such higher law persists. Or are we merely "living in the declining momentum" of natural rights theory (McKinnon, 1953)? Polls have shown that many Americans do not really accept the principles of the Declaration of Independence or First Amendment (Chase, 1962:152-57). Positivists and Marxists alike take a hard view of this "metaphysical" doctrine of "bourgeois ideology." The United Nations Declaration of Human Rights (1948) is still far from unanimously accepted; indeed, human rights are brutally ignored in many parts of the world, and even slavery persists. How long will it take for such a "natural" truth to be perceived, or is it merely a Utopian doctrine? Such extremes are only part of the larger question which comes from the *variability* of observable manifestations of rights within different cultures. If one cannot find rights equally distributed in a culture, let alone the species, one must hold in abeyance the question whether they are naturally encoded in humans. Many would hold, on the contrary, that rights are simply what society is willing to bestow, that they depend on consensus. The Nobel prize winning biologist, Jacques Monod, said: "If you analyze this idea of natural rights of man, it doesn't stand up for a minute. There's no such thing as the natural rights of man" (New York *Times*, November 8, 1971). In other words, consensus gives rise to the rights, not the rights to consensus. In such a view, rights are not naturally encoded but depend upon the environment and what one has been taught. Others argue that the objective proof of "natural rights" is irrelevant, since no one has invented a better way to protect man from himself. But, on the other hand, if natural rights do not really exist, then the Constitution becomes merely a bulwark of culture—or class interest, not an encouraging thought.

DEVELOPMENT OF
CONSENSUS THEORY

Once natural rights are doubted, the question immediately arises as to the source of shared sentiments like loyalty, morality and justice, by which groups assert their claims on individuals. Even contract theorists argued that society is more than a contract. Edmund Burke, for example, argued that "the state ought not to be considered as nothing better than a partnership agreement in a trade of pepper and coffee." It should be looked on with "reverence" because all relationships enter into it, including people "who are dead and those who are to be born"

(1790). So besides the difficulty of showing natural encoding, contract theory was also unsatisfactory as an explanation of human social order: it was too rationalistic and atomistic. It did not account for the full range of human togetherness, or for what is really included in the "general will." Much more was needed to explain the facts of human cohesiveness. Even in the eighteenth century, theorists began to invoke other principles to supplement reason as a source of social cohesion. In 1759 Adam Smith wrote his *Theory of Moral Sentiments*, discussing sympathy as a natural human bond, a concern shared by Hume and other "Scottish moralists" (Schneider, 1967).

The nineteenth century saw many efforts to explain the non-rational unity of men. An analogy drawn from biology was widely accepted: Society was a kind of "super organism," according to Herbert Spencer, Comte, Lester Ward, and the social Darwinists. Instinct theories, which view man as innately gregarious or herdlike, are favored even today (Trotter, 1917; McDougall, 1921; Ardrey, 1970). Such supposed biological encoding of a social bond, however, has been as hard to prove among humans as the idea of natural rights.

A more promising start on explaining human togetherness was by those who thought they could find its basis in some kind of interaction other than rational agreement. One of the most notable was Le Bon, who found in crowd suggestibility evidence of a "group mind" which could not be reduced to rational decisions, even feelings, of individuals (1895). Another promising line was followed by theorists who thought that imitativeness would explain the nonrational togetherness of humans (Tarde, 1903; Giddings, 1896; Ross, 1908). Such theories were the forerunners of what is now called symbolic interactionism.

Cooley, however, deserves a place by himself for showing that communication, including imitation, gives rise to a human nature which includes sociability, sympathy, we-feeling, conscience and a "looking glass" self, especially in primary, or intimate face-to-face, groups (1902, 1909).

Meanwhile, in 1887, Ferdinand Toennies in Germany had developed his enormously important theory of *Gemeinschaft* and *Gesellschaft* (Loomis, 1940). ("One might almost say German sociology is founded upon that book." said Robert E. Park). *Gemeinschaft*, said Toennies, is a community based on living together under one roof or in a small community, where social bonds are built and maintained through easy and frequent meetings. Such communities are bound together by a sentiment which he called "natural will," or understanding based on sympathy and intimate knowledge of each other. Natural will is "direct, naive, and therefore emotional volition and action," as distinguished from "rational will."

> Out of ... such relationships ... there results the recognition ... that definite mutual action ... is expected and demanded of each by the other.... In this lies the embryo of "rights" which each claims for himself but also concedes to the other, as well as "duties" to which one feels obligated but which one puts upon oneself....
>
> However, when I become conscious of my most urgent needs and find that I can neither satisfy them out of my own volition nor out of a natural relation, this means that I must do something to satisfy my need ... soon I perceive that I must work on other people in order to influence them to deliver or give something to me.... However, ... when one is not receiving something in a *Gemeinschaft*-like relationship ... one must earn or buy it by labor, service, or money ... I now enter ... into a social relationship, but it is of a different kind. Its prototype is barter or exchange ... (TOENNIES AS QUOTED IN LOOMIS, 1940:17-21).

Out of this need to deal with people on whom one has no natural claim comes the contract relationship which earlier theorists supposed was the basis of all society. With his concept of *Gemeinschaft* Toennies established a different and much stronger basis for the social contract.

French sociology provided another basic formulation superseding contract theory. Emile Durkheim's theory of "collective representations" asserted that something was going in the social contract besides rational individual ideas like natural rights. The unity of a society is based on concepts (representations) which have moral authority "without regard for any consideration relative to their useful or injurious effects." From such concepts, collective, as opposed to merely individual, decisions become possible:

> The ways of action to which society is strongly enough attached to impose them upon its members, are, by that very fact, marked with a distinctive sign provocative of respect. Since they are elaborated in common, the vigor with which they have been thought of by each particular mind is retained in all the other minds, and reciprocally. The representations which express them within each of us have an intensity which no purely private states of consciousness could ever attain; for they have the strength of the innumerable individual representations which have served to form each of them. It is society who speaks through the mouths of those who affirm them in our presence; it is society whom we hear in hearing them; and the voice of all has an accent which that of one alone could never have (DURKHEIM, 1915, 1947:207-208).

Although collective representations surely do not come from legislative or other such rational decisions, Durkheim remained vague about the "strengthening and vivifying action of society" which he claimed did give rise to them:

> In the midst of an assembly animated by a common passion, we become susceptible of acts and sentiments of which we are incapable when reduced to our own forces; and when the assembly is dissolved and when, finding ourselves alone again, we fall back to our ordinary level, we are then able to measure the height to which we have been raised above ourselves.... This is why all parties, political, economic or confessional, are careful to have periodical reunions where their members may revivify their common faith by manifesting it in common. To strengthen those sentiments which, if left to themselves, would soon weaken, it is sufficient to bring those who hold them together and to put them into closer and more active relations with one another (1915:209-210).

146

Nor are collective representations always conservative:

> There are periods in history when, under the influence of some great collective shock, social interactions have become much more frequent and active. Men look for each other and then assemble together more than ever. That general effervescence results which is characteristic of revolutionary or creative epochs (1915:210-211).

Durkheim's debt to Le Bon's "crowd mind" is apparent here.

He elaborated this concept of collective consciousness into his famous distinction between two kinds of solidarity: "*mechanical*," based on common representations, making members imitative and cohesive and creating a "collective conscience" whose break constitutes a crime; and "*organic*," based on differences and division of labor (similar to the organs of the body), which among humans is expressed in civil law (1893:70, 123, 129-32). He defined *anomie* as a gap or pathological breakdown in either organic or mechanical solidarity (353-73). Like Toennies, Durkheim distinguished the non-rational consensus forming "collective conscience" of cohesive groups from the more rational consensus of contractual relations of the larger society.

Robert E. Park and Ernest W. Burgess drew such strands together into theory of consensus as the basis of society. "Consensus even more than cooperation or corporate action is the distinctive mark of human society" (1924:165-67). All consensus and society exists in and by communication (quoting Dewey, 1916). They clearly distinguished the social from the ecological, or symbiotic, level of cooperation.

> It is not ... a division of labor, but the fact of social control that characterizes human society. It is not, in other words, the unconscious competition and cooperation of individual men and women within the limits of a human habitat that has impressed upon human nature and human society their most distinctive traits. It is rather the conscious participation in a common purpose and a common life, rendered possible by the fact of speech and by the existence of a fund of common symbols and meanings. The lower

animals have neither words nor symbols; nothing, for them, has what we may describe as meaning. The lower animals have, in the words of Durkheim, no "collective representations." They do not organize processions and carry banners; they sing, and sometimes, we are told, even dance, but they do not celebrate; they acquire habits which are sometimes transmitted as a kind of social tradition, but they have no customs, and for them nothing is either sacred or lawful. . . . By suggestion, by imitation, by expressions of sympathy and antipathy, men invade one another's lives and participate one with another in their efforts to direct, control, and give expression to their own conflicting impulses (PARK, 1927).

Consensus has three main aspects: *esprit de corps* (group or we-feeling); morale as collective will; and collective representations, which make for unified behavior of the members (1921) The group exists, as it were, in its consensus. Physically gathered (for example, a fleet), the group is "in being"; but even dispersed it still exists in consensus.

The "organization of differences" (as Cooley called it—Durkheim's organic solidarity) had to be explained. How could different kinds of people with different value-orientations (for example, doctor and patient, boss and employee, even policeman and thief) work together? Park held that it was by consensus on the relationship, whatever else was different. For example, a Brahmin and an "untouchable" in India could agree on how to act toward one another. Other sociologists pursued the question of how much consensus was needed and how much difference was tolerable in relationships (for example, Hartung, 1953; Gross, 1956; Turk, 1963).

A major development followed Park's synthesis. G. H. Mead developed a sweeping theory of mind, self and society arising out of symbolic interaction. The entire social reality was a matter of the individual creating and using "significant symbols," within his own mind and with others, to create a "generalized other" which was the internalized basis for morality and justice in the larger social order. Mead's term for consensus was "taking the attitude of the other," a skill which comes from language learning and the play-acting of children.

Language in its significant sense is that vocal gesture which tends to arouse in the individual the attitude which it arouses in others, and it is this perfecting of the self by the gesture which mediates the social activities that gives rise to the process of taking the role of the other. . . . We see the process . . . where the child's play takes different roles. . . . The very fact that he is ready to pay out money, for instance, arouses the attitude of the person who receives money; the very process is calling out in him the corresponding activities of the other person involved. The individual stimulates himself to the response which he is calling out in the other person, and then acts in some degree in response to that situation. In play the child does definitely act out the role which he himself has aroused in himself. . . . The content of the other that enters into one personality is the response in the individual which his gesture calls out in the other. . . . If we say 'This is my property, I shall control it,' that affirmation calls out a certain set of responses which must be the same in any community in which property exists. It involves an organized attitude with reference to property which is common to all the members of the community. . . . When one says such a thing he calls out in himself the response of the others. He is calling out the response of what I have called a generalized other. That which makes society possible is such common responses . . . (1934:160-161).

Mind and self were merely "reflexive" aspects of such a process:

The self is not so much a substance as a process in which the conversation of gestures has been internalized within an organic form. This process . . . is simply a phase of the whole social organization of which the individual is a part. The organization of the social act has been imported into the organism and becomes then the mind of the individual (178).

Mead's key contribution here was showing more clearly how consensus (the attitudes of others) got internalized within the individual, and how that in turn made possible a social order of role-playing and justice (taking the attitude of the "generalized other"). He came closer to solving the "egocentric predicament" that consensus theory must resolve: How is it possible ever to know through the symbols of language whether the inner experience of individuals really match? For example, how do I know what you mean by your "toothache" unless I can get inside your head? Mead showed that the continual sympathetic response of role-taking adults to children in teaching them language *did* identify and label even subjective experiences. (For more on this, see Lindesmith and Strauss, 1968.) All meanings, said Mead, are supplied by responses of others: The meaning of an act is another's act performed in imagination. This pragmatic theory, in which there is no gap between what an individual means by a gesture and the social response it evokes, went a long way toward answering the question about what consensus really consists of.

Robert Redfield's model of the folk society (1947) added further insight into the components of high consensus. He pictured a small society which had been isolated for a long time, a tribal village like Tusik in Yucatan. Under such conditions, one would expect to find the highest possible agreement. Tradition, unwritten but encoded in collective memory, would be unquestioned and sacred, while there would be little or no input from the outside world as information or change. One effect of lack of communication with outsiders would be "intimate communication among the members." Because oral tradition "has no check or competitor," knowledge is curiously curtailed—behind "the time of our grandfathers" all is legendary and vague. But in this limited knowledge, the old are wise and have authority. Both because of so much intercommunication and interbreeding for so long, the people are much alike: They "see their own resemblances and feel correspondingly united;" they "say of themselves 'we' as against all others, who are 'they'." On the organizational side, "all the ways are folk ways:" There are no formal contracts or other agreements; status, fixed at birth, determines rights. There is little division of labor: "What one person does is what another does." Almost everything is organized by kinship, "a constellation of familial relationships." Hence, all relationships are personal. Indeed, the relation to the whole world is personal—there is no objectivity. The society is sacred and its world is also sacred. In such a world, of course, there is no scientific thinking nor secular values of the market place. Redfield considered such a sacred, high consensus society the extreme opposite of a large urban society, with its large mass of strangers, market, news and information input from media, contractual and legal relationships, and secular values.

So Redfield drew together strands of Durkheim and Toennies about the natural unity of groups. He gives us a picture of consensus in a media-free world where personal relations predominate and formal coercive law or government does not exist. Here we see consensus theory at the opposite pole from power theory and diverging widely from social contract theory: The folk society is "anarchic" in Hobbes' terms, yet well governed by tradition and we-feeling. Of course, it was the consensus of a closed oral system, leaving open to speculation the form high consensus would take in the "global village" or "new tribalism" of the media system as described by McLuhan (1964), though perhaps suggesting what the tribalism of the counterculture was seeking.

Louis Wirth summed up the position of consensus as no less than the central concept of sociology:

> I regard the study of consensus as the central task of sociology, which is to understand the behavior of men in so far as that behavior is influenced by group life. Because the mark of any society is the capacity of its members to understand one another and to act in concert toward common objectives and under common norms, the analysis of consensus rightly constitutes the focus of sociological investigation (1948).

Mass society, Wirth felt, presents special difficulties to consensus. About the best that democracies can hope for is "not so much agreement on all issues" as "the established habit of intercommunication, of discussion. . . ." The future depends upon processes by which "consensus on a world scale is created."

A great deal of research was pursued on consensus processes in small groups (for example, Bales, 1950; Coch and French, 1948; Festinger, Schachter and Back, 1950; Roethlisberger, 1941), and in the role-relationship (Gross, Mason, and McEachern, 1958), and the self and its reference points (Kuhn and McPartland, 1954). The two-way nature of communication became of great concern (Matson and Montagu, 1967). Following Mead's insight, symbolic interactionism gained greatly in popularity (Blumer, 1969). A more sophisticated conception of consensus developed, including depth of reciprocity (mirroring) and levels of consensus: monolithic, pluralistic ignorance, and false consensus (Scheff, 1967). The concept of consensus as a manipulative or bargaining relationship was also developed (Goffman, 1959; Goode, 1960), which implied a considerable degree of "role strain" or "distance" between perspectives of the parties. There was also considerable concern with strain arising from the development in organizations of "double standards," informal norms different from formal rules (Homans, 1950; Blau, 1956).

Symbolic interactionists, however, were tending to part company over the question of whether consensus really exists as an outcome of negotiation, or is merely a power relationship (as explained in Chapter VI). Power theorists continued to see social order as a vast series of influential and manipulative relations merely resembling consensus, while consensus theorists persisted in looking for common norms and "core values,' which bound people to each other and made them willing to be ruled. Beneath this gap, there yawned another: The problem of the "reality" of the group persisted (Warriner, 1956; Tiryakian, 1962), with some claiming that the concept of man was "oversocialized" (Wrong, 1961). All of this suggested that the "egocentric predicament," which some thought Mead had solved, was by no means banished. There was little assurance that people who used the same reference groups (Merton, 1968:279-440; Sherif, 1964) really had much in common with each other.

COLLECTIVE IDENTITY

Meanwhile, developments in system theory gave promise that some of such gaps might be bridged. Wiener's discovery of feedback as a general characteristic of living systems led to efforts to translate social structure into feedback loops and nets. For example, Deutsch applied it to the problem of defining a nation (1953). An even broader formulation was made by J. G. Miller (1971). Sociology moved from emphasis on equilibrium toward morphogenesis as a characteristic of open systems (Buckley, 1967). Shibutani applied the cybernetic concept of feedback to Mead's theory of the self (1968). Hulett devised a feedback model of the self (1966). Later, a feedback model of collective identity was developed (Klapp, 1972). That model can be outlined as follows:

1) *Collective identity* (CI) is more than mere subjective agreement on a rational "contract" or a common culture. It is a motivating image in the minds of members, who conceive of themselves as together forming a whole, with favorable attitudes towards "we." That the image is shared must be verified: If individuals cannot demonstrate a common "we," they do not belong together. Depending as it does on historical experience such a collective memory may be unique for each group.

2) Collective identity comes into being and is maintained through a network of communication which gives feedback to members. The flow of information maintains consensus, that is, the overlap of messages encoded and decoded by validating responses of others, "we" feeling and group morale, and personal identity (Klapp, 1969). To maintain collective identity, loops must be sufficiently closed to assure that images are repeated often enough to be remembered, and that messages will not just flow out into nowhere without feedback, direct or indirect.

3) Collective identity is not the same as common reference to similar group standards, usually called *reference group orientation* (RGO). All CI is RGO but much RGO is not CI, for much RGO occurs with-

out a closed net. For example, A and B both might call themselves "Buddhists," though neither shared a net with other Buddhists nor with each other. The adoption of life-styles through the influence of mass media involves innumerable group references without corresponding nets; indeed, mass media (inherently monological) make possible numerous unreciprocal identity-claims—even the notion of a global village without a net. But *collective* identity is only that kind of group reference which is sustained by a real net and characterized by awareness of common involvement.

4) Collective identity develops from the encoding of we-related information, which occurs in three main ways: historical experience (such as the defeat of the Armada by the English), ritual (such as the Fourth of July), and personal interaction. When successful, such transactions provide a gain of information (loss of entropy) for the "we" concept (see numbers 6 and 7 below). Such gains lead to a mutual *ordering* of relationships, a coming together as people feel they can communicate better and are bound to a collective memory. They begin to refer to a *charter* or template (Miller, 1971:309). They are not bound to follow such a charter rigidly, but they must refer to it in their decisions about "our" life, "our" past, "our" constitution, with a feeling of responsibility. A modern society differs from a folk society in this respect mainly in degree and number of possible conflicts of "we." Thus collective identity (as Durkheim said of collective conscience) is more than a mere individual preference. It is truly a group product and obligation, yet it is an "open" transaction which can be renegotiated; to use Mead's term, the "generalized other" can have conflicts and undergo a dialectic, it is a little debating society within ourselves. So collective identity is not static encoding but receives continual inputs from new experience and choice. There is no contradiction between such freedom and loyalty to a charter. The only ordering requirement is enough flow and closure of the net to sustain the charter and accountability to it within the minds of most members. This, if we could trace it, would be the wiring diagram for Durkheim's collective conscience.

154

5) As a net, collective identity has its own social structure within institutional structure. The CI net must perform certain symbolic functions (by the same or different individuals), including those of gatekeeper (reading incoming signals; screening and interpreting intake); elaborator (retouching, embellishing, and constructing the group image, performed, for example, by the epic poet, artist, biographer); custodian of collective memory (arbiter, archivist, story-teller, etc.); the decider; and the actor (effector, agent) acting on the environment in real life or as hero in drama (Klapp, 1964). The institutional structure (kinship, tribe, nation, bureaucracy, etc.) requires *at some level* (usually a small group) a CI net to maintain a charter or template—of who "we" are and why "we" are engaging in group action. Without such a net, one can expect alienation and disintegration of the group.

6) Collective identity is maintained through opening and closing processes. As noted in Chapter 1, all living systems open and close as part of their struggle against entropy. A system which does not do so is probably dead. Such a balance is not static but oscillating. An open system, whether static or moving, must open and close as circumstances require, in order to deal with entropy. Social closing occurs by ingrouping at many levels (cliques, parties, crowds, cults, etc.). It includes engaging in defensive action (closing ranks, emphasizing boundaries against outsiders, or inimical messages, hence reducing dissonance); increasing internal communications (reinforcement, ritual, group memory, fraternalization); and conservative action (emphasizing group memory, reducing new input and decision, hence change). Opening means increasing communication with outsiders, for the sake of a net gain in information (trade-off of entropy from noise and intrusion for greater payoff in synergy and new patterns): the decision of the United States to open contacts with Peking in 1971 is an example. Even in war, exchange of messages during truce may be mutually beneficial. Opening, of course, risks an overload of noise, intrusion, and dissonance, as well as of leakage of secrets all of which may presumably destroy the collective identity. Hence no viable society can be entirely open.

7) Certain kinds of messages are threatening, if not damaging, to collective identity, including, for example, "bad news," betrayal of trust, conflict and ambiguity of rules, semantic corruption (as in advertising), and insincerity with friends. Euch entropic communication might be called "information pollution." Any group has a range of tolerance to entropy, but beyond a point (which may be different for each group) increase in entropy leads to a crisis in collective identity, often called anomie. Beyond that range, entropy becomes irreversible: "we" breaks down, alienation increases to loss of morale and membership, and the group is likely to break up.

8) Crucial to collective identity is the content and quality of information flowing in net channels. Is information relevant and useful? Is it encouraging- Does it contribute to "we"? Is it noisy, deceptive, polluted? Is there a net gain over entropy? What is the mix or balance? Many kinds of entropic communication need to be identified before such questions can be answered.

9) In terms of communication theory, consensus (including collective identity) represents the great fact of *redundancy*, what we already know about the message of those who are signaling to us. Redundancy is information already within a system which enables members to recognize, "read," and use information from messages. Were all the information of a message entirely new, including the language in which it is encoded,* we should be unable to decipher it. Redundancy is taken-for-grantedness in messages, roles, situations, institutions, and meanings. Another way of saying this is that redundancy is that part of messages referring to the charter of a system. Plainly communication cannot be concerned only with new information, for without redundancy messages would be unintelligible. Indeed, a kind of insanity would exist: We would be unable to make sense (order) of the incoming chaos, nor could

---

*Redundancy must even be established for a temporary relationship of communication, as when a mathematician says, "Let $X = \ldots$" for the sake of a proof.

we recognize our own thoughts. In short, redundancy gives us a symbolic world. Without ability to recognize its familiar codes, we should be dead.

For this reason, all social systems devote a large portion of their communication to building, maintaining and sharing redundancy, as a vocabulary of symbols (much more than verbal language), and as a tradition including collective memory. *Ritual* is that kind of communication institutionalized to state and revitalize redundancy. But for all its benefits, redundancy is not fully appreciated in modern societies, whose "progress" ideology overvalues the new and discounts the old (see Chapter 10). Traditional consensus is deprecated because it is assumed that new consensus can be drawn from scientific input, or endlessly negotiated from scratch by voting or other means. But the fact seems to be that in such societies change simply outraces consensus, which never does catch up, as expressed in phrases like "cultural lag," "unbalanced growth," "future shock."

There is no justification for assuming that symbolic systems can run on less than a certain minimum "mix" of the familiar to the new. Languages seem to need about 50 percent redundancy (Colby, 1958). Ritual, aiming to conserve and deepen redundancy, presumably needs an especially rich mix to infuse other symbols and persons with new strength, leading us to wonder how much it could be streamlined and still be effective (Klapp, 1969:116-137). The optimal mix of general cultural redundancy is yet to be determined, but surely progress will have to be redefined to include redundancy-optimization. Recognition of such a need is hardly to be dismissed as mere conservatism. Only the most sanguine radical would claim that society moves most productively by a break with the past, from total conflict and zero redundancy to communal utopia.

CONCLUSION

We have sketched the development of consensus theory from the social contract to collective identity. The collective identity model offers some answer to the question of how obligation gets internalized and a fuller view of what is meant by consent.

Once again, however, power theory must be dealt with. As we recall, power theory sees order as essentially some kind of constraint (coercion, influence, manipulation) from the outside. This is especially true when human relations are very binding, as in the case of a martyr who gives his life for a group purpose. A power theorist sees such a phenomenon as the result of propaganda or brainwashing.

In contrast, a collective identity model can have some of the voluntary character of a contract while binding members to the group. The binding power does not hinge on contract enforcement, willpower, or loyalty but on a functioning net whose messages keep the collective identity alive. This is where social unity is and happens. With such a model, consent must be continually negotiated through the net of feedback, and is not reducible to mere manipulation or constraint. Within this net people are continually constructing new definitions of their group and new loyalties. It is quite possible for the group image to emphasize traits such as natural right, freedom and dignity.

To settle the question, however, of whether power or collective identity supplies the binding force for social order, it would be necessary to find conditions where power is not operating or is ineffectual, so that what happens is clearly due to collective identity. The voluntary martyr (Joan of Arc, Nathan Hale) is a perfect case in point: A person sacrifices himself freely for a social cause, despite the chance to escape his fate. Such cases are the supreme test of consensus as distinguished from power. And this of course is why the role of the martyr is so important for collective identity.

Another aspect of the freedom of collective identity is that if people freely give good will and trust to each other, and do not withhold information, an enormous synergy is possible. The output of work and morale increases, while creativity and personal growth result from information exchange and new syntheses (brain-storming, peak experiences, revivalism, and so on). So collective identity does give rise to new patterns of order as well as maintaining the old.

If such freedom and creativity are possible within collective identity, then it belongs in the picture of social order along with power theory, but largely as a countervailing force. It is only when entropic communication badly damages the net and destroys collective identity —when secrecy and pseudo-communication falsify consensus—that we should expect Machiavellian power relations to seem the only realistic picture of human affairs.

8

Order
from
Market

Market is one of the greatest sources of order ever discovered by man. From an Arab bazaar to an international securities exchange, market tends to bring people together who might otherwise be enemies and bind them into enduring relationships, not only for exchange of goods but for other benefits of communication. Market can keep truce among enemies—indeed, it is so important that warring armies often avoid destroying central trading areas, such as Switzerland or Hong Kong. One of the most remarkable features of market is that in spite of being free, it gives rise to an order that could not be established by force. A market derives its greatest importance not only from offering people things (including contact with one another), but from serving as the source of a competitive pricing system. An economist describes the order-making function of the market in this way:

161

> A competitive system is an elaborate mechanism for unconscious coordination through a system of prices and markets, a communication device for pooling the knowledge and actions of millions of diverse individuals. Without a central intelligence it solves one of the most complex problems imaginable, involving thousands of unknown variables and relations. Nobody designed it. It just evolved, and like human nature, it is changing; but it does meet the first test of any social organization—it can survive (SAMUELSON, 1970:38).

It works as a "vast system of trial and error, of successive approximation to an equilibrium system of prices and production," which by matching supply and demand solves three problems: what will be produced, how it will be produced, and for whom (40).

This chapter is not an excursion into economic theory, but a broad and simple treatment of exchange relationships when they work as a market of any kind, that is, when parties offer things to each other where there is bargaining against a background of others who offer and who buy. In this broader sense market might include a political candidate bidding for votes, an artist performing before an audience, the debut of a marriageable girl, or a message offered in the market of ideas. Market includes any competitive offering which leads to the fixing of a value by collective response, which allocates resources and which commits people to action and organization as the result of their willingness to "buy." Such collective response leads to an order that is not simply the sum of the individual wills of the "buyers," but has equilibrium characteristics or other such higher level result. Market then, is one of the basic ordering principles of social systems. It rests on the promise of mutual benefit and is what Boulding calls a "positive sum game," that is, "a series of events in which all parties can be better off." It contrasts with the "threat system"—"You do something nice to me or I'll do something nasty to you"—or (what we would call a conscious power relationship), and also with the consensual system, the "integrative" relationship based on status recognition, love, trust, and legitimacy which we treated in the last chapter as the bond of consensus. The exchange relationship, as Boulding describes it, is neither coerced nor is it a bond of consensus but a free relationship in which "*both* parties feel at the time of the decision to exchange that they will benefit" (1970:44-47, 63). To sharpen the difference of market from consensus, we may say that market is a competitive situation in which bargaining and contracts lead to results beyond the purposes visualized—establishing a market price, for example, is not ordinarily the goal of buyers and sellers. Nor does a free market express power, except when it loses its freedom, i.e., when monopoly conditions exist.

Our purpose here is to appreciate market as an information system leading to an ordering beyond that attained by consensus or power, and to appreciate it in its social aspects, both favorable and unfavorable. The saying, "You can buy anything—even a murder—in New York," sums up both the blessings and the afflictions of market. Plainly it is not a mechanism that always works for good.

THE INVISIBLE HAND OF MARKET

The year 1776 is of special significance for Americans because of the publication of two momentous works—the *Declaration of Independence* and the *Wealth of Nations*—both on the theme of freedom. One was a declaration of the political rights of man, the other amounted to a bill of rights for free enterprise. Together, they made a complete political economy, and still do for many people.

Let us consider Adam Smith's contribution. What he discovered was a gigantic cooperation taking place through a worldwide market, which achieved results such as the division of labor through what are now called the laws of supply and demand. His was the first great statement of the equilibrium theory of the market. The market, said Smith, has an automatic balancing mechanism, like a thermostat; it will adjust itself if left alone. Further, this beautiful mechanism achieves results that no man ever planned, indeed that are beyond human planning.

In the economics of Smith's time, the notion of "laissez-faire" was staggering: Instead of mercantilism (what is now called protectionism), in which governments interfere with trade for its own good, Smith suggested that humans should keep as much as possible out of the market except as economic participants.

No one has been so eloquent as Smith on behalf of the independence of businessmen. He did not claim a special privilege for them, but argued from the beauty of the mechanism, asking if, by analogy, one would tamper with the inner workings of a watch? The mainspring, the moving force of this mechanism, was selfishness. On this one could rely to get the world's business done:

> It is not from the benevolence of the butcher, the brewer or the baker that we expect our dinner, but from their regard to their own interest. . . . I have never known much good done by those who affected to trade for the public good. It is an affectation, indeed, not very common among merchants, and very few words need be employed in dissuading them from it (1776).

The self-interest of the businessman leads to a chain of productive and trading actions that work beyond the participants' knowledge toward a higher result:

> The natural effort of every individual to better his own condition, when suffered to exert itself with freedom and security, is so powerful a principle, that it is alone and without any assistance, not only capable of carrying on the society to wealth and prosperity, but of surmounting a hundred impertinent obstructions with which the folly of human laws too often incumbers its operations (1776).

So, argued Smith, the businessman is "led by an invisible hand to promote an end which was no part of his intention."

Smith was praising the profit motive, one of the strongest and most reliable forces ever let loose in the world. With the idea of the hidden hand guiding self-interest into social harmony, Smith achieved almost a miracle of logic, explaining how a motive which the church had regarded as usurious—the sin of greed—could be the unseen and hitherto unrecognized benefactor of man.

A contemporary example, the automobile "import war" of the 1970s, will illustrate Smith's thesis as well as any. During the 1960s the United States found its domestic automobile market invaded by small foreign imports, such as Volkswagen, Toyota, and Datsun. Volkswagen sales, for example, soared from 390,000 in 1962 to 1,200,000 in 1970. The Detroit auto makers became alarmed over this threat to their "leadership." In 1971, the government levied a protective ten percent import surtax, of which Smith would have strongly disapproved. But the foreign exporters successfully maintained their beachhead in the American market. The Detroit manufacturers' final answer to the "import war" was to make smaller cars themselves as an answer to consumer needs. Thus the competition produced a better variety of cheaper cars than American consumers could have obtained from one manufacturer acting on his own self-interest.

But Smith might have reasoned that it would be better in a free market to let the foreign producers make the small cars, while Americans specialized in large ones. This would have been *division of labor*. With each producer doing what he is best fitted to, the efficiency and prosperity of the entire system is greater. Smith used pin factories as an example of the power of division of labor to increase productivity:

> One man draws out the wire, another straights it, a third cuts it, a fourth points it, . . . I have seen a small manufactory of this kind where ten men only were employed . . . make among them upwards of forty-eight thousand pins in a day. . . . But if they had all wrought separately and independently . . . they certainly could not each of them make twenty, perhaps not one pin in a day (1776).

It all hinged of course on access to a market large enough that if one produced only pins, one could trade them for everything else one needed. Smith was the first to show the great advantages of world free trade combined with the division of labor.

Such was his explanation of how the profit motive, unhampered, could be such a benefactor: It was the chain of consequences which could turn the sow's ear of self-interest into the silk purse of prosperity. The great idea of Adam Smith was the germ of social equilibrium theory.

Classical economics (Ricardo, Marshall) elaborated Smith's ideas into a theory of price adjustment under conditions of "pure competition." If prices and profits rise too high, more producers are drawn into the market, thereby increasing supply, while the resultant competition to sell leads to price-cutting until a "natural" (equilibrium) price is reached. Likewise, if prices and profits fall too low, suppliers are driven from the market, shortening the supply, which leads competing buyers to offer more. This rising of price in turn draws more supplies into the market, until an equilibrium is reached. This was the core idea for a century and a half of development of economic theory about laws of supply and demand under more or less perfect competition, as one might see them in standard works (Samuelson, 1970; Boulding, 1970:102-111).

The famous phrase "invisible hand" summed up this doctrine of the ultimate harmony of selfish, competing interests. This picture of the benign result of unobstructed self-interest caught on and became an almost mystical optimistic faith in the nineteenth century. In 1830 the historian Macaulay, for example, wrote that it is only necessary to leave

> capital to find its most lucrative course, commodities their fair price, industry and intelligence their natural reward, idleness and folly their natural punishment, by maintaining peace, by defending property and by observing strict economy in every department of the state. Let the government do this and the people will assuredly do the rest.

166

Such faith in the "hidden hand" guiding self-interest persisted well into the twentieth century and is reflected in the statement by Charles Wilson while Secretary of Defense that "what's good for General Motors is good for America"; or in the claim by the president of an oil company in 1968 that

> Business should harness the enormously effective force of self-interest and put it to work in the social market place. I can personally discern no moral conflict between enlightened self-interest and corporate actions which benefit society.

It was not in Adam Smith but in Ricardo (1817), however, that one really met the capitalists, the servants of mankind; they were, said Heilbroner,* a

> gray and uniform lot, whose entire purpose on earth is to accumulate—that is, to save their profits and to reinvest them by hiring still more men to work for them; and this they do with unvarying dependability.... His capitalists are nothing but economic machines for self-aggrandizement (1953:87).

So was born the "economic man." "Would you want your daughter to marry one?" Boulding asked humorously (1970:134).

For some time self-aggrandizement seemed to work well. It brought about the worldwide expansion of markets, the industrial revolution, and "the great transformation" of primitive societies into market economies (Polanyi, 1944). Market development was seen as the key to world progress. Economists looked for the "takeoff" point at which underdeveloped countries could produce their own capital and hold their own in the world market (Rostow, 1960). But there was another side to the great transformation which could be glossed over by the mystical doc-

---

*One of the best and most readable sources on the historical background of economic theory is Robert L. Heilbroner, *The Worldly Philosophers* (New York: Simon & Schuster, 1953).

trine of harmony of interests. The nineteenth century could be looked at either as a thrilling expansion of trade and prosperity or as a proliferation of pollution, ugliness, and exploitation. Intelligent men saw it both ways. Those who saw the sixteen-hour work day, child labor, and the poverty of the workers stressed the horrors of the factory system. Men such as Ruskin, Carlyle, and Owen called for a life based more on More than Malthus.

Out of such conflicts of reality with the ideal of harmony of interests and Christian brotherhood developed the debate over ideology, that is, the question of where ideology comes from and what role it plays in social relations (See Mannheim, 1936.) One part of this debate was over whether economic development should occur without any ideological guidance at all, other than that implied by laissez-faire, or whether it should, as socialists held, occur within a planned economy, with the general welfare as a central goal rather than a by-product. Another question was whether theories like laissez-faire or natural rights merely screens and rationalizes ("mystifies") economic realities but do not cause them (as Marx held), or whether beliefs like laissez-faire, Christianity, and the difference between Catholicism and Protestantism really affect capitalistic market development, whether by helping or limiting it, as the Weber-Tawney thesis held. According to them, for example, the doctrine in Protestant countries of "freedom of conscience" would make a businessman less anxious about losing his own soul and help him in gaining the world (Weber, 1930; Tawney, 1954). Because such debate is still unsettled, it seems fair to allow some credit to both sides.

North America remained largely committed to laissez-faire until 1929, when the economic shock of the stock market collapse, culminating in the depression of 1932, finished belief that an economic system could take care of itself. Laissez-faire policy changed to a policy of government intervention in the limited free enterprise, or managed capitalism, of a welfare state. The year 1932 was a watershed in many ways. It was the last time a United States president (Hoover) advocated rugged individualism. President Roosevelt adopted the "pump priming" theories of John M. Keynes, who held that the economy cannot work by itself but requires government intervention to revive and stimulate it through jobs, taxation, price regulation, and control of monopolies. Berle and Means published their study of corporations, which showed that oligopoly was destroying free competition: One-half of all corporate enterprise was in the hands of two hundred giant companies (1932). John Dewey wrote of the "new corporateness" which was displacing rugged individualism (1930). Government responsibility for the individual became official policy with the Social Security Act of 1935.

By the 1960s and early 70s, such strange views of free competition had developed that it was hardly recognizable. Government was habitually intervening in such sectors of the economy as money flow and labor relations. A military-industrial "complex" or partnership had developed, so influential that one could not tell whether government was managing or being managed by the economy—one writer called it the "warfare state" (Cook, 1962). The economist John Kenneth Galbraith concluded that America did not have free enterprise any more, but "prices administered" by "countervailing powers"; free market was a "theology" rather than a description of reality. The notion that the economy serves the consumer through the mechanism of a relatively free market was myth, since the economic apparatus sells the consumer products whether or not he needs them (Galbraith, 1967). Even the conservative Nixon administration adopted price and wage controls in 1971. Laissez-faire remained a position advanced only by the extreme right. Trying to sort this out, an economist concluded there were several different ideologies of American capitalism: classical, that is, close to laissez-faire, disseminated by groups like the National Association of Manufacturers; managerial, emphasizing professional control of corporations and recognizing government intervention; countervailing power, following Galbraith; "people's capitalism," stressing widening stock distribution and decision-making; and "export ideology," a blend associated with foreign aid, which may seem somewhat unrealistic to the folks at home (Monsen, 1963).

During this time, another crisis emerged which seemed to have been brought on by market, namely, environmental deterioration. Cities were sprawling, air and water were polluted, insecticides had become dangerous, wilderness was disappearing under the axe and the tractor. Many of the most destructive intrusions were brought about by technology, but does not market control the decisions as to the use of technology? Where was the "invisible hand"? When would "social costs" enter cost/benefit computations?

OTHER ASPECTS OF MARKET

Anthropologists tell us that the boundaries of economics are nowhere nearly so sharp in traditional societies as they are in ours, where certain transactions are entered in ledgers and others are ignored, or scored as politics, or perhaps analyzed in psychology books. So market as we know it is a vast system of specialized signals about money, credit, and goods, which might ignore such social costs as an accumulation of tension or a loss of good will. But in traditional societies, market includes such feelings and whatever else humans can hold mentally in account. Marriage, for example, is often a market process, a matter of dowries and bride-prices transacted by brokers. Among the Dahomey of West Africa, even children are given into service as "pawns" for debt. Indeed, most of the circulation of goods may be in a "non-economic matrix" of gift and ceremonial exchange (Herskovits, 1952:229, 155-179). Veblen was the first to show how large was the scale of "non-economic" considerations in such things as conspicuous consumption and capitalistic trophy-taking in modern society (1899, 1904).

Primitive trade helps us to see how wide is the scope of market, actual or potential. When brides are sold or goods are given at ceremonies, far more is exchanged than money, if, indeed, money is exchanged at all. Gifts are a major part of primitive trade, for they fulfill complex reciprocal obligations of respect, kinship, or customary duty (Mauss, 1925). "Prestige economics" looms large in primitive exchange, as among the Kwakiutl, Melanesians, and Polynesians, where distribution or even destruction of wealth is for prestige rather than material equivalence or gain. Anthropologist Ruth Benedict mentions a chief who burned his home and all his goods in a potlatch, for no other purpose than showing up his rivals who were unable to afford such a thing (1934). Group pride plays a large part in hospitality, work, and exchange. Greek villagers, for example, give lavishly from *philotimo* (in-group pride), for a return that is not measurable materially. In Tikopia, much effort is expended in ritual shark-fishing when other kinds of fishing would be more productive; credit is informal; and there is a "system of friendly borrowing," in which those in need are allowed to pay back less than the equivalent (Firth, 1965:359-360). Economic relations are personalized and governed by a code of reciprocity which is "but part of a wider code which obtains for all types of social relationship" (Firth, 1965:354-355).

Such a market is very different from what we understand by economics. An outstanding feature of primitive markets is that they deal in generalized values of reciprocity (you do X for me, and I or my kinsman will do Y or Z for you or your kinsman), whereas our undimensional market tends to price everything according to one standard, money. In the primitive market, not merely credit, goods and paid services circulate, but an entire network of social relations reflected in favors, gifts, patronage, and nepotism; it is difficult to say where such obligations stop. Nor do people enter the market to buy, sell, or labor as free individuals but as groups attached to one another by ties beyond contract. Above all, primitive exchange, as in Kula-trading in the South Pacific, is, however far it extends, an unbroken oral network, providing feedback through a chain of face-to-face encounters, whereas the modern market is impersonal and interrupted by media. The customer may never see the producer, even the middleman, so that while market information may be very accurate, the oral network is broken. Thus primitive markets are important for social integration, both within and between groups. They are an important part of festivals, and as ceremonies, are capable of being desecrated or polluted (Thurnwald, 1952:163). Because of their richness of personal relationships, the exchange of primitive markets is intrinsically satisfying, rather than just for a sale, as anyone can agree who has watched an Arab bargaining. The laws of supply and demand and fluctuations of value are not the same in primitive economics as in our own society, because of such personal ties and integrative functions. Also, goods may be so scarce or painstakingly produced by hand for one's own use, that there is no inducement to trade on a large scale, especially with strangers (Herskovits, 1952:15).

Primitive economics suggests that a broader definition of market might be applied to our own society, to include many kinds of exchanges such as telling a joke, offering oneself in candidacy, courtship, religious preaching and prophecy, presenting a work of art or talent performance — any public offering leading to fixing of a value by collective response, which draws on resources and commits people to action when they "buy" it, especially when a kind of order results which has equilibrium characteristics. For example, a study of dating among college students by Willard Waller (1937) showed that a kind of collective pricing (rating) system was in operation, setting values of "dating desirability" by competitive performance and how students were talked about in fraternities and sororities (establishing what might be called a product reputation). The result of this particular kind of price system was that it established a status order, indeed a kind of class system, among students, that was not without parallel in the economic classes established by economic market.

Some sociologists are inclined to view all interaction in terms of exchange—bargaining for something—which, in its larger ramifications, could be market:

Interaction between persons is an exchange of goods, material and non-material. This is one of the oldest theories of social behavior, and one that we still use everyday to interpret our own behavior, as when we say, "I found so-and-so rewarding"; or "I got a great deal out of him (HOMANS, 1958).

A pigeon in a laboratory pecks at a target, for which a psychologist feeds it corn. So the pigeon is reinforced (paid) for the "cost" of his input into the exchange. The mutual outcome of successful exchange (equivalent of the pigeon's corn) is values. In human groups such successful outcomes bring about practical equilibrium.

If every member of a group emits at the end of, and during, a period of time much the same kinds of behavior and in much the same frequencies as he did at the beginning, the group is for that period in equilibrium. . . . A person stabilizes his behavior, at least in the short run, at the point where he is doing the best he can for himself under the circumstances. . . . Change in behavior is greatest when perceived profit is least (1958).

"Distributive justice" develops when the market distributes rewards in such a way that "profits" (excess of reward over cost) "tend to equality." This "may be one of the conditions of group equilibrium." Homans concludes his analogy of all social behavior to market with the comment:

Of all our many "approaches" to social behavior, the one that sees it as an economy is the most neglected, and yet it is the one we use every moment of our lives (1958).

The American sociologist Peter M. Blau showed how a social equilibrium could arise out of consultations of law enforcement agents as they chose each other for exchange of information and values: Both gained something, but had to pay a price in prestige, flattery, and so on. The status order which emerged reflected the effort of all to maximize gain and minimize costs (1955:99-116). Blau sees exchange as the primary relationship, out of which grow the status order and power relationships. Exchange consists of "voluntary actions of individuals that are motivated by returns they are expected to bring . . . from others." The need to reciprocate serves as a "starting mechanism" for interaction and social structure. The advantages foster a network and norms to regulate it, while differentiated power relations and structure arise out of inequalities in exchange. For example, unilateral dependence is the ability to withhold services and status rewards from another more than he can in return (1967:91-93, 118-125). Another view of interaction as exchange, Goode's treatment of adjustment as a "role-bargain" has already been cited (1962). Gamson treats power in terms of exchange, defining "cost of influence" as "resources committed to an influence transaction" (1968:83-91). From the economic side, Boulding applies "terms of trade," and "ratio of exchange" broadly to "all persons and organizations in the social system;" with "role" considered as a "node" in an input-output network for three kinds of relationships: threat, exchange and integrative (1970b:9, 21). Thus we see a convergence between the economic view of market as a mechanism for material distribution, and the sociological view of it as a structure of exchange through which all the values of a society may be realized. Of course, exchange is not necessarily market, for market is an extended network of exchange relations transmitting information which sets values and feeds an overall equilibrium.

To avoid extending market to all exchanges in interaction, let us limit it to that system of signals dealing with whatever is consciously reckoned as inputs and outputs (debit-credit, expenditure-income), which information, passing through the network, establishes equilibria registered in signals that are used as feedback to further reckoning of input. Examples of such feedback would be a stock ticker tape or a racetrack tote board. In broader terms, it could well be that a kiss or a favor could be part of market, but not, say, the blink of an eye, nor an act of aggression not entered as a score in some collective account.

How far market can be extended is shown by C. W. Mills' description of personality market, "the great sales room" of the middle class. Motivated by status anxiety, rather than economic need, its commodities include personality traits, life style, and fashion. One enters the market by putting oneself on the line in sales, interviews, contracts, and deals, and improves one's product by grooming and charm schools, rather than technical training:

> In a society of employees, dominated by the marketing mentality, it is inevitable that a personality market should arise. For in the great shift from manual skills to the art of "handling," selling, and servicing people, personal or even intimate traits of the employee are drawn into the sphere of exchange and become of commercial relevance, become commodities in the labor market. Whenever there is ... a sale of those traits which affect one's impressions upon others, a personality market arises. ... The sales-person ... uses her "personality." ... The smile behind the counter is a commercialized lure. ... "Self-control" pays off. "Sincerity" is detrimental. ... Tact is a series of little lies. ... In the normal course of her work ... the salesgirl becomes self-alienated. ... She wears a fixed smile on her made-up face. ... When a customer approaches, she immediately assumes her hard, forced smile ... such calculation given to the timing of a smile. ... The personality market is subject to the laws of supply and demand: When a "seller's market" exists and labor is hard to buy, the well-earned aggressions of the sales people come out and jeopardize the good will of the buying public. When ... jobs are hard to get, the sales people must again practice politeness. Thus ... the laws of supply and demand ... regulate the intimate life-fate of the individual and the kind of personality he may develop and display (1951:182-184).

Show business is the personality market on a large screen, just as life becomes like show business on a smaller scale. Under such conditions the entire electoral process comes close to show business: Image predominates over issues and candidates are packaged by public relations experts.

175

Mills sees the personality market as a source of personal alienation, a notion similar to the Marxian analysis, which described the alienation of the worker from his own work when he enters the labor market and becomes himself a commodity. Other modern theorists also see the alienation of man from himself and others as a result of impersonal market conditions, in which the person is treated as a commodity (Buber, 1950; Fromm, 1955). Market also fosters the mobility which gives rise to identity problems as loss of roots, meaning and personal value (Klapp, 1969).

We now turn to another extremely important market, that of information itself.

THE FREE MARKET OF IDEAS

John Stuart Mill in his great essay, *On Liberty* (1859), fashioned the ideas of Milton, Voltaire, and Jefferson about freedom of opinion into the most powerful argument for free speech that has ever been made. His essay made a sweeping claim of freedom for the individual in all spheres where society had no explicit right to intrude to protect itself: (1) "absolute freedom of opinion and sentiment on all subjects," including liberty of expressing and publishing same; (2) "liberty of tastes and pursuits ... framing the plan of our life to suit our own character ... doing as we like, subject to such consequences as may follow;" (3) "freedom to unite, for any purpose not involving harm to others." Mill did not call such an area of freedom a market, but recognized its parallel with Smith's free trade:

> It is now recognized, though not till after a long struggle, that both the cheapness and the good quality of commodities are most effectually provided for by leaving the producers and sellers perfectly free, under the sole check of equal freedom to the buyers

for supplying themselves elsewhere. This is the so-called doctrine of Free Trade, which rests on grounds different from, though equally solid with, the principle of individual liberty asserted in this Essay (1859:v).

But what brought him into league with market thinkers was his emphasis on *utility*:

I forego any advantage which could be derived to my argument from the idea of abstract right, as a thing independent of utility. I regard utility as the ultimate appeal on all ethical questions (1859:1).

He accepted the presupposition of "absolute right," but rejected the motion of a social contract (IV), and built his argument on the utility of free competition, of which truth was a utility-value. Without fully intending to, he created a price theory of truth.

Above all, it was the way in which utility of ideas was to be tested that put Mill's doctrine into market theory. First, let us consider his famous principle that:

If all mankind minus one were of one opinion, and only one person were of the contrary opinion, mankind would be no more justified in silencing that one person, than he, if he had the power, would be justified in silencing mankind (II).

Why all this concern for different—including many crackpot—ideas? It was the same concern one would feel about a small promising new enterprise in the market, say that of Thomas Edison.

The peculiar evil of silencing the expression of an opinion is, that it is robbing the human race. . . . If the opinion is right, they are deprived of the opportunity of exchanging error for truth; if wrong, they lose, what is almost as great a benefit, the clearer perception and livelier impression of truth, produced by its collision with error.... We can never be sure that the opinion we are endeavoring to stifle is a false opinion; and if we were sure, stifling it would be an evil still (11).

Mill has such contempt for prevailing opinion because without competition from dissent, we have no way of telling which part of the current opinion is true and useful, since it all comes from the public, that miscellaneous collection of a few wise and many foolish individuals. Even good ideas, unless challenged continually, deteriorate (like market goods untested by competition):

> Not only the grounds of the opinion are forgotten in the absence of discussion, but too often the meaning of the opinion itself.... Instead of a vivid conception and a living belief, there remain only a few phrases retained by rote (11).

Such a "mischievous operation of the absence of free discussion" is what economists would call monopoly exerting its hand to stifle competition and set prices, in this case truth-values.

> There must be discussion, to show how experience is to be interpreted. Wrong opinions and practices gradually yield to fact and argument.... The whole strength and value ... of human judgment, depending on the one property, that it can be set right when it is wrong, reliance can be placed on it only when the means of setting it right are kept constantly at hand.... Hearing what can be said ... by persons of every variety of opinion, and studying all modes in which ... looked at by every character of mind. No wise man ever acquired his wisdom in any mode but this.... The steady habit of correcting and completing his own opinion by collating it with those of others, so far from causing doubt and hesitation ... is the only stable foundation for a just reliance on it ... knowing that he has sought for objections and difficulties, instead of avoiding them, and has shut out no light ... he has a right to think his judgment better than that of any person, or any multitude, who have not gone through a similar process (11).

So an invisible hand brings progress and truth from the clash of biased and selfish opinions. It hinges, of course, on the ability to recognize truth when one has tested it through rational arguments under open, temperate conditions. Without these, there is little hope:

> The dictum that truth always triumphs over persecution is one of those pleasant falsehoods which men repeat after one another. ... History teems with instances of truth put down by persecution. ... Christianity might have been extirpated. ... It spread, and became predominant, because the persecutions were only occasional, lasting but a short time, and separated by long intervals of almost undisturbed propagandism. It is a piece of idle sentimentality that truth, merely as truth, has any inherent power denied to error of prevailing against the dungeon and the stake. ... The real advantage which truth has, consists in that ... it may be extinguished once, twice, or many times, but in the course of ages there will generally be found persons to rediscover it, until one of its reappearances falls on a time when from favorable circumstances it escapes persecution (11).

At the opposite pole from persecution are optimum conditions of competition for improving knowledge: constant debate, temperateness, Socratic dialectics, searching out the strongest opponent of an opinion—even a devil's advocate—to test it. Will this lead to disorder and confusion? On the contrary, knowledge will accumulate and society will progress:

> As mankind improve, the number of doctrines which are no longer disputed or doubted will be constantly on the increase: and the well-being of mankind may almost be measured by the number and gravity of the truth which have reached the point of being uncontested (11).

But all truths must be continually protected by dialectics in education from the "incurable defect" of being accepted from authority, not from reason.

Like Smith, Mill had to base his argument for freedom on the assumption that if society wants progress, it must grant freedom. Otherwise it must enjoy the dubious comfort of conformity to poor ideas and products. In this way progress in wealth is paralleled by progress in knowledge. The pricing system in one case is competitive sale of goods, and in the other, open debate, the outcome in either case being a moving equilibrium of progress toward a better society. The great power of Mill's idea, as of Smith's was that it placed freedom on a utilitarian instead of a metaphysical basis, the latter being shaky in an age of positivism. In the free market truth-value and price are parallel notions of utility.

Mill's splendid argument should be read in detail and at leisure. It is the core of liberalism any time, anywhere. Attacks on liberalism today show the discomfort of some at free competition of ideas, just as some of their counterparts in the business world dislike free trade. As Karl Popper (1952) pointed out, even Plato did not appreciate the importance for rationality and justice of a free market of ideas as implied by Socrates' roving dialectic. But his concept of Utopia was after all a static rather than a moving equilibrium.

According to Mill's argument, an open society must constantly face the challenges of new ideas or it will lapse into conformity. To avoid suppressing valuable ideas, it must tolerate deviant, even dangerous opinions and life styles, so long as they do not result in social injury. Censorship is abhorrent, for it implies the assumption of infallibility. The liberal must even tolerate ideas which threaten the free institutions on which he relies. Suppose he faces in debate an opponent who talks openly of establishing concentration camps. His dilemma is that if he denies his opponent the privilege of urging such proposals, he himself suppresses the free market of ideas. If he grants his opponent a hearing, freedom may be imperiled. A true follower of Mill must at this point rely on the probability of the free market of ideas working in the long run, over the certainty of damaging it by his own act of suppression. He must believe that an uncertain evil done by another is better than committing a certain one himself.

The question that Mill did not answer was how the market of ideas would function when opinions were not tested by rational debate. In dogmas he saw merely stagnant conformity. But modern sociologists are studying the growth of religion and other ideology as a "market of legitimation" under non-monopolistic conditions, in which consumers of ideas choose among legitimating systems, say Buddhism, Vedanta, psychoanalysis, or Presbyterianism, in building—one might say buying— their pictures of the world, instead of being forced into a particular choice by the monopolistic market of traditional society (Berger and Luckmann, 1963).

MARKET AS AN INFORMATION SYSTEM

Having looked at market in its varieties, we are in a better position to see its scope as an integrative social process, as a distributing system for goods and services, matter-energy and information (Miller, 1971: 314-316). It is as an information system that the characteristic functions of market are performed. As an information system market supplies parties with feedback which they *cannot see from direct relations* of exchange. This feedback, in the form of concepts like "price" helps market participants determine what they should do to maximize returns from their own inputs. Market feedback provides a reading of a total state of affairs, an entire systemic balance, from an extended network of communication, in which no one party knows or controls his own input-output completely, but has only generalized feedback from relations occurring over the whole net, whether from many sources or a centralized "tote board." From this feedback he derives a picture of the state of the market ("soft," "bearish," etc.), for which he can devise strategies. Prompt feedback may require a central scoreboard, or price listing. In broader terms, truth, esthetic, and religious values are respectively registered by such agencies as scientific journals, reviews, academies, or scholarly opinion generally; art criticism, shows and galleries; mass media pundits and authoritative pulpits. In this aspect of registering "price" of various kinds, market is an *encoding* mechanism, converting a vast amount of information into a few signals. So market serves as a sensitive indicator of human wants, an adjuster of what otherwise might be conflicts, and a strong incentive to enterprise and cooperation.

Such an information system brings parties into cooperation and balance through concepts like "fair price," but also contributes to negative results beyond their intention, such as booms, panics, and misleading rumors. Parties seek to dictate, but cannot dictate, the outcome of the market. This integrating information process is distinguishable from mere power relations, on the one hand, and consensus on the other. Power is calculated investment of influence in a result desired by the wielder of power. But a free market typically denies such power over itself. Power thrives on secrecy, market thrives on publicity.

An important distinction exists between market and power as forms of order resulting from rationality. Rational use of power leads to *plan*, which is fundamentally different from *market*. Though they coexist, they are incompatible in principle; indeed, their "clash provides the substance of the central social and political conflict of our time." "Plan-rational orientation" requires "substantive social norms" and "use of power to determine in advance who does what and who gets what;" there is "no room at all" for individual or conflicting decisions. Nonliberal societies are organized according to plan, whereas liberal societies are organized on market principles, where in competition and exchange "all comers do their best to improve their own lot." To preserve market, power and planning must leave it alone, except to define and enforce "rules of the game," although when major adjustments of market are needed, for example, taxation, protection from monopoly, or granting outsiders the right to participate, "planned intervention of government is indispensable." So we have what seems a paradox: though often in

182

conflict, both market and planned systems of order need and supplement each other. A plan-rational or authoritarian society is in danger of revolutionary upheaval unless it allows market-rationality the freedom to work out the needs and interests of pluralistic society. On the other hand, a pure free market, or a society without plan-rationality, is a fiction, a "utopia of powerlessness." In real life "the game always takes place in front of city hall." Though pure market is a fiction, the metaphor "still guarantees more freedom than any other idea in the history of political theory. Its strength lies in its recognition of social conflicts, and thus of the fundamental changeability of any good society. . . . Only one thing remains certain: If the new rationality is to be compatible with human freedom, it must be market rationality." (Dahrendorf, 1968:218-231).

In contrast to the random working of market or the planned operations of a power model, consensus is typically a direct understanding among parties, as in contract, marriage, or collusion. Though it is necessary to many exchanges making up market, too much consensus tends to resemble power monopoly in its clogging effect on free competition and flow of goods and information. Market needs consensus as to the rules of the game, but consensus about outcomes would stop the game as surely as in any sport. As Mill pointed out for ideas, constant challenge to consensus is necessary—competitive bargaining, even a little conflict. Opinion leaders and gatekeepers, exerting power here and molding consensus there, have their part in both power and consensus systems affecting market.

In short, market is ideally an integrated system of larger scope than either power or consensus, but works in balance with them. Table 5 shows the flow of information and role of power and consensus in market. (See Table 5, next page.)

Plainly, market requires balanced inputs. Too much noise could drown out rather than stimulate innovation. Although some control is needed to preserve the game, too much control, whether from consensus or power, could stifle the market. Too much power or too heavy an authority of tradition could put such a cost on the supply of innovation

Table 5   INFORMATION MODEL OF MARKET—POWER—CONSENSUS SYSTEM

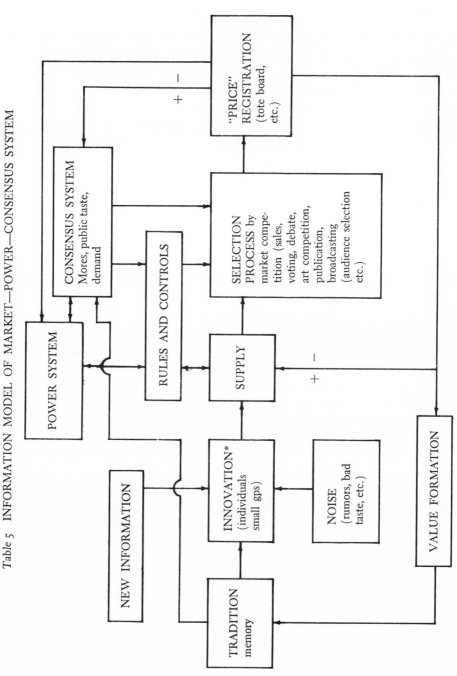

*Includes deviation

or make the odds of competition so unfair that it would dry up. Nevertheless, "price" registration feeds consensus, and rises and falls reflect changes in the power system.

So we see a complex network of feedback loops among three components: power, consensus, and market. If any of these were to maximize themselves, others would be minimized or eliminated. It is to the advantage of society to see as clearly as possible where its markets are, what they deal in, how well they are working, or why they may be failing. Society should also be aware of the balance of exchange between power, consensus, and market. Information theory may ultimately be able to provide a general model for all kinds of information flow in society, including market.

DISAPPOINTMENTS AND DEGRADATIONS OF MARKET

The self-adjusting market discovered by Adam Smith and John Stuart Mill has served man remarkably, with respect to both goods and information. Socialist countries have tried to curtail the free market, but found they could not do so successfully (Libermanism in the USSR). A black market of rumor also flourished, offsetting official news and propaganda (Bauer and Gleicher, 1953; Inkeles and Bauer, 1966). But in countries where market was allowed to work most freely, complaints were heard about its apparent inability to balance itself, about the encroachment upon it of power and selfish interest (oligarchy), and about its irresponsibility for and unresponsiveness to human needs. History has made plain that economic market, however free, however attuned to conditions of supply and demand, is not inherently just and does not distribute justice.

> Even if the system worked perfectly ... many would not consider
> it ideal. In the first place, goods go where there are the most votes
> or dollars. A rich man's dog may receive the milk that a poor child
> needs to avoid rickets. Why? Because supply and demand are work-
> ing badly? ... Not from the standpoint of what the market mech-
> anism is geared to accomplish. Functionally, auction markets are
> doing what they are designed to do—putting goods in the hands
> of those who can pay the most, who have the most votes (SAMUEL-
> SON, 1970:41-42).

Rewards of the game go to those who enter best fitted by ability, training, and fortune to play. One cannot expect from market concern for
values beyond the pricing of market. So in 1971, American auto makers
were preparing to invade foreign markets since domestic were nearly
saturated. With almost one car for every two people, future expansion
had to lie in the pool of unsatisfied demand abroad. There was no concern, however, with whether the rest of the world—its air, surface or
resources—could stand similar saturation, say about two billion more automobiles. Let people try to sell other proposals in competition with automobiles. Then we will see what market says the world needs.

In the United States some people were asking whether the market
and its corporate participants were supplying private rather than public
luxury (Galbraith, 1958), and whether it was responsive to consumers'
needs and to the social costs of pollution. The consumers' crusade led
by Ralph Nader tried to force corporations to be more responsive to
their customers, resorting to power machinery outside market, such as
courts, legislative processes, investigative exposés, and protests and con-
frontations.

Yet the notion of market as unresponsive was only a partial truth.
Actually, the giants were very responsive to what they wanted to see.
Boulding says market is "a sensitive system" which "has a capacity for
going very badly wrong" (1970a:105). Rather than lack of response, the
problem is better called over-response and under-response, depending on
partial vision.

186

A filtering mechanism seems to be at work in market, encoding certain kinds of information into legitimized "price," and disregarding all other considerations, opinions and feelings except as priced in that market. Such blindness is expressed in the saying, "He knows the price of everything and the value of nothing." Should the market happen to be logical argument, then feelings become invalid unless rationalized. Should it be priced in terms of symbols of social front, fashion, or personality, then personal worth without such symbols is devalued relatively, by having no recognized voice. On the other hand, a black market (Clinard, 1952) shows how responsive market can be to new demands properly priced, in this case an illicit demand for something for which people are willing to pay high prices, even break laws, to buy in a market whose very illegitimacy raises the price and draws in more supply. Here an insensitive or overcontrolling power structure seems to be thwarted by a highly sensitive and venturesome market. So Al Capone described himself as a public benefactor during Prohibition.

Because of its very sensitivity combined with partial blindness, market is capable of degradations, whether these occur as a swing toward debased values, or entropic side-effects on society. Economists recognize such a degradation in Gresham's law, where "cheap money drives out good." For example, when two metals are used as a basis of coinage (bimetallism), coins of the cheaper metal will enter circulation and those of the more valuable metal be withdrawn into saving, until, for all practical purposes, a monometallic standard at a lower level has been reached. Any market may not only filter out "good" values but pick up and emphasize "bad" ones, pandering to "lower" tastes by downgrading the quality of goods, by overpricing the base, or by failing to give market value to some higher good. For example, every instructor knows that if student demand for entertainment is allowed to dictate teacher ratings, intellectual content might well decrease while entertainment values and even salaries increase, as students flock to the more popular performers, who may also offer interesting premiums such as no grades or all "B" or "A" grades. If an academic power structure did not dictate the terms and standards of such a market, supported by consensus of instructors, a popularity market of education could deteriorate into fiasco or fraud.

The dispute as to whether such degradations of market come more from input (media, products offered) or popular demand (indiscriminate or debased mass tastes) need not be settled here, since either constitutes a filter for market, and somehow together they make "price."

One of the most familiar examples of this unhappy price-fixing is the battering down of esthetic standards under the pressures of commercialism. An architect, for example, complains:

> Why should the nation with the highest living standard, the best program for mass education, and the highest degree of ingenuity in solving scientific problems make such a mess of its physical environment? ... The approaches [to cities] are befouled by billboards, garish signs, utility poles, overhead wires, junkyards and blighted business buildings.... Waterfronts, potentially places for recreation, are littered with junk and industrial debris (DREW, 1966).

An American real estate developer takes some responsibility for poor design and passes the rest of it on to market demand, "If it's more profitable to make garbage, you'll get garbage." Again, we find an artist who can make fine things manufacturing gewgaws, knowing that he is corrupting his own work. Or there are the phenomena known in the academic world as "publish or perish," and "grants chasing," in which true scholarship is sacrificed for money or prestige. Whatever the primary cause, we can see a vicious circle of debased or blind demand leading to increased low quality production to meet this demand, further debasing, numbing, or polluting taste and leading to less demand for good quality and more willingness to accept poor. A more tragic example of demand resulting in greater entropy than service to participants is the worldwide, escalating competition for armaments. Public and private arms merchants typically blame not themselves but demand, the market itself, for supplying the world with the instruments of death. The head of Interarms, the world's largest private arms broker, claims that political agreements to restrict nuclear weapons would not decrease the total supply of arms but simply increase the movement of conventional types. Speaking for his fellow arms merchants, he said:

> We are merely, in my view, a reflection for better or worse of the times in which we live.... The whole arms business ... is essentially based on human folly and as such is self-perpetuating. It increases in direct proportion to human folly as the world's population increases (COOLEY, 1972).

Without trying to pinpoint the start of the degradation cycle, we may suppose that a contributing factor is the sheer emphasis on market itself, to the exclusion of other values. The overemphasis on selling in American mass media is a striking example of the intrusion of market values: Television channels are overloaded with sales pitches and even the content of programs is dictated by commercial interests. Indeed, consumption has become a symbol of the good life, a way of solving all problems from heartaches to heartburns, which Goodman satirized in his design of a city as a cluster of apartments centered around a supermarket (1947). How market values can intrude where they have no proper place is illustrated by a New York *Times* editorial deploring "history for sale":

> An industrial development opposite Mt. Vernon, power lines at Antietam, an intrusive viewing tower overlooking Gettysburg, the prospect of a supermarket at the entrance to the Roosevelt home at Hyde Park—the threats to the nation's hallowed ground are seemingly endless. Congress could ... provide ... protection for the scenic approaches to all the nation's historic sites (1971).

In these cases the sheer presence of market is inappropriate.

Margaret Mead suggests that some of the mistrust of and alienation from the mass media, the political system, and venerated American symbols is due to debasement of information by commercial interests. Suppose a dishonest correspondence course used a name like Florence

Nightingale or Abraham Lincoln to gain students. Would experience with such a phony course corrode these venerated symbols?

> In our American system of communications, any interest, wishing to "sell" its products or messages to the public, is able to use the full battery of available communication techniques, radio, and film, press and poster. It is characteristic of this system that the symbols used to arouse emotion . . . have come into the hands of those who feel no responsibility toward them. In a society like Bali there is simply no possibility that such a symbol as "The Village," also spoken of as "Mister Village" and as "God Village," could be used by a casual vendor or rabble rouser. The symbols which evoke responses are used by those whose various positions in the society commit them to a responsible use. But in the United States, most of the value symbols of American tradition are ready to the hand of the manufacturer of the most trivial debased product, or the public relations counsel of the most wildcat and subversive organizations (M. MEAD, 1964).

Information-pollution and overload (Miller, 1971:383) give a broader view of such degradation in the market of ideas: The communication process itself is polluted by noise of various kinds, including semantic corruption, deception, bias, excessive violence or negative feeling from media and from the irrational inputs of rumor and emotional contagion. Partly because of its very openness, society suffers from a high noise situation, in which "good" voices have to yell to be heard, debate may be silenced, and media technology amplifies the signals of anyone who has access to it, so that the open market of information often results in increased entropy.

Such were some of the social costs attributed to the use or misuse of market in modern society. The concept of social costs was enlarged in the 1970s into a statement of all human values—abused by power structures and neglected or degraded by market mechanisms. No longer were people sure, as Smith and Mill were, that open market necessarily meant progress, or that it was fairer than political mechanisms.

Market's responsibility for degradation seemed due in part to inherent characteristics of *filtering*; that is, in whatever terms market sets its own univalent "price," it cannot reckon social costs not expressed in that price. For example, it cannot transmit what an anthropologist would call social reciprocity. Nor, by its pricing, can it keep out goods judged worthless by another standard (especially when its own sensitivity is to some "sinful" common denominator of human nature as described by St. Augustine or Freud).

Another intrinsic weakness of market is that its participants rarely know until after feedback even the price outcomes of their actions in market, let alone the effects on society as a whole. Yet another inherent weakness is that merchandising and propaganda, voices of market, tend to be louder and more powerful than non-market voices, if only because the wherewithal to buy such power is accumulated by market voices. Finally, market often exploits weak consumer judgment through dishonesty, direct marketing to children, or creating distortions of demand (Hechinger, 1962), all of which only add to whatever degradation is underway.

Perhaps the moral of this discussion of free market's failure to recognize the need of the whole man and to keep out "garbage" is that when conscience and wisdom are required, market should not be allowed to govern policy decision. In other words, however efficient and self adjusting market may be, there is no assurance that any higher value like justice or beauty will result, nor even that its proper products will not be degraded. Efficient though it may be in filling ordinary demands, market is no substitute for wisdom and conscience. Because of its filtering characteristic, we could never expect it to be wise enough to solve the world's problems, nor remove the need for good deeds and wise men at the helm, as the Greeks realized. At the moral level, we remain with Plato: The hope of the world rests less on its ability to mobilize resources, supply, demand, or power structures than on wisdom—the one thing market can not register.

CONCLUSION

As a system, market consists of an information net created by exchanges, through which feedback flows to create equilibrium and to provide information about it. As such, a free market goes beyond whatever power is invested in it, unless such power is enough to destroy competition by creating monopoly, in which case market is destroyed. Market also goes beyond whatever consensus is brought to it, being impaired by too much (as might a horse race if there was an agreement among jockeys), although it does feed back a higher consensus in terms of "price." Market normally works in balance with consensus, power, and rational planning. As we have already suggested, it could not be enough for societal guidance, even if it were possible to eliminate rational planning, power, and consensus. Doubtless, also, a pluralistic society benefits from many kinds of markets, so that many kinds of "prices" are available to various needs and abilities.

A total systemic view requires that market be seen as only one of the information systems which work together to integrate the total system. [Hajda suggests that there are four kinds of subsystems: community, consensus, market, and hierarchy, working in pairs as polar opposites to integrate the total system (1971).] However many subsystems there may be, market can only hope for freedom for information about market conditions and for freedom to buy and sell according to rules. It must operate within a context of power and consensus, in which ideology may screen the realities of the relationships between market, power, and consensus. In the larger system view, there is doubtless a balance sheet of payoffs and exchanges, costs and benefits, broader in scope than any market price could register (Klapp, 1972). By study of such a balance sheet, system theorists may hope ultimately to solve the problem of optimizing a system—whether along lines envisioned by Plato, or Marx, or Mill, or Machiavelli.

9

Order through Struggle

In the Garden of Eden all was well. The trees gave forth fruit and man lived without struggle, either with nature or his own kind. Then an element of disorder crept in, giving rise to a clash that thrust man into the struggle for survival and what St. Augustine called the yoke of servitude.

A school of social thinkers—which includes Machiavelli, Hobbes, Freud, Marx, the social Darwinists, and modern sociologists like Dahrendorf (1959) or Lyman and Scott (1970) are known as *conflict theorists* because in their view of social reality man's earthly lot is naturally filled with conflict and difference of interest, not cooperation and consensus. Such thinkers may also be power theorists, holding that order is the result of one person or group having enough power to impose his or their will on others. But power theorists or not, all conflict theorists observe that conflict and change take place at all levels, and reject the notion of society as an "equilibrium" or a "structure" held together by consensus. Dahrendorf speaks well for modern conflict theory:

> Many sociologists seem convinced that in order to explain... change they have to discover certain special circumstances that set these processes in motion; the implication here is that change is an abnormal, or at least an unusual, state, one that has to be accounted for in terms of deviations from a "normal," equilibrated system.... We must realize that all units of social organization are continuously changing unless some force intervenes to arrest this change.... The great creative force that leads to change... is social conflict.... Not the presence but the absence of conflict is surprising and abnormal, and we have good reason to be suspicious if we find a society or social organization that displays no evidence of conflict.... Conflict can be temporarily suppressed, regulated, channeled... but... neither a philosopher-king nor a modern dictator can abolish it once and for all.... From the point of view of this model, societies... are held together not by consensus but by constraint, not by universal agreement but by the coercion of some by others. It may be useful... to speak of the "value system" ... but in the conflict model such characteristic values are ruling rather than common, enforced rather than accepted, at any given moment of time. And as conflict generates change, so constraint may be thought of as generating conflict.... It is always the basis of constraint that is at issue in social conflict (DAHRENDORF, 1968: 126-127).

Conflict theorists do not usually go so far as to say that everything in society is conflict and constraint, that all peace and harmony is either fraud or illusion. Rather, they are inclined to grant, as Machiavelli might, that a just consensus might exist somewhere, but they would consider it an unstable and unusual Utopian condition. Dahrendorf says structural-functional theory describes "a social system that has never existed and is not likely ever to come into being." "Revolutions are exceptional events, but are they more exceptional than the perfect equilibrium of stagnation?" (147). He adds, however:

I do not intend to make the mistake of many structural-functional theorists and advance for the conflict model a claim to comprehensive and exclusive applicability. As far as I can see, we need both models. . . . It may well be that society . . . has two faces of equal reality: one of stability, harmony and consensus, and one of change, conflict, and constraint (128).

Obviously, constraint can lead to order achieved by suppression or monetary truce, but our concern in this chapter is with two especially interesting theories which hold that out of turmoil can come a higher order than anyone could have anticipated from its immediate results. These two models of social order through struggle, one worked out by Karl Marx and the other by Charles Darwin provided secular salvation schemes, (Burke, 1937, II:137, 218-224) redemption through struggle itself. Marx's model starts from exploitation and is called the dialectic of class conflict. Darwin's starts from overpopulation, and is called evolution through natural selection.

Both men wrote major works largely from British Museum sources and published them within eight years of each other (*The Origin of Species*, 1859; *Das Kapital*, 1867). These models have a common emphasis on change, whereas power, consensus, and market emphasize stability. Both stressed progress through struggle, not just against but toward something. Out of destructive processes, whether called struggle for existence or revolution and crisis, could come unexpected fruits. Both models were alternative views of the same reality, and controversy about them dominated the scholarship of the nineteenth century.*

It was a bleak world indeed that these theories tried to account for, as reflected in phrases like "child labor," "wage-slavery," and "predatory capitalism" which appear in the novels of Dickens, Upton Sinclair,

---

*By such a focus on two major models of order-through-struggle, we do not mean to ignore the other views competing with Marxism in the nineteenth century. An excellent review of the historical polemical context of Marx's thought is provided by Irving M. Zeitlin, *Ideology and the Development of Sociological Theory* (Englewood Cliffs, N. J.: Prentice-Hall, 1968).

or Zola. To account for such inhumanities, one should explain evil and, if possible, wring some benefit from it. Both Marx and the social Darwinists, as "realistic" optimists, attempted to do so.

CLASS CONFLICT

Marx's concept of class struggle was inspired by Darwin's concept of "struggle for existence." Indeed, Marx even proposed to dedicate his book to Darwin (Potter, 1971:47). But he avoided organismic analogies, for his "scientific laws" of social development were basically linear thrusts. A criticism by Bertrand Russell, in debate with the socialist Scott Nearing, makes the issue clear. The Marxian

> outlook comes from a time before biology had got the hold upon our thoughts that it has in our time.... There was ... a habit of following the philosophy of Hegel. Now Hegel's philosophy was logical and it went by sharp transitions from this thing to that thing and then to the other thing and it was all a matter of hard outlines, sharp and rigid outlines, such as you get in logic. Well, later, after Marx's thoughts were fully formed, came the biological outlook which is associated with Darwin, a habit of viewing society as a thing that grows, a thing that develops like a tree, a thing that has a life by itself, a thing that moves in a certain manner not prescribed by the laws of logic or reason but prescribed by the law of life.... Human societies are of that sort.... You cannot get human societies to move in the manner of a logical transition, but only in the manner of a change in the way of life that must come gradually and bit by bit.

In debate with Leon Trotsky, John Dewey (1938) also denied that there is a fixed law of class struggle from which outcomes can be predicted and absolute goals set up in advance. Rather, such things must be discovered pragmatically from their actual consequences. The contrast here is between the idea of a linear thrust into human affairs, whether by command or law, by which happenings can be programmed into a more or less straight and dependable line; and the idea of uncertain, highly unpredictable evolution, whose balance is more often harmed than helped by linear intrusions, however well planned. Boulding warns us to beware of "trying to confine history to any particular strait-jacket." In the evolutionary process, there are many possible lines of development; there is "no blueprint that we can perceive; and why should it be so different with economics than biology?" (Boulding, 1970:12-18).

Marx was confident he could, indeed, perceive a line of development which, based on inexorable natural law, made a distant outcome certain. Despite the bleakness of the world he saw, Marx was optimistic that the social condition would eventually improve and that the basic source of injustice was not man but the system and environment in which he found himself. So he belonged among those whom we may call "bright side" theorists, such as Rousseau, Locke, Dewey, and Ashley-Montagu, who hold that human nature is good if not spoiled by a bad environment. They are opposed by "dark side" theorists, such as Hobbes, Machiavelli, St. Augustine, Freud, and Konrad Lorenz, who find human nature inherently troublesome and in need of control. Marx believed in the ultimate perfectibility of man, if the unjust and corrupting conditions surrounding him could be removed.

Marx rejected the optimistic picture of market which Adam Smith had established a century before. The world he saw was a dark one, in which conflict, not fair competition, prevailed. Industry is a "war of conquest" between economic interests in which "decisions of war assign defeat and death to one side and victory to the other. . . . This war is called competition" (Marx, in Bottomore, 1964:83-84). This contrast of world-views between Adam Smith and Marx is worth noting: Both were concerned with the just distribution of wealth and the causes of poverty, but their thinking diverged widely after that premise, as Table 6 shows.

Table 6   CONTRASTING VIEWS OF MARKET:
ADAM SMITH AND KARL MARX

Smith (1776)	Marx (1867)
Free trade is desirable.	Free trade is rapacious acquisition.
Fair economic competition prevails.	Economic conflict and exploitation prevail.
Small, fairly equal, enterprises participate in market.	Monopolies, concentrations of capital and power, dominate market.
Restriction of trade is a major cause of poverty.	Unrestricted profit-making is a major cause of poverty.
Market promotes harmony of social interests above the differences between buyers and sellers, labor and employers.	Market widens differences between rich and poor, increasing strains and conflicts.
Free enterprise tends toward equilibrium of prices and fair returns.	Free enterprise tends toward increasingly intolerable inequities which lead to crisis and breakdown.
Progress occurs through peaceful trade, division of labor and economic development.	Progress occurs through class war and revolution, which will abolish capitalism and move through socialism to the ideal state of communism.
The free market is a permanent feature of the modern state.	The free capitalistic market will be abolished.

In short, Smith saw market as leading to fair competition, prosperity, harmony of interests, and a moving equilibrium; Marx saw it leading to exploitation, economic depression, class war, and revolution.

Marx's radical critique of capitalism challenges market itself, and its ability to prompt the general welfare, when based on private property and profit-seeking: For Marx market was the original source of evil: Production for exchange was alienating; after exchange men became more alienated from and unequal to each other. Marx saw *classes*, not individual men, as the cause of market's failure to do what Smith promised. He also saw market as the source of modern classes: The moment that men sold their services to others under unequal conditions, the troubles began. For this reason, all socialistic theories are somewhat inhospitable to capitalistic market, from More's Utopia, which abolished money, to the Stalinist command-economy.

Marx's "dialectic of history," sees change produced by inevitable class conflict. The following proposition from the *Communist Manifesto* sums up his position:

> The history of all hitherto existing society is the history of class struggles. Freeman and slave, patrician and plebeian, lord and serf, guild-master and journeyman, in a word, oppressor and oppressed, stood in constant opposition to one another, carried on an uninter- rupted, now hidden, now open fight, a fight that each time ended either in a revolutionary reconstitution of society at large, or in the common ruin of the contending classes (1848).

He saw classes in intransigent opposition, the thrusts and counter-- thrusts of which led to a progressive movement like a *dialectic*, that is, a thesis overthrown by an antithesis, resulting in a synthesis which in turn becomes a thesis. Thus Marx view of history is agonistic, seeing opposition and struggle rather than flow and growth.

As Smith pointed out, market leads to division of labor, but after that the outlook is grim because:

1) Market leads to accumulation and concentration of capital, purchasing power, and "the power of command over labor . . . which nothing can withstand" (Marx, in Bottomore, 1964:85).

2) Such concentration of capital and power divides society into classes who own and rule, versus a property-less class, the proletariat, with little or nothing to sell but its own labor:

> The constant tendency, the law of development of the capitalistic mode of production, is to separate the means of production increasingly from labor ... transforming labor into wage-labor and the means of production into capital (1964:178).

This Marx calls "expropriation."

> The large capitalists ruin the small ones, and ... a part of the working class falls into a condition of beggary or starvation ... (1964: 72-73).

3) This is the source of *alienation* and forced wage-labor, in which men must sell themselves because they have no access to any other means of production. Market works unfairly by producing *surplus value*, which, according to Trotsky, was "the single law that Marx discovered and explored to the end" (1939:6). An example was:

> the prolongation of the working day beyond the point at which the laborer would have produced just an equivalent for the value of his labor-power, and the appropriation of that surplus-value by capital, this is production of absolute surplus-value. It forms the general groundwork of the capitalist system ... (MARX, 1906:559).

Anyone who has stayed overtime at the office to please the boss knows something of surplus-value. Marx has an imaginary laborer complain to his boss:

> That which on your side appears a spontaneous expansion of capital, is on mine extra expenditure of labor-power. ... What you gain in labor I lose in substance (TROTSKY, 1939:98-99).

Marx compares capital with a wolf hungry for surplus-value, taking the worker's leisure, haggling over a meal-time,

> shortening the extent of the laborer's life, as a greedy farmer snatches increased produce from the soil by robbing it of its fertility (101-102).

Once surplus-value has been extracted, the worker suffers further from market:

> No sooner is the exploitation of the laborer by the manufacturer so far at an end, that he receives his wages in cash, than he is set upon by other portions of the bourgeoisie, the landlord, the shop-keeper, the pawnbroker, etc. (MARX, 1848).

Almost everywhere some kind of exploitation could be found; Marx might even have agreed with the claim of modern feminists, that the greatest instrument for extracting surplus-value is the home.

The other side of surplus-value is a greater evil, *alienation* of the worker from his work, his fellow man, and himself:

> The work is *external* to the worker . . . not a part of his nature. . . . He does not fulfill himself. . . . feels himself at home only during his leisure, whereas at work he feels homeless. . . . It is not the satisfaction of a need, but only a *means* for satisfying other needs. . . . As soon as there is no physical or other compulsion it is avoided like the plague. . . . It is not his work but work for someone else, . . . in work he does not belong to himself but to another person (MARX, IN BOTTOMORE, 1956:169-170).

Added to which is the alienating effect of money:

> In modern civil society all relationships are in practice subordinated to the single abstract relationship of money and speculation. . . . Through this *alien intermediary* . . . man sees his will, his activity and his relation to others as a power which is independent of him and of them. His slavery therefore attains its peak (1956:161, 172).

The owning class feels the same alienation, but "is satisfied with its situation, feels itself well established in it," and so is the conservative while the proletarians are "the destructive party" (231). Alienation and surplus-value are the "inherent contradictions" of capitalism, which move class conflict along what Marx thought was its path of change:

201

> Proletariat and wealth are antinomies. . . . Private property . . . is forced to *maintain* itself and consequently to *maintain* its opposite, the proletariat. . . . The proletariat, on the contrary, is forced, as proletariat, to work for its own abolition, and thus for the abolition of the condition which makes it a proletariat—private property. It is the *negative* side of the antinomy, private property in a state of unrest . . . (1956:231).

4) Awareness of such antinomies leads to hostile *class consciousness*:

> Society as a whole is more and more splitting up into two great hostile camps, into two great classes directly facing each other— bourgeoisie and proletariat (1848).

Class-conscious antagonism is aggravated by crises and repressive reactions of the owning class. Struggle organizes the proletariat into a class, then into labor unions and ultimately into a political party, which draws recruits even from the upper class as it grows (1848). In the meantime the ruling class stabilizes itself by co-opting able men from the ranks below (compare Pareto's circulation of elites).

> The more a ruling class is able to assimilate the most prominent men of the dominated classes the more stable and dangerous is its rule (1867:III).

5) Class conflict worsens, divisions widen, misery increases, until finally "the knell of capitalist private property sounds" (1867:I). At the decisive hour

> a small section of the ruling class cuts itself adrift, and joins the revolutionary class, the class that holds the future in its hands (1848).

The last act is "a brutal contradiction, in a hand to hand struggle" (Bottomore, 1956:239).

6) If successful, the proletariat will seize the power of the state, become the ruling class, and use all means, some necessarily despotic, to abolish private property and bring about the social reorganization of labor (1848). Marx felt that this could not be done peacefully, that a revolution was needed to accomplish reforms:

> It is necessary for men themselves to be changed on a large scale, and this change can only occur in a practical movement, in a *revolution*. Revolution is necessary not only because the ruling class cannot be overthrown in any other way, but also because only in a revolution can the class which overthrows it rid itself of the accumulated rubbish of the past and become capable of reconstructing society (1956:65).

Lenin was more explicit about the need for forceful revolution and dictatorship of the proletariat. He despised parliamentary methods as a waste of time; for "The replacement of the bourgeois by the proletarian state is impossible without a violent revolution" (1918).

To understand this emphasis on force, it is crucial to see that Marxism regards the conflict of interest of classes as impossible to resolve by compromise or reform, as a struggle, in which each party can only lose by concession. One might visualize situations like the denial of civil rights to Blacks in South Africa. But are class relations inherently that incompatible? Marx based his theory on the hypothesis of an ineradicable zero-sum game between classes with and without property and power. He believed it was only mystification to talk about "common interests" or "equal rights," so long as a conflict of class interest was combined with difference in power, especially when one class controlled the state. Then the game could be changed only by the usurpation of power by the oppressed.

7) After attaining dictatorship of the proletariat, the final stage would be reached by a transition from the 'bourgeois' idea of distribution of goods according to the amount contributed, to the "higher phase communist society," when alienated labor will be eliminated and people

will cooperate happily because they want to. No longer will there be concern about amount of payment: Distribution will be "from each according to his ability, to each according to his needs!" This is the meaning of Marx's statement that "communism . . . is humanism" (1956: 244). Marx relaxed a little describing that happy state: When the forced division of labor would be abolished, one could

> do one thing today and another tomorrow . . . hunt in the morning, fish in the afternoon, rear cattle in the evening, criticize after dinner, in accordance with . . . inclination, without ever becoming hunter, fisherman, shepherd or critic (1956:97).

In summary, Marx saw all history as a dialectic of class struggles, in which a ruling class (thesis) is opposed by a proletariat (antithesis), until a revolution brings about a synthesis in which class contradiction ends. For example, if the divine right of George III to tax the American colonists was a class thesis, then their assertion of natural right to rule themselves was an antithesis, and peaceful relations after 1812 would be a synthesis. Unfortunately, this synthesis did not abolish class distinctions, and according to Marx the process must be repeated until a classless, communal society is attained.

If the term "dialectic," remains puzzling, take comfort in the fact that it has puzzled many thinkers who are not orthodox Marxists (Schneider, 1971; Rytina and Loomis, 1970). Popper calls its claims of being a law of history "historicism," a "myth of destiny" (1952, I:7-10), suggesting that Marx himself was a mystifier.

Perhaps the clearest non-Marxist explanation of dialectical change has been given by Boulding, who distinguishes two major kinds of historical change: *developmental*, which are "cumulative, evolutionary, and continuous," in which conflict is only incidental; and *dialectical*, which involve oscillations between claims of "us" versus "them," and tend to be violent, short-run, more costly, and ultimately less important than evolutionary changes, "only waves and turbulences." National wars and class revolutions provide many examples. According to Boulding, the French Revolution was "an actual hindrance to French development;" the American Revolution was more successful because it was "so cheap;" but the Russian Revolution was:

> perhaps the highest-cost revolution known to date. It took more than thirty years for real wages in Russia to recover to the 1913 level. It took even longer for per capita income to recover. These losses arose directly out of the revolutionary philosophy of Lenin and Stalin. . . . It is hard to tell whether the Chinese Revolution will turn out to have a higher cost . . . it may indeed turn out to be an example of a fairly low-cost revolution, even though the disaster of the "great leap forward" suggests that all the costs are not yet in (1970b:103).

Boulding shows by charts the comparative costs of successful and unsuccessful revolutions, the main point being that the point where gains exceed costs is so far in the future that it may be a long time before society gets to where it would have been without a revolution, and "we may easily have a situation in which the revolution was not worth the cost" (100). In any case:

> Revolution in the sense of political upheaval usually accompanied by violence, in which an existing class or clique of rulers is displaced by another, is almost invariably an interruption of the process of development. . . . While one cannot say . . . that revolution is never justified, one can say with some confidence that revolutionism is likely to lead to a proliferation of costly and unjustified revolutions. The developmental philosophy, while not ruling out the possibility of desirable revolutions, will put its stress on accelerations rather than revolutions . . . (100, 104-105).

Why are dialectical processes so costly? Boulding answers this question by showing four kinds of relations between two parties. One is "benign," in which both parties gain, two are "zero-sum," in which one must lose from what the other gains, while the fourth is "malign," or "negative-sum," in which both parties lose. In fact, Boulding notes that malign outcomes are much more common than benign ones (for example an arms race versus a disarmament race), because

> Dialectical philosophy ... encourages conflict, hatred, class, race, national consciousness, and malevolence ... [and puts] high value on conflicts as such and on "defeating the enemy" (49-52).

Another economist suggests that Marxism has a built-in need for contradictions and crises, and stagnates in times of peace and prosperity:

> Communism is a system designed primarily for revolution; once the revolution is accomplished, the troubles really begin. To maintain support, communism needs enemies. I suggest that the United States should not supply this need by playing the role of the foreign imperialist devil.... Our intervention in Vietnam has been unfortunate because it has strengthened the position of orthodox, hard-line communists and ... done a good deal more to help communism than to hurt it (YNTEMA, 1969).

So does Marxism describe inevitable conflicts within a class society, or does it *create* them by its "dialectical" view of reality? In fairness, one must recognize and respect the despair reflected in the belief—which may be fact—that some vested interests are so intransigent that they will not be reformed except by force. The general costliness of dialectic as a method of change does not rule out the possibility that there may be circumstances in which violence is called for, as the American colonists felt in 1773.

Other social scientists, instead of challenging the intransigence-force doctrine (which would, perhaps, be supported by many conflict theorists), deny the relevance of Marx's observations to the modern world, whatever truth they may have had in 1867. Why indeed, they say, should generalizations made over a hundred years ago be valid today? One such critic is Seymour M. Lipset:

In the century since Karl Marx died, his most fundamental assumption about politics and social change has been decisively refuted by history. Marx said that in advanced industrial societies, where possibilities for further economic growth were exhausted, the working class would replace capitalism with a socialist system. Revolutionary socialist movements have not come into power in any industrial society. In a number of preindustrial societies, of course, revolutionary socialist [Communist] movements have seized power, but they have largely been dominated by members of the intelligentsia and backed by the peasantry. Marx specifically denied that the peasants could constitute a self-conscious revolutionary class.... Given the inappropriateness of much of Marx's basic theory of change to latter-day conditions, what explains his place as the charismatic figure of the revolutionary movements of this century? Marx has performed the same function ... [as Christian millenarism] ... "Scientific socialism" projected the "inevitable" triumph of the proletarian revolution. Marx assured all who would listen that the materialistic god of history was on their side (1972:53, 58).

In short, Marx was serving as a Messiah, not a scientist. Another important reinterpretation of Marx's doctrine by sociologists was to shift the emphasis away from economic exploitation to alienation (loss of feelings of belongingness and personal meaning), which might have little relationship to property distribution and conditions of work (Bell, 1961:355-367; Klapp, 1969:3-70).

We have tried here to show the content of Marx's model of social change, without, presuming to test it against reality. His villain was capitalism itself as a market system, which he felt had to be defeated rather than reformed or bargained with. However, even if the dialectical view of change were proven false, or merely a "turbulence" on the wave of change, sociology would still be indebted to Marx for the following contributions: (1) the first incisive analyis of social classes; (2) recognition of the problem of ideology as mystification or false-consciousness (Mannheim, 1936); (3) definition of alienation in material, especially economic, settings; (4) a much closer look at exploitation, wherever it exists; and (5) a view of social problems and strains as systemic faults instead of individual failings.

Let us turn now to the evolutionary model of social change, which opposed Marx during the nineteenth century and still does.

SOCIAL DARWINISM: NATURE'S PRUNING HOOK

An alternative to dialectic for explaining the harshness of nature and economic systems came from likening societies to organisms and conceiving of change as an evolutionary development which, even in gradual stages, was difficult for individuals.

Charles Darwin was the inspiration for this concept, although he drew the suggestion originally from Malthus' "Essay on the Principle of Population" (1798), which asserted the tendency of all living things to breed beyond environmental resources until checked in some way, such as starvation, disease, war, or "moral restraint." The implication was that at some point there would be intense competition, and from this Darwin drew his theory that the struggle for survival could lead to the improvement of existing species and the origin of new species, as mutations were tested against established varieties, to see which would survive and outbreed the other, and so prevail by natural selection, or the survival of the fittest. Darwin said:

> Let us take the case of a wolf, which preys on various animals, securing some by craft, some by strength, and some by fleetness; and let us suppose that the fleetest prey, a deer for instance, had from any change in the country increased in numbers, or that other prey had decreased in numbers, during that season of the year when the wolf was hardest pressed for food. Under such circumstances the swiftest and slimmest wolves would have the best

chance of surviving, and so be preserved or selected.... I can see no more reason to doubt that this would be the result, than that man should be able to improve the fleetness of his greyhounds by careful and methodical selection.... If variations useful to any organic being ever do occur, assuredly individuals thus characterized will have the best chance of being preserved in the struggle for life; and from the strong principle of inheritance, these will tend to produce offspring similarly characterized. This principle of preservation, or the survival of the fittest, I have called Natural Selection. It leads to the improvement of each creature in relation to its organic and inorganic conditions of life; and consequently, in most cases, to what must be regarded as an advance in organization. Nevertheless, low and simple forms will long endure if well fitted for their simple conditions of life (1859:IV).

Of course, the application of such an idea to society was another step, and Darwin did not make it. It required the assumption that societies were like organisms: They too had to struggle against rivals to survive; and they also could adapt biologically or culturally and so win out against competing societies. The criterion of evolution at the societal level was, however, not so much sheer fitness to survive (as might very well have been attained by the Eskimos) but advance in civilization and complexity of organization. Thinkers who advanced this theory were called social evolutionists (including even Marx), and when they stressed survival of the fittest, social Darwinists.

No fitter example can be found than Herbert Spencer, who, along with Comte, helped to establish sociology as an "evolutionary" science, as well as laying the foundation for equilibrium and functional theory. He worked out a mind-boggling scheme of evolution from the simplest molecules to the most complex societies. "Progress" of humanity was merely the upper levels of "an advance from homogeneity of structure to heterogeneity," as one might see it in a growing embryo:

By endless such differentiations there is finally produced that complex combination of tissues and organs constituting the adult animal or plant. This is the history of all organisms whatever....

209

This law of organic progress is the law of all progress. Whether it be in the development of the Earth, in the development of Life upon its surface, in the development of Society, of Government, of Manufactures, of Commerce, of Language, Literature, Science, Art, this same evolution from the simple into the complex, through successive differentiations, holds throughout. From the earliest traceable cosmical changes down to the latest results of civilization ... the transformation of the homogeneous into the heterogeneous is that in which Progress essentially consists (1857).

So have differentiated the races and cultures of man from a single stock. Americans and Australians are late varieties from English (1880:296-297).

Society in its first and lowest form is a homogeneous aggregation of individuals having like powers and like functions; the only marked difference of function being that which accompanies difference of sex. Every man is warrior, hunter, fisherman, tool-maker, builder; every woman performs the same drudgeries; every family is self-sufficing, and, save for purposes of aggression and defense, might as well live apart from the rest. Very early, however, in the process of social evolution, we find an incipient differentiation between the governing and the governed. Some kind of chieftainship seems coeval with the first advance from the state of separate wandering families to that of a nomadic tribe. ... At first ... it is ... unaccompanied by any difference in occupation or style of living; the first ruler kills his own game ... does not differ from others of his tribe. Gradually ... the contrast between the governing and the governed grows more decided. Supreme power becomes hereditary ... the head ... begins to assume the sole office of ruling. At the same time there has been arising a co-ordinate species of government—that of religion. ... Another controlling agency [is] that of manners or ceremonial usages. ... Each of these kinds of government is itself subject to successive differentiations. ... There arises ... a highly complex political organization of monarch, ministers, lords and commons, with their subordinate administrative departments, courts of justice ... supplemented ... by municipal governments, county governments, parish or union governments. ... By its side there grows up a highly complex re-

ligious organization, with its various grades of officials, from arch-
bishops down to sextons, its colleges, convocations, ecclesiastical
courts, etc. . . .

Simultaneously there has been going on a second differentiation
. . . by which the mass of the community has been segregated into
distinct classes and orders of workers. . . . Long after considerable
progress has been made in the division of labor among the different
classes of workers there is still little or no division of labor among
the widely separated parts of the community; the nation continues
comparatively homogeneous in the respect that in each district
the same occupations are pursued. But when roads and other means
of transit become numerous and good the different districts begin
to assume different functions and to become mutually dependent.
The calico manufacture locates itself in this county, the woolen
manufacture in that; silks are produced here, lace there. . . . Every
locality grows more or less distinguished from the rest by the
leading occupation carried on in it. . . . This subdivision of functions shows itself . . . among different nations. That exchange of
commodities which free trade promises . . . will ultimately have
the effect of specializing . . . the industry of each people. . . .

Not only is the law thus clearly exemplified in the evolution of
the social organism, but it is exemplified with equal clearness in
the evolution of all products of human thought and action. . . . Let
us take language . . . the gradual multiplication of parts of speech
. . . differentiation of words of allied meanings . . . the multiplication of languages (1880).

What, then, distinguishes evolution from disorder and breakdown, which
are also increases in heterogeneity?

Along with an advance from simplicity to complexity there is an
advance from confusion to order—from undetermined arrangement to determined arrangement. Development, no matter of
what kind, exhibits not only a multiplication of unlike parts, but
an increase in the distinctness with which these parts are marked
off from one another. . . . A political outbreak implies a loosening
of those ties by which citizens are bound up into distinct classes
and sub-classes. Agitation, growing into revolutionary meetings,

fuses ranks that are usually separated. Acts of insubordination
break through the ordained limits to individual conduct, and tend
to obliterate the lines previously existing between those in authority and those beneath them. . . . Disease and death, individual or
social . . . from the very outset . . . destroy this definiteness, and
gradually produce a heterogeneity that is indeterminate instead of
determinate . . . from orderly arrangement to disorderly arrangement . . . (1880:314-315).

Along with the tendency toward determined as opposed to disorderly
arrangement is another universal tendency toward equilibrium. Any
difference of forces had to resolve into a steadier state. So the ultimate
picture of the universe was the steadiest possible state of utmost
complexity.

In all cases . . . there is a progress toward equilibration. The universal co-existence of antagonist forces which . . . necessitates the
universality of rhythm, and . . . decomposition of every force into
divergent forces, at the same time necessitates the ultimate establishment of a balance. . . . The moving equilibrium . . . tends to
arise in an aggregate having compound motions as a transitional
state on the way toward complete equilibrium. . . . The evolution
of every aggregate must go on until . . . *equilibrium mobile* is
established; since . . . an excess of force which the aggregate possesses in any direction must eventually be expended in overcoming
resistances to change in that direction, leaving behind only those
movements which compensate each other and so form a moving
equilibrium. . . . The structural state simultaneously reached . . .
must obviously be one presenting an arrangement of forces that
counter-balance all the forces to which the aggregate is subject. So
long as there remains a residual force in any direction. . . the
redistribution of matter must continue (1880:418-424).

Would all evolution finally come to rest in total equilibrium? Spencer
avoided this question by speculating that there was a rhythm between
forces of attraction and repulsion throughout the universe which, after

"an immeasurable period" would bring about "alternate eras of evolution and dissolution" (465).

Within this vast scheme, social evolution rested on an *organismic analogy*, about which Spencer was quite literal. Imagine a colony of bees: Queen, workers and drones work together as interdependent parts, they are of the same heredity; it is just as true to call the whole colony an organism as any individual. Spencer applied this conclusion to human society, and claimed that it also grew in size and complexity, that its parts were functionally interdependent, and that as a structural whole it outlives the individuals who make it up. The main differences between individuals and social organisms, whether one is speaking of human society or a beehive, are that: (1) the group lacks an external skin or resistant boundary; (2) The members of a group are separate, unlike the tissues and organs of the body; (3) Members have freedom and mobility far beyond that of the cells of an organism; and (4) Groups have no social sensorism or brain without which the society cannot function—each individual thinks for himself as well as in cooperation with others. By such an analogy, a parliament would correspond to the brain, transportation to blood circulation, law enforcement and communication to the "regulating system" of nerves, industry to the alimentary system, and the military to biological equipment like the tooth of the tiger or the ink of the squid (Spencer, 1914). Such *adaptations* came about by survival of the fittest. Adaptation is the means an organism uses to establish equilibrium with its environment, including competitors. The *function* of any interdependent part consists in what it contributes toward helping an organism survive, in other words, adapt, and reach equilibrium.

The final goal of social evolution is an equilibrium in which everyone gets what he wants while performing all functions required by the social organism—a harmony between society and the individual that is surprisingly like that of Marx, and less surprisingly that of Durkheim:

The arrival at a state of human nature and social organization, such that the individual has no desires but those which may be satisfied without exceeding his proper sphere of action, while society maintains no restraints but those which the individual voluntarily respects.... The ultimate abolition of all limits to the freedom of each, save that imposed by the like freedom of all, must result from the complete equilibrium between man's desires and the conduct necessitated by surrounding conditions (1880:444).

Though such an organicist, Spencer found a place for intense individualism in the service of the struggle for existence, which was to lead finally to such beautiful equilibration. Conflict had its service to perform, not as Marx thought to advance classes, but to select the individual and societies fittest to survive. If one looks at history, a "startling truth" appears: Higher stages of civilization are not less violent, nor are primitive men more brutal; Christianity has not greatly reduced cruelty and warlikeness; savages, as we call them, may be "gentle and affectionate." How is all this to be explained, except that without unceasing warfare there would have been little development and organization, either individually or socially? The

merciless discipline of Nature, "red in tooth and claw," has been essential to the progress of sentient life.... Myriads of years of warfare ... have developed ... powers now used ... for countless objects besides those of killing and avoiding being killed ... limbs, teeth, ... nails ... mind ... similarly with social organisms.... Social cooperation is initiated by joint defense and offense; and from the cooperation thus initiated, all kinds of cooperations have arisen. Inconceivable as have been the horrors caused by this universal antagonism which, beginning with the chronic hostilities of small hordes tens of thousands of years ago, has ended in the occasional vast battles of immense nations, we must nevertheless admit that without it the world would still have been inhabited only by men of feeble types, sheltering in caves and living on wild food (1897, II:229-242).

However, the "predatory period" will not be permanent; a new industrial organization will arise, in which natural competition will displace war, and military autocracy will give way to democracy. But society must face a harsh fact: Such progress does not abolish the process of natural selection. And there is no justification for interfering with it. The humanitarian ethic of gratuitous aid, appropriate within the family, must not be allowed to operate in society at large to interfere with "reward in proportion to desert," which is the ability in competition with others to fulfill requirements of life, get food and shelter, and escape enemies. If benevolent, "world-rectifying schemes" like socialism help the feeble and the poor, it will favor "the multiplication of those worst fitted for existence" and hinder multiplication of those best fitted. It is not only unscientific but unfair to pass welfare laws which force the public to pay that "good-for-nothings might not suffer:"

> Men who are so sympathetic that they cannot let the struggle for existence bring on the unworthy the sufferings consequent on their incapacity or misconduct, are so unsympathetic that they can, deliberately, make the struggle for existence harder for the worthy, and inflict on them and their children artificial evils in addition to the natural evils they have to bear! (1914:357-369).

So Spencer turned self-help in the "struggle for existence" into an elaborate justification for everything that Marx and the socialists were deploring. "Nature red in tooth and claw" took the place of class exploitation, and who can quarrel with nature?

Walter Bagehot (1826-1877) was another important political economist who applied Darwinism to the progress of society. He, too, claimed nature as a justification for war as part of the struggle for existence and for competition as the way in which the best are selected:

> Those nations which are strongest tend to prevail over the others; and in certain marked peculiarities the strongest tend to be the best. . . . Within every particular nation the type or types of character then and there most attractive tend to prevail; and the most

attractive, though with exceptions, is what we call the best character (1872).

Laws and institutions evolve by proving their "survival value." The most conspicuous example in history is military:

> The strongest nation has always been conquering the weaker.... Every intellectual gain, so to speak, that a nation possessed was in the earliest times made use of—was *invested* and taken out—in war; all else perished. Each nation tried constantly to be the stronger, and so made or copied the best weapons.... Conquest improved mankind by the intermixture of strengths; the armed truce, which was then called peace, improved them by the competition of training and the consequent creation of new power (1872).

The cause of progress is always competition; those societies without it—in Africa, Asia, the Pacific—remained "arrested civilizations."

Arrested civilizations had what Bagehot called a "cake of custom" consisting of rigid law, group discipline, and faith, all of which had proven their survival value, but become too rigid for full expression of the individual. Such societies are concerned with "nation-making," and it is "war that makes nations." A higher stage of evolution occurs when society breaks out of the cake of custom by free discussion (Mill's market of ideas), intellectual and other "new virtues" appear, war ceases to be the moving force in the world, and men become more tender one to another . . . because they have no longer the daily habit of war."

More ferocious applications of Darwinism appeared in Germany. According to Ludwig Gumplowicz (1838-1910), struggle between the races (*der Rassenkampf*) is the basis of social evolution, in which groups war for survival and conquest. Beginning with primitive hordes having an instinctive hatred of other hordes, warring groups conquer one another, creating larger systems with classes of victors and vanquished. Unlike Spencer, Gumplowicz minimized the individual. Whenever

216

collectivities form, individuals become "sheeplike." Self-government as advocated by contract theory is impossible. The state forms in war for the sole purpose of establishing sovereignty and exploitation (1883, 1899). Gustav Ratzenhofer (1842-1904) also developed a sociology based on the innate hostility of each individual to all his fellow-men. Cooperation in community and economic life lessens this innate hostility, but the appearance of a rival community or nation is the signal for a battle which ends only when one group has vanquished or enslaved the other, thus entering a "higher stage of the social process" in which order is based on domination by means of the state (1898). Ratzenhofer's emphasis, however, was on interpersonal rather than inter-group conflict. Friedrich Nietzsche, however, outdid them all. He saw a mystical will to power working through evolution, which would give rise to a super-race with its own religion and values. These "supermen" would displace decadent Christian humanitarianism, defeat democracy, and rule: "Ye shall love peace as a means to new wars ... not to work, but to fight. ... It is the good war which halloweth every cause" (1885:62-63).

For all their warlikeness, such theorists of progress were not talking about a dialectic of polarized opposition, as was Marx. Natural selection is not a fight to the finish between two opposed patterns, but a gradual winnowing over time of the best out of a field of many competitors. Imagine one of those marathon dance contests of the 1920s: Week by week the field dwindles until finally only two are left. Is this a duel of opposites? Not quite: The survivors may be almost alike in style and ability. Aside from emphasis on struggle, the resemblance between natural selection and polarized class war ends here. An evolutionist might say there is no polarization in nature outside the minds of men. The reason is simple: Human imagination and symbols are necessary to create polarized relations such as absolute principles, dialectical contradictions, intransigent demands, crusades, villain-images, etc. The deer and the wolf are not enemies, only competitors to live. They are adapted to struggle with each other. There is no dialectical movement in their lives nor intensification of the war between the species. So evolution emphasized the general process of competition. No particular group was at fault, nor could any one group be overthrown to bring about a better ordering of things. Marx felt Darwin's work supported his own thesis, and said, "Darwin's book is very important and serves me as a basis for the class struggle in history" (Hofstadter, 1959:115). But evolutionists did not return the compliment. They felt evolution was larger than anything that might occur in an economic market.

By its very vastness, evolution pleased social thinkers of the positivistic cast such as Comte and Durkheim, who wanted to see laws of nature (like "organic solidarity") behind economic development. They tended to put sociology as the science of social progress (a kind of super-biology), above all other scientific knowledge, as noted in Chapter 3. Since sociology was an infant science, an alliance with the field which had produced Mendel, Darwin, and Pasteur seemed highly advantageous. This helped explain the appeal of evolution as scientific theory to sociologists.

Another reason for the popularity of evolutionary theory in the nineteenth century was that it served as a scientific rationalization for laissez-faire economics. As Spencer had argued, it provided a reason why government should not intervene in business or welfare: Let "survival of the fittest" take its course. Well-to-do conservatives enthusiastically accepted a doctrine which explained, why they deserved their privileges while it nullified the socialists' argument for social change. When biology seems to oppose radical economics, which is the more "scientific"?

To many of those unattracted by the concept of class conflict, the organismic analogy became an acceptable explanation of societal disease and health. Writings like Durkheim (1893), and Lilienfeld (1896), introduced the idea of "social pathology," describing diseases of the social body in clinical terms. For example a market crisis or civil war were seen as diseases of the social nervous system, while a bank loan was compared to the function of red corpuscles.

Vaster schemes or organismic evolution were envisioned by thinkers who took whole cultures rather than nations as competing units.

So Spengler (1918) described the rise and fall of civilization as an organic cycle of birth, growth, maturity and death. And Toynbee (1947) used natural selection to explain how civilizations grow by "challenge and response," or failing to respond, become "arrested" (as in Polynesia) or die (as in Egypt).

In America, the reception of social Darwinism was perhaps even more enthusiastic than in Europe. For one thing, no strong socialistic encampment existed to oppose it. It quickly became entrenched in conservative ideology, for America, in rapid and rugged economic change after the Civil War, was a vast "caricature" of the struggle for existence (Hofstadter, 1959:5-6, 17, 44). Spencer had a vogue even exceeding that of Darwin; Rockefeller, Carnegie, and Hill invoked "survival of the fittest" to explain large fortunes (31, 45). Sociology, of course, was affected. Cooley wrote, "I imagine that nearly all of us who took up sociology between 1870, say, and 1890 did so at the instigation of Spencer" (33). W. G. Sumner became the most vigorous and influential social Darwinist in America. He went to Malthus for principles, and returned to report that competition was a glorious law of nature, millionaires were a product of natural selection, and equality and natural rights were ridiculous (51-59). His book, *Folkways* (1906), explained how customs arose unwittingly and were selected as adaptations, "unconscious experiments," in the struggle for existence. Keller went farther, applying to custom the Darwinian concepts of variation, selection, transmission, and adaptation (1915).

Among the important American theorists who responded to Darwinism were some who dissented in various ways. One was Lester Ward, who rejected the idea of human progress as governed by purposeless evolution. Since nature is wasteful and uneconomical, intellect, education, and planning, instead of laissez-faire, should carry evolution beyond nature, Ward called such social purposefulness *telesis*. It required a class of planners (similar to Comte's "new philosophers"), and a "sociocracy." (1883, 1906). In other words, the encoding of progress, Ward said, was in the mind, its knowledge and goals—not in the genes, a point which many evolutionists did not make clear. (Bagehot, for example, believing in the Lamarckian thesis, that adaptations learned could be inherited.) Indeed, only after Kroeber's definition of the "superorganic" (1917) was the dividing line clearly recognized in social science. Another dissident Darwinian was Thorstein Veblen, who in his book, *The Theory of the Leisure Class* (1899) and *The Theory of Business Enterprise* (1904), granted the "predatory" ability of those who were successful in pecuniary competition, but denied that such virtues, compared with craftsmen or engineers, for example, benefitted society; indeed, business-men caused almost more disruption of the business cycle than they were worth.

The flood of irresponsible racist, imperialistic, and eugenic argu-ments which came as side-effects of social Darwinism, together with its negative view of social reform and welfare, was bound to provoke a reaction. After a time, the American middle class shrank from Darwin-istic brutality, says Hofstadter (1959:202). In another study he described the liberal conscience at work to repair the damage of too much individ-ualism (Hofstadter, 1955). Even some Darwinists were appalled. Kro-potkin is notable for having argued that conflict is not even the most characteristic mode of the struggle for existence. Mutual aid, whether symbiosis or conscious cooperation, and the ethics reflecting it, are the most important factor in survival. Man's true struggle was not against other men, but with others to control nature (1902).

The end of biologism in sociology came from efforts of sociologists and anthropologists to find something for themselves that could not be reduced to the data of biology. Notable efforts along these lines included Durkheim's definition of "social facts" (1895:1-14); and Kroeber's con-cept of the "superorganic" (1917), which separated the laws of cultural change from those of biology and psychology, while others studying cultural diffusion (Wissler, Lowie, and others) quarreled continually with the evolutionary notion that societies developed along a line of cultural inheritance rather than by exchange. A crucial blow to the notion that there was an evolutionary sequence of stages was dealt by

Hobhouse, Wheeler and Ginsberg (1915). Well before that sociology was struggling to disengage itself from the organistic analogy. One of the earliest and most influential American textbooks said:

> The sociological concept "organism" is a wider generalization of the term already generic in biology.... The enlarged concept "organism" ... omits traits peculiar to vegetable or animal organisms, and contains only relationships common to these and also to societies of human beings.... Modern sociologists who have employed the organic conception of society to the best purpose have used it as an instrument of discovery or exposition, not as a means of exhibiting social facts in fanciful arrangements ... with forced analogies.... When we speak of the "life" of the social body, we do not imply that, in addition to the stomachs and hearts of the individual members, there is a physical organ to digest food for society, and another to force blood into social arteries. We mean that there is discoverable among associations of human beings that "continuous adjustment of internal relations to external relations" (Spencer).... While we distinctly repudiate a literalism which identifies the social body with physical organisms ... we are ... unprepared to assert positively how far actual analogies hold.... We assume that every act in society, like every process in the animal organism, has a causal explanation, and a functional significance. We treat society just as we might imagine the anatomist treating the human body, if all the vital processes could be exposed.... He would at once proceed to verify hypotheses about vital cause and effect.... Sociological analysis, by use of the organic conception ... is a method of examining social facts so critically that their essential relations with all other social facts will be detected.... To render the general facts of society in terms of their functional values ... should sharpen the perception that social activities are to be judged according to their causal relations to the proper aims of the social whole and of the individual parts (SMALL AND VINCENT, 1894:88-96).

No clearer explanation of the difference between functionalism and organicism could be expected.

FUNCTIONALISM

Out of organicism grew *functionalism*, the theory that society is a system held together and maintained, not by "vital" connections but by services of parts to each other and to the whole, without which it would collapse and the component activities fade away, as a building would if the girders were removed. The function of anything, whether in architecture or society, is what it contributes to the whole, or as Parsons and Shils said, what it does to promote the maintenance of a system, whether a society or a personality (1951:35).

> The *function* of any recurrent activity, such as the punishment of a crime, or a funeral ceremony, is the part it plays in the social life as a whole and therefore the contribution it makes to the maintenance of the structural continuity . . . a structure consisting of a set of relations amongst unit entities . . . (RADCLIFFE-BROWN, 1935).

Function implies a systemic need, which must be met if the system is to endure. As Durkheim said, "We must determine whether there is a correspondence between the fact under consideration and the general needs of the social organism." For example, punishment not only controls crime but "has the useful function of maintaining . . . (collective) sentiments," which "would soon diminish if offenses against them were not punished" (1938:89-97). According to functionalism, the main task of sociology was to study such relationships. Obviously, this tended to focus on stability (homeostasis) and recurrence, rather than change, in systems.

Much of the pioneering in functional theory work came from anthropology, especially Radcliffe-Brown and Malinowski, who held that all culture exists by virtue of meeting needs—biological, psychological, individual, and social. No part of culture, however useless it might seem —magic, superstition, the incest taboo—should be presumed to be without function. Myth, for example, is

... not simply a piece of attractive fiction which is kept alive by the literary interest in the story. It is a statement of primeval reality which lives in the institutions and pursuits of a community. It justifies ... the existing order and it supplies a retrospective pattern of moral values.... The function of myth is to strengthen tradition and to endow it with a greater value and prestige by tracing it back to a higher, better, more supernatural and more effective reality of initial events (MALINOWSKI, 1931).

Malinowski tended to stress function as a service to individual needs, whereas Radcliffe-Brown held it was a contribution to social structure. In the celebrated controversy about magic, Malinowski claimed it serves to relieve anxieties, while Radcliffe-Brown maintained that it teaches people to be anxious, in order to reinforce obedience to social norms— and so creates, in part, the very anxiety that it alleviates (Homans, 1950: 330-331).

Recognizing the difficulty of studying subtle functions, Robert K. Merton developed a "paradigm for functional analysis," in which he distinguished between *manifest functions*, "those objective consequences contributing to the adjustment or adaptation of the system which are intended and recognized by participants in the system," and *latent functions*, "those which are neither intended nor recognized." Both types serve "functional requirements" of systems, and require careful study. *Dysfunctions* are structural strains, which give rise to a "pressure for change," which leads in turn to the development of variations in the direction of a new equilibrium providing "functional alternatives" to the old system (Merton, 1968:104:108). So functionalism urged sociologists to search for relationships which were neither conscious nor obvious.

Cultural lag theory (Ogburn, 1922) may be considered a kind of equilibrium theory, since it assumes that unequal rates of change will produce a strain or maladjustment, which in turn produces a "lag," until the slower-changing, usually nonmaterial, culture catches up. For example, if technology changes, schooling may be out of date, students will be less able to get jobs. Unemployment may then be a problem until education is modernized.

> The thesis is that the various parts of modern culture are not changing at the same rate, some parts are changing much more rapidly than others; and since there is a correlation and inter-dependence of parts, a rapid change in one part of our culture requires readjustments through other changes in the various cor-related parts of culture.

Dysfunction (Merton) is another way of describing serious strains of cultural lag. So also is Durkheim's term anomie.

But even conflict (whether called lag or strain) was not merely destructive but often had some important functions. So Durkheim had noted that crime contributes to social solidarity by strengthening the collective conscience in law enforcement. Gluckman (1955) saw feuds working for social cohesion in primitive society. Coser explored many functions of conflict for both close-knit groups and pluralistic societies, including "safety-valve" institutions which drain off hostility from within the group and provide substitute objects for it, hence often slow down change (1956:151-156).

One of the disadvantages of functionalistic theory, soon recognized by sociologists, was that it unduly emphasized equilibrium and stability. Indeed, Talcott Parsons regarded stability or equilibrium as "a defining characteristic of structure," which might, however, be either "static" or "moving" (1964:84). According to Parsons, every social system must cope with four sets of problems: "integration" (keeping itself together), pattern-maintenance (keeping the same arrangements going), "goal attainment," (setting and achieving purposes), and "adaptation" (adjusting to new conditions). Strains arise in every system, not only because of changing external conditions, but because the requirements of these sets of problems are not necessarily compatible. For example, stressing loyalty (integration) might interfere with getting new ideas (adaptation) (1966). Systemic change is unlikely to move outside the scope of these functional goals, so long as one assumes that systems tend inherently to be homeostatic, that is, self-preserving.

But newer general system theory, stressing openness and morphogenesis (creation of structure) rather than adaptation (Buckley, 1967), took the emphasis off equilibrium. Such theory offers a new look at function, by requiring the tracing of all loops of feedback, positive and negative, which preserve or constructively change a state of affairs. Continual action of a system to attain new goals or generate new structure comes under the aegis of function. Modern theorists apply functional explanation even to equifinality, i.e., the capacity of systems to pursue a goal under various circumstances, by different routes, undergoing different changes of state (say A—C—E, rather than B—D—E) in the transition. Stinchcombe traces such a functional causal structure of explanation:

> There is nothing any more philosophically confusing, nor anything less empirical or scientific, about functional explanations than about other causal explanations (1968:90).

In information theory, the focus on equilibrium so prominent in functionalism is gone. Functions would be matter-energy and/or information flows, within or across system boundaries, contributing to the reduction of entropy for the relevant system.

> Matter-energy and information always flow together. Information is always borne on a marker. Conversely there is no regular movement in a system unless there is a difference in potential between two points, which is negative entropy or information. Which aspect of the transmission is most important depends upon how it is handled by the receiver. If the receiver responds primarily to the material or energic aspect, it is a matter-energy transmission; if the response is primarily to the information, it is an information transmission. For example, the banana eaten by a monkey ... has its informational aspect, but its use to the monkey is chiefly to increase the energy available to him (MILLER, 1971:281).

225

The functions of communication are empirical facts that can be observed. Communication can also, of course, be a zero or negative sum game. Open living systems gain in their struggle for existence (Chapter I) by losing entropy ("life feeds on negative entropy"). They are not merely homeostatic (in the old Spencerian sense) but always building, always searching for a better ratio of exchange. Equilibrium would be optimal in a "closing" phase, such as fatigue or old age.

Although the debate continues among sociologists on just what is the function of conflict in social systems (Horton, 1966; Schneider, 1971; Goodwin, 1971; Lyman and Scott, 1970; Ellis, 1971; Dahrendorf, 1959), we have at least traced the roots of two major models of change through struggle—Marxist dialectics and Darwinist evolutionary theory.

SOCIETAL SEARCH THROUGH NATURAL SELECTION

Whatever may be said about conflict, interest in social evolution through natural selection remains strong. A major spurt of interest came from a paper by a biologist, an anthropologist, and a mathematician, reporting on their work as an interdisciplinary group at the Center for Advanced Study in the Behavioral Sciences (Gerard, Kluckhohn, and Rapoport, 1956). They had begun with the conviction that "the question of similarities between biological and cultural change deserved re-examination from a somewhat fresh angle." Presenting a table of parallels between biological and cultural evolution, they said:

> We suspect ... that the "inner logic" of the organism is paralleled by the "inner logic" of a culture. ... Organisms and cultures may be "ready" for radical innovations so that when these come on the scene through biological or cultural mutation or diffusion, the

evolution, whether of an organism or of a culture, may be greatly accelerated.

They traced the parallel between the evolution of genes and that of *phonemes* (unitary sounds of language), finding, for example, variations comparable with mutations, natural selection, and migration; and linguistic differentiation similar to cellulation, *selection pressure* as it might operate on speech. They concluded that

> a definition of survival advantage of a speech unit analogous to the survival advantage of a gene could be constructed. . . . If . . . the spoken word is taken as the individual organism, and its repetitions . . . as its progeny. . . . Modification of the "progeny" may be of two kinds: . . . "internal" . . . based, perhaps, on the needs of the speaker; . . . "external" . . . analogous to an exchange of "genetic material."

They also designed an experimental program to simulate the evolution of cultures.

> If by evolution we mean the cumulative process of small changes, it is a truism that this term can be applied not only to the history of organisms but equally to many other histories of development. One speaks of evolving institutions, evolving languages, evolving ways of thought. Often the history of an artifact presents a striking similarity to that of an organism: witness the changing appearance of the automobile, in which we can trace "vestigial parts."

The experimental program was to create microcultures (small groups) whose evolution could be observed and experimentally manipulated. As they performed various tasks, members were rotated, the evolving culture was transmitted to new generations, mutations met various selection pressures, and communication patterns and language changed. It might be possible to encourage cultural differentiation, breed cultures, establish lines of descent, cross strains, and otherwise do with cultures what a breeder might with animals. It was supposed that selection pressure would have much influence on innovations. For example, if the environment were very severe, so that the group would "die" if its performance fell below a certain level, the premium would be on conservation rather than experimentation.

Thus the Gerald-Kluckhohn-Rapoport paper opened up again the whole question of social evolution: A revival of evolutionary theory in the social sciences occurred (White, 1959; Campbell, 1965; Appelbaum, 1970:36-64). The natural selection of business firms was studied and natural selection was applied to the learning process and to the scientific method, in a model, for example, of "artificial intelligence" (Fogel, 1965). From such synergy much more could be expected.

As described in Chapter I, the separation of sociology and biology was further reduced during the 1960s by the application to sociological thought of general system, or information, theory, which indicated new parallels between social and other living systems (Miller, 1971; Back, 1971).

Natural selection provides an admirable model for explaining how variety and disorder can be introduced into a system at the risk of chaos, but with the long run gain of creativity and better adapted patterns, amounting to a gain in order (negative entropy) and loss of less successful patterns. The basic paradigm for an evolving open system has four elements: (1) a tension of action and reaction to environment; (2) a source of variety acting as a pool of new adaptations; (3) selective criteria or mechanisms against which variations may be sifted to choose the more successful; and (4) an arrangement for preserving and propagating these successful patterns (Buckley, 1967:63).

Evolution, in spite of its tendency toward conflict and struggle in eliminating less successful forms, is probably less entropic (more negentropic) in its net outcome for society than dialectical conflict, with its destruction and forced choice between two patterns. Dialectic is like a two-horse race in which winner takes all, while natural selection is like a many-horse race, in which there is a range of possible winners, each slightly different—a normal curve, if you like, with extremes but most at the center. In such a selection, the survivors may be only slightly different from the losers, and successful adaptations are likely to be in the middle range rather than in the extremes of possibly freakish variation. Development occurs gradually through a series of trials approaching some goal not clearly seen in advance. On the other hand, dialectical changes tend toward extreme changes disruptive of continuity, the outcome of which is a huge gain or huge loss, as described in Table 7. Natural selection avoids this by small but steady gains or promptly curtailed losses. Finally, the dialectical "great leap forward" creates its own adjustment problem: Socialization is difficult, perhaps requiring a "new man" along heroic, collectivist, or fanatical lines, whereas the evolutionary process offers easy adjustment, since the new pattern is not all that different from the old, as in the transition from a welfare state to socialism. This contrast suggests that natural selection has advantages over polarized conflict as a way of encoding new order into a system.

"Fang and claw" struggle is not usually implied in evolutionary theory. A model of societal search should encompass any kind of variation in pattern or symbol which a group might find useful, for example, a fashion (Klapp, 1969; 1972), or a rumor (Shibutani, 1966), or a communal experiment in living (Kanter, 1968). Such a model can be outlined in five main stages: (1) Increasing strain leads to increasing variations of behavior and communication, some of which are deviations from norms, others of which are hardly perceived; (2) Such variations are tried out as plans, styles, symbols, rebellions, living experiments, and so on; (3) Competition and conflict ensue, whether in market,* appealing to mass tastes, communication (competition with noise), ecology, or political struggle, and this conflict leads to winnowing of more viable patterns, while the less successful fade away; (4) Survivors having found viable patterns try to legitimize themselves (for example, "Gay Liberation," having developed as a homosexual community, tries

*Natural selection is taken to include market, being a more general class of competition, including ecology, without a pricing system.

Table 7   DIALECTICAL MODEL OF SOCIAL CHANGE*

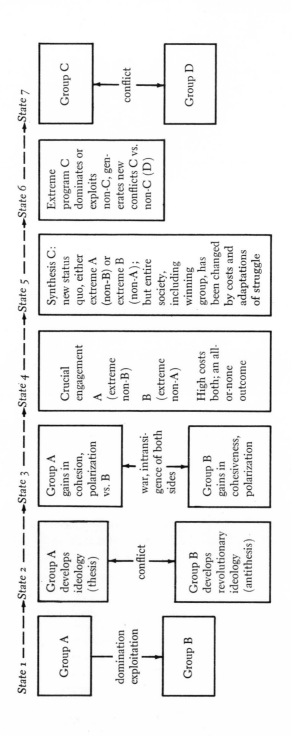

State 1 - - - → State 2 - - - → State 3 - - - → State 4 - - - → State 5 - - - → State 6 - - - → State 7

| Group A | Group A develops ideology (thesis) | Group A gains in cohesion, polarization vs. B | Crucial engagement A (extreme non-B) B (extreme non-A) High costs both; an all-or-none outcome | Synthesis C: new status quo, either extreme A (non-B) or extreme B (non-A); but entire society, including winning group, has been changed by costs and adaptations of struggle | Extreme program C dominates or exploits non-C, generates new conflicts C vs. non-C (D) | Group C |
| Group B | Group B develops revolutionary ideology (antithesis) | Group B gains in cohesiveness, polarization | | | | Group D |

domination exploitation (Group A → Group B)

conflict (Group A ↔ Group B)

war, intransigence of both sides (Group A ↔ Group B)

conflict (Group C ↔ Group D)

*See K. Boulding, A Primer on Social Dynamics (Free Press, 1970), for further analysis of a polarized conflict model.

Table 8 EVOLUTIONARY NATURAL SELECTION MODEL (applied to biological and cultural forms) *

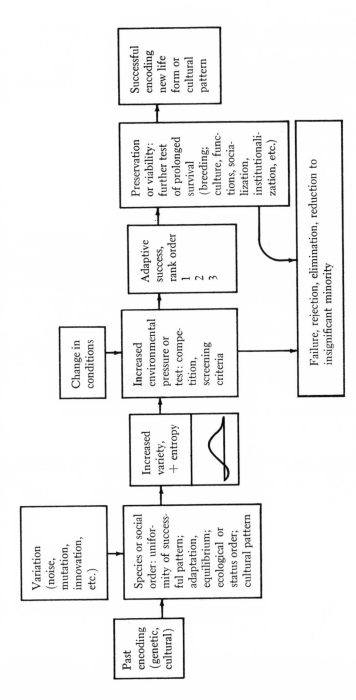

*See Gerard, Kluckhohn and Rapoport, 1956; D. T. Campbell, 1965; W. Buckley, 1967; T. Shibutani, 1966; K. Boulding, 1970; Back, 1971.

to win political legality and social respectability); (5) Legitimation leads to institutionalization, as people, recognizing services and claims, give more support to the pattern and come to rely on its functions, while at the same time perhaps withdrawing participation from older institutions. So society can change by a search which is at the same time a struggle, but with polarization and "backlashes" subdued and outlived, avoiding the entropy of a fight to the finish between two patterns, as shown in Table 8.

So there was a resurgence in seeing evolution as a way of reaching societal goals. Applying natural selection more boldly and broadly, modern thinkers claimed they could see a higher ethic and social type evolving (Huxley, 1957; Teilhard de Chardin, 1964; Potter, 1971). The astronomer Harlow Shapley said:

> I think we've finally come to the place where we see that the same principles apply to the evolution of every blasted thing, including the universe.... It's a very penetrating, deep process that touches the universe in many different ways (1970).

Within this perspective, Marxist dialectics and even the "cold war" of the United States with the Soviet Union appear to be turbulences which the world can ill afford. What seems needed is a broad range of societal experiments in viability, allowed to compete and settle the question of which are best for the best kind of man.

10

Order
from
Progress

All the trend curves we may examine show rates of acceleration which underline the unprecedented nature of things to come.
—BUCKMINSTER FULLER

The geodesic dome invented by Buckminster Fuller is a symbol of the promise of the future, of man's ability not only to supply housing for all but perhaps an entire climate for bubble-covered cities, in short, to make the world as he pleases. But however hopeful Fuller's technological contributions, his statement above gives little assurance about the end results of such progress. Even using old ways can have results that are not expected. Take the homely example of salt: In 1971 the Massachusetts Audubon Society noted that too much salt in the drinking water was causing water supplies to be closed down in many New England towns. Used as a de-icing agent on public roads, about six million tons were spread in 1970. Unfortunately, so much salt endangered the water supply, injured or killed tremendous numbers of roadside trees, killed fish and wildlife, and corroded bridges and underground pipelines, even concrete roads and walks. Only after all this did it become apparent that it would have been cheaper to have used sand. Similar adverse side-effects might be illustrated for DDT or the automobile. Even the tractor, friend of the farmer, can be used to destroy forests, level hills, or put an airstrip in the Everglades. Man shows a curious dullness about the larger effects of what he does.

Partly it is a matter of scale. With a bow and arrow in a forest, man might shoot as he pleased. But with a high-powered rifle, even ability to defoliate an entire forest, the outlook changes. The case is similar to self-medication: In the old days it was fairly safe because most remedies were weak; but now with pills as powerful as LSD, can one rely on his own judgment? In information theory terms, the magnitude and thrust of inputs has increased enormously, but knowledge of outcomes hardly at all—or too late to avoid negative consequences. It is ironical, then, that much of the human race is still living with the assurance from the nineteenth century that something called "progress" is bound to be the net result of "useful" innovations, though he knows less than ever what in fact is coming in a world whose regularities he has interfered with. Man's faith in progress has dimmed considerably, however, since the optimism of the Enlightenment.

IDEOLOGY OF PROGRESS

The idea of progress arose, "on the ruins of the concept of providence." It was the belief that the "world as a whole was proceeding onward indefinitely to greater and greater perfection" (Park and Burgess, 1924). It was a secular conception of the world in man's hands, depending upon his ability to control it, and was reflected in writings like those of Machiavelli and Locke. Man's trump card in the game was reason,

by which he could remedy the faults of nature and devise Utopias if
need be. Bacon's *New Atlantis* (1627) was one of the first bold pictures
of what science could do. Faith in progress reached an almost mystical
optimism in the eighteenth century, as we have seen in Adam Smith's
faith in the market and the rationality of self-interest to bring good to
man, or in Locke's belief that reason working through democratic consensus would produce ever widening spheres of freedom and government
by consent. Condorcet, an eighteenth century French social thinker,
sums up the faith in progress through reason as follows:

> Are we not arrived at the point when there is no longer anything
> to fear, either from new errors, or the return of old ones; when
> no corrupt institution can be introduced by hypocrisy.... Every-
> thing tells us that we are approaching the era of one of the grand
> revolutions of the human race.... The present state of knowledge
> assures us that it will be happy ... that the human race shall not
> again relapse into its ancient barbarity ... eternal oscillations be-
> tween truth and falsehood, liberty and servitude.... Our hopes,
> as to the future condition of the human species, may be reduced
> to three points: the destruction of inequality between different
> nations; the progress of equality in one and the same nation; and
> lastly, the real improvement of man. Will not every nation one
> day arrive at the state of civilization attained by those people who
> are most enlightened, most free, most exempt from prejudices, as
> the French, for instance, and the Anglo-Americans? Will not ...
> slavery ... and the ignorance of savages gradually vanish? Is there
> upon the face of the globe a single spot the inhabitants of which
> are condemned by nature never to enjoy liberty, never to exercise
> their reason? ... Among those causes of human improvement that
> are of most importance ... must be included, the total annihilation
> of the prejudices which have established between the sexes an
> inequality of rights.... People being more enlightened ... will
> learn by degrees to regard war as the most dreadful of all calamities,
> the most terrible of all crimes.... The perfectibility of man is
> indefinite.... It cannot be doubted that the progress of the sana-
> tive art, that the use of more wholesome food and more comfort-
> able habitations ... that the destruction of the two most active

causes of deterioration, penury and wretchedness on the one hand, and enormous wealth on the other, must necessarily tend to prolong the common duration of man's existence, and secure him a more constant health and a more robust constitution.... Improvement of the practice of medicine ... must in the end put a period to ... contagious disorders, as well as to ... general maladies.... Would it even be absurd to suppose ... that a period must one day arrive when death will be nothing more than the effect either of extraordinary accidents, or of the gradual decay of the vital powers; and that the duration of the middle space, ... between the birth of man and this decay, will itself have no assignable limit? Certainly man will not become immortal; but may not the ... term ... be ... protracted? ... Lastly, may we not include ... the intellectual and moral faculties? ... Is it not probable that education, by improving these qualities, will at the same time have an influence upon, will modify and improve this organization itself? ... How admirably calculated is this view of the human race, emancipated from its chains, released alike from the domination of chance, as well as from that of the enemies of its progress, and advancing with a firm and indeviate step in the paths of truth, to console the philosopher.... This prospect ... rewards him for all his efforts to assist the progress of reason and the establishment of liberty. He dares to regard these efforts as a part of the eternal chain of the destiny of mankind (1795).

Condorcet saw no reason why by endlessly encoding the fruits of reason, man could not make limitless progress in virtue and longevity. On the heels of the French Revolution, this was hope indeed!

This faith of the eighteenth century became entrenched in the thought of the nineteenth century, indeed, it was a firmly fixed assumption upon which theories were built. In his book *Madame Bovary*, the great French novelist Gustave Flaubert sketched an unforgettable caricature of the nineteenth century rationalist. The character is a small-town druggist who proclaims that his religion is that of Socrates, Franklin, and Voltaire, who opposes priests for teaching "things absurd in themselves, and completely opposed ... to all physical laws," who keeps "pace with science by means of pamphlets and public papers . . . always on the alert to find out improvements," who knows "all the latest inventions in economic stoves, together with the art of preserving cheeses and of curing sick wines," and who persuades a poor club-footed youth to submit in the name of science to an operation which cost the boy his leg. Even this result doesn't shake the druggist's faith in progress, nor does he give a second thought to the damage he is willing to inflict upon people in its name. Although he was a fanatic thoroughly armed with facts and experiments, his practical faith in ingenuity was not of an entirely different kind from that of Thomas Jefferson, Benjamin Franklin, or Thomas Edison.

Such confidence in progress was expanded into philosophies like those of Hegel, Marx, and Comte, who argued that history was moving by an invincible logic toward greater perfection. Providing support to many, such philosophies became ideologies, systematized social beliefs. Comte stated his "law of progress," in three stages, which Levy-Bruhl (1927) later amplified by claiming that there was a difference between the "prelogical" mind of traditional peoples (such as aborigines and ancient Hindus and Chinese), and the logical mind of modern man, which had to be overstepped before scientific progress could occur. Evolution seemed to guarantee a grand outcome, however rough the struggle along the way. From their elevated position on the evolutionary scale, Western men drew strength to carry the "white man's burden" and set about interpreting imperialism as the uplifting of backward peoples for their own good, even though this meant denying them self-government. No less a thinker than the great liberal J. S. Mill argued that representative government was not for people who had

> still to learn the first lesson of civilization, that of obedience. A race who have been trained in energy and courage by struggles with Nature and their neighbors, but who have not yet settled down into permanent obedience to any common superior, would be little likely to acquire this habit under the collective government of their own body. A representative assembly drawn from among

themselves would simply reflect their own turbulent insubordination (1861).

It was, then, possible to argue that if a foreign civilization was superior to that of people whom it ruled, such government was

> often of the greatest advantage to a people, carrying them rapidly through several stages of progress, and clearing away obstacles to improvement which might have lasted indefinitely if the subject population had been left unassisted to its native tendencies and chances (MILL, 1861: CHAPTER IV).

Protests by such men as Owen, Carlyle, and Ruskin, over the inhumanities of industrialization did not shake faith in progress. Even the dire logic of Marx foretold Utopia after the proletarian revolution. Some followers of Marx despaired, claiming that the idea of progress was only an optimistic illusion, a weapon of bourgeois class interest (Sorel, 1908), but the main wave of Marxist faith carried on into the Soviet Union:

> The very concept of progress—of the forward movement of society —is in itself revolutionary. It presupposes that society develops along upward lines, in other words that its movement is predominantly neither backward nor proceeding in a circle, neither a treadmill nor stagnation, nor yet mere conservation of existing social forms; it is rather an inevitable replacement of old or obsolescent institutions with new, growing young ones. This means that just as early slave society gave way to feudalism and feudalism to capitalism, so modern capitalism must inevitably make way for a new, infinitely more perfect social system for which the whole of society's earlier development has prepared us—namely, socialism (ZHUKOV, 1961).

For socialist and liberal alike, the goal of history seemed to be, as Tennyson wrote, "one far-off divine event, to which the whole creation moves." Or, as Spencer put it: "The establishment of the greatest perfection and the most complete happiness" in a final state of cosmic equilibrium (1880: Section 176).

238

Such views help us to define the notion of progress. It refers not just to particular changes, but to the overall improvement of society as a whole. Temporary ups and downs may occur, but in the long run there would be a continuous change for the better, from one century to the next. Progress is a march, not a staggering or wandering; it is a general betterment, not just a gain in one value such as employment at the expense of another such as liberty.

The problem in defining progress scientifically comes from this very overall character. While it is indisputable that there has been in Western history "progress" by indices such as literacy, life expectancy, GNP, or other measures of material well being, there is no proof these are necessarily correlated with broader and more intangible goods such as happiness, wisdom, or virtue. The English followers of Mill tried to define progress as increased happiness for the greatest number. The American sociologist L. F. Ward followed this, saying:

> Human progress may be properly defined as that which secures the increase of human happiness. Unless it do this, no matter how great a civilization may be, it is not progressive. If a nation rise, and extend its sway over a vast territory ... this alone does not constitute progress. It must first be shown that its people are happier than they would otherwise have been (1883:II, 174-77).

Yet the moment one focuses on happiness, it becomes impossible to exclude higher ethical and spiritual values, as Aristotle and Thomas Aquinas insisted. Plainly, material well being is only a circle within a much larger and less well-defined one of general well being. And even on the material side, the picture of progress is far from reassuring, as we shall see.

But for the nineteenth century obsessed with the grand outcome, such doubts could not be seriously entertained. They believed there were too many forces for good at work. Progress came to be thought of as a kind of genie working through technology to bring a better life for all through the market.

Only such a belief in progress could explain that curious attitude called *modernism*, which puts low value on tradition, rates everything by how new it is, regards the present as better than the past and the future as better yet, and sees time as an endless conveyor belt bringing good things to man.

CRISIS OF PROGRESS

The crisis of progress might be dated roughly from World War I; at least this was a turning point, a loss of naiveté for Americans and Europeans alike, as many historians have observed (Hofstadter, 1955). The war interrupted the flow of Victorian optimism and set the stage for Spengler's *Decline of the West* (1918). In this work Spengler maintained that whole cultures could go to ruin for reasons he could only define as organic. By contrast, the muckrakers of the turn of the century —such as Lincoln Steffens, Upton Sinclair, Ida Tarbell, Theodore Dreiser, Gustavus Myers—were crusaders like Theodore Roosevelt. Although they saw "vested interests" as enemies of progress, they had not lost faith in an inherent trend toward betterment, but were merely impatient to get on with it (Filler, 1961).

In 1921 a Cambridge historian, J. B. Bury, published a modest book which examined the idea of progress as a cultural product. It had devastating impact, not because it disproved progress but because it showed so objectively its historical growth. It explained why the Greeks with their ideal of fixed order had not needed it, how St. Augustine's idea of life on earth as a punishment for original sin precluded it, and why Oriental civilizations had not developed it. Only in Europe had it flourished, under the great precursorship of Francis Bacon, who gave an "entirely new value" to the augmentation of knowledge and "sounded the modern note" that "the end of knowledge is utility" for increasing men's happiness and lessening their sufferings (1921, 50-52). No civilization, Eastern or Western, had ever before seriously considered such a possibility on a broad scale. But by stressing how special was the development of the idea of progress, Bury made scholars acutely aware of its ideological character. While not intending to destroy the notion of progress, he destroyed the claim of progress to the naturalness of a scientific law, like evolution. For one thing, progress contains a *value* judgment, which evolution does not:

> Evolution itself . . . does not necessarily mean, applied to society, the movement of man to a desirable goal. It is a neutral, scientific conception, compatible either with optimism or with pessimism. According to different estimates it may appear to be a cruel sentence or a guarantee of steady amelioration. And it has been actually interpreted in both ways (335-36).

Indeed, progress was a *dogma*, with no more finality than those it had replaced. Quite possibly, a new idea would "usurp its place as the directing idea of humanity" (351-52).

Another side of progress was becoming more visible to sociologists. Lists of social problems were getting longer, especially after the Great Depression. The leading textbook on social disorganization in the 1940s listed no less than twenty-six types of problems to which it devoted chapters:

> social disorganization; individual disorganization; adolescence; juvenile delinquent; the criminal; sex; prostitution; mobility, migration; drink, men in industry; women and children in industry; unemployment; the mentally deficient; the mentally deranged; suicide; family disorganization; the changing family; the romantic fallacy; family tensions; desertion; divorce; community disorganization; the small town; leisure; political corruption; crime and the community; revolution (ELLIOTT AND MERRILL, 1934).

The third edition in 1950 added chapters on religious minorities; racial minorities; totalitarianism, and war. Doubtless some of this proliferation was due to the assiduity of sociologists, and a certain "Parkinson's law" in development of subjects; still, a battery of ills below the political and economic level was being revealed as never before. Nor with passing years did sociologists' stock of problems show any signs of decreasing. There was a certain monotony in reports of increasing crime. It seemed possible to counter every index of material progress with another on the gloomy side, such as suicide or divorce.

The good genie, technology, came under closer scrutiny as a source of such evils as dehumanized speed-up (Taylorism) and technological unemployment. W. F. Ogburn made pioneering studies of the social effects of technology, noting that the automobile, not the socialist, was "radical number one" (1946). The anomie thesis was applied to industrialism (Mayo, 1953; Roethlisberger, 1941), and to the freedom which went with loss of a sense of organic community (Fromm, 1941; Nisbet, 1953). What had begun as concern about "lags" and side-effects of progress grew into sweeping indictments of technology and cities as inimical to man (Mumford, 1970; Ellul, 1965). Sorokin said it was the "crisis of our age," including loss of altruism and the decadence of "sensate" culture (1941). All this was progress? It took strong faith indeed!

Meanwhile, anthropologists were developing their own list of charges, based on respect for cultures that were not "progressive." Their list began with a deepening contempt for the "missionary spirit" in dealing with primitive cultures. Viewing the white man's contact with Zulus or Zunis, one could well ask, who is civilizing whom? There was also the question of cultural relativism posed concisely in 1934 by Benedict who asked: By what right can a standard drawn from one culture be used to measure another which has a vastly different value-emphasis? Without a culture-free standard, to call one society "higher" and another "backward" is mere ethnocentrism. The issue is illustrated by a letter written to a Western social scientist by a Moslem, who responded to a request for information about his community as follows:

> My Illustrious Friend and Joy of My Liver:
> The thing which you ask of me is both difficult and useless. Although I have passed all my days in this place, I have neither counted the houses nor inquired into the number of inhabitants; and as to what one person loads on his mules and the other stows away in the bottom of his ship, that is no business of mine. But above all, as to the previous history of this city, God only knows the amount of dirt and confusion that the infidels may have eaten before the coming of the sword of Islam. It were unprofitable for us to inquire into it. . . .
> Listen, O, my son! There is no wisdom equal to the belief in God. He created the world and shall we liken ourselves unto him in seeking to penetrate into the mysteries of his creation? Shall we say, Behold this star shineth around that star, and this other star with a tail goeth and cometh in so many years? Let it go. He from whose hand it came will guide and direct it. Thou art learned in the things I care not for, and as for what thou hast seen, I spit upon it. Will much knowledge create thee a double belly, or wilt thou seek paradise with thine eyes?
> The meek in spirit,
Imaum Ali Zado

(THOMAS, 1902:170)

By the 1960s another awkward problem had emerged, resulting from the impact of progress on developing countries. Exposed to the standards of the West through increasing literacy and mass media, people who had previously not thought much about the hardships of being "backward" developed a feeling of "relative deprivation" as they compared their own style of life with that reflected in Sears Roebuck catalogs or American movies. Their "want-get ratio" of frustration thus increased as they entered the mainstream of progress (D. Lerner, in Hoffman, 1968:134-5). Such transitional countries also underwent population booms that wiped out material gains, and were prone, from political instability, to lose what freedom they had to military dictatorships. This new version of the "white man's burden" plainly raised grave questions about what was meant by progress. The problem was not just in closing the serious gap between the "have" and "have not" nations, but in dealing with the problem which arises if well-being is measured by fulfillment of *expectations*, which are themselves variable. If that is the case, then a rise in expectations can lead to a feeling of going down hill even if one is in fact gaining a little ground. Suppose an inhabitant of Latin America gets more corn but expects an electric refrigerator too. Then he is mentally worse off from such progress. There is no use saying that such a sense of losing ground is illusory. Humans, unlike all other animals, live in symbolic environments; if images do not register progress, then neither does reality. For a human, progress is either in the mind or not at all. So we have the paradox that the very idea of progress can increase misery. This outcome could not have been anticipated by the Enlightenment, but it might have been by St. Augustine.

So we have traced a change in the view of progress which began harmlessly enough with lists of social problems and questions about cultural lag. Attacks upon problems in the name of progress gradually became attacks on progress itself. The first round had been fired by the muckrakers outraged at the failure of society to live up to its democratic ideals. But by 1970, change itself had become a villain causing "future shock" (Toffler, 1970). Ogburn's student, Phillip Hauser, characterized the "manifest confusion and disorder" of contemporary life as "the chaotic society," suffering a "social morphological revolution" (population explosion, population implosion, population diversification, and change acceleration) which threatened its viability (Hauser, 1969). Some anthropologists were even reaching the bitter conclusion that not only was culture not progressive, it was malign, "against man." There was no reason to suppose, according to Jules Henry (1964) that culture in general (any more than technology in particular) is always the servant of man. Culture can impose itself on people, by mythology, by methods of training (socialization) that create artificial needs. This is no more true of the ancient Norse culture, that had men rushing to die in battle in order to quaff a brew with blonde maidens in Valhalla, than of modern American culture which has become a trap of material consumption, using self-indulgence for bait. A "culture against man" also creates obsessive fears of failure to succeed, of communism, and war. One cannot banish such ghosts because the economy hinges on these very things. The personality fostered by such a system is self-indulgent, anxious, lacking in concern for others, misrepresentative in roles, shallow in involvement, confused and vague, tending to "read life off in terms of a dominance-submission struggle" (Henry, 1964:349)—in other words, to be the kind of creature most likely to be quiet in such a cage.

But for all this disappointment with the results of progress, we have not yet touched on perhaps the deepest source of such disillusionment: the instrument that was supposed to guarantee freedom and progress, the human mind itself.

ANTI-INTELLECTUALISM

Along with the piling up of the dubious fruits of progress following World War I, was a clearer view on the part of sociologists of the kind of organization which provided, so to speak, the cage for modern man's existence. It was a system of work organized by plans, rules, and procedures, which seemed to be modeled after a machine—indeed, it was a human machine, commonly called bureaucracy. Max Weber deserves most of the credit for revealing the character of bureaucratic structure. He showed how it was everywhere a late product of social development destroying other, less efficient kinds of organizations. Its prime characteristic and the source of its strength is *rational discipline*:

The consistently rationalized, methodically trained and exact execution of the received order, in which all personal criticism is . . . suspended . . . (WEBER, 1946:253).

It was rational discipline, not gunpowder, that gave superiority to modern armies—that allowed Cromwell, for example, to defeat the Cavaliers. In the long run, bureaucracy wins out everywhere over gallantry and other nonbureaucratic qualities. This is to a large degree the basis of progress:

> No special proof is necessary to show that military discipline is the ideal model for the modern capitalist factory. . . . Organizational discipline in the factory is founded upon a completely rational basis. With the help of appropriate methods of measurement, the optimum profitability of the individual worker is calculated like that of any material means of production. On the basis of this calculation, the American system of "scientific management" enjoys the greatest triumphs. . . . The decisive reason for the advance of bureaucratic organization has always been its purely technical superiority over any other form of organization. . . . Precision, speed, unambiguity, knowledge of the files, continuity, discretion, unity, strict subordination, reduction of friction and of material and personal costs—these are raised to the optimum point in the strictly bureaucratic organization (WEBER, 1946:222).

We are concerned with the picture of the man that emerges in Weber's description of the "official," the cog in the bureaucratic machine: trained, obedient, impersonal, matter-of-fact, respectful of rules more than men, secure in tenure but replaceable by any average worker with similar experience. The bureaucratic office called for men of mediocre ability and produced what Veblen called "trained incapacity" to see the larger task and make judgments in terms of the whole—the small-mindedness of the petty official. This kind of person is the opposite of what Weber called the charismatic personality. Imagine, if you will, Richard the Lion Hearted in an office; the predicament would be no

246

less laughable for Picasso. In short, the very triumph of the rationality of bureaucratic organization was achieved at the price of diminishing the stature of the man who held a position within it. So progress had come to this: Organization was stronger but man was less! Two thousand years of rationalization had produced a type of man the opposite of Socrates. Sensitive intellectuals like Franz Kafka began to mistrust the rationality of highly organized systems, and their criticism was enlarged into massive indictments of the "unsane" society (Fromm, 1955), the "megamachine" (Mumford, 1970), and the "banality of evil" (Arendt, 1963).

A kind of mistrust of reason or anti-intellectualism grew up which was different from that of the prejudiced crowd which condemned Socrates. The common type of anti-intellectualism has always been with us, as a simple dislike of ideas, books, eggheads, by people who may pride themselves on being practical men of action. In the twentieth century however, the greatest challenge to intellect was coming from highly educated thinkers who had drunk from Faust's cup, so to speak, and found it bitter. This led to the phenomenon of the "intellectual anti-intellectual," such as Henri Bergson. This French philosopher (1859-1941) made a highly reasoned argument against putting faith in reason. His case hinged on the claim that in forming concepts the intellect is abstracting from reality rather than capturing it. To illustrate the difference he compared knowledge to a movie film, a cinematograph:

> Suppose we wish to portray on a screen a living picture, such as the marching past of a regiment. . . . One way . . . is to take a series of snapshots . . . and to throw these instantaneous views on the screen, so that they replace each other very rapidly. This is what the cinematograph does. With photographs, each of which represent the regiment in a fixed attitude, it reconstitutes the mobility of the regiment marching. . . . If we had to do with photographs alone, however much we might look at them, we should never see them animated: with immobility set beside immobility . . . we could never make movement. In order that the pictures may be

animated, there must be movement somewhere. The movement does indeed exist ... it is in the apparatus. It is because the film of the cinematograph unrolls ... that each actor of the scene recovers his mobility. ... The process then consists in extracting from all the movements ... an impersonal movement abstract and simple, *movement in general.* ... We put this into the apparatus and we reconstitute ... each particular movement. ... Instead of attaching ourselves to the inner becoming of things, we place ourselves outside them in order to recompose their becoming artificially. We take snapshots, as it were, of the passing reality, and ... string them on a becoming, abstract, uniform and invisible, situated at the back of the apparatus of knowledge. ... Whether we would think becoming, or express it, or even perceive it, we hardly do anything else than set going a kind of cinematograph inside us. ... The mechanism of our ordinary knowledge is of a cinematographical kind (1911: 331-332).

Such knowledge, then, is devoid of contact with inner reality, or "becoming." We must "give up the cinematographical habits of our intellect" (339) and replace them with another way of knowing, *intuition*, based on instinct or sympathy.

Intelligence and instinct are turned in opposite directions, the former toward inert matter, the latter toward life. ... Science ... goes all around life, taking from outside the greatest possible number of views of it ... but it is to the very inwardness of life that *intuition* leads us. ... Intuition may enable us to grasp what it is that intelligence fails to give us (194-195).

Action also helps to break the bonds of intellectual knowledge:

If we had never seen a man swim, we might say that swimming is an impossible thing. ... Reasoning, in fact, always nails us down to the solid ground. But if, quite simply, I throw myself into the water without fear, I may keep myself up well enough at first by merely struggling, and gradually adapt myself to the new environment: I shall thus have learnt to swim. So, in theory, there is a kind of absurdity in trying to know otherwise than by intelligence; but if the risk be frankly accepted, action will perhaps cut the knot that reasoning has tied and will not unloose (211).

So Bergson showed how seriously reason limits our understanding of the *elan vitale* (life-force). He implied that more freedom would come from greater trust in action and intuition, however illogical they might appear. Though to Americans this might seem very sensible and pragmatic, it was to many a romantic invitation to place feeling and intuition above thought.

The second major salvo against the house of intellect was fired by Sigmund Freud, who based his depth psychology on the theory of the unconscious, that part of the mind which is hard to know because there is "resistance" against it:

> When we undertake to cure a patient of his symptoms he opposes against us a vigorous and tenacious resistance throughout the entire course of the treatment. . . . It is precisely those associations against which innumerable doubts and objections are raised that invariably contain the material leading to the discovery of the unconscious (FREUD, 1938:253-254).

Freud likens the mind to a house of two rooms: The first is a large anteroom into which various impulses crowd; adjoining this is a smaller reception room, on the threshold of which stands a door-keeper who examines the various impulses, censors some, and admits others. The impulses of the anteroom are not visible in the reception room where consciousness resides; when turned back by the door-keeper, they are "incapable of becoming conscious; we call them repressed" (1938a:260).

> The theory of repression is the pillar upon which the edifice of psychoanalysis rests. It is really the most essential part of it. . . . The theoretical value of the fact, that this resistance is connected with an amnesia, leads unavoidably to that concept of unconscious psychic activity which is peculiar to psychoanalysis . . . (FREUD, 1938b:937).

The mind then, can never know much of what it thinks and feels; consciousness is like the tip of the iceberg above water. What we consciously will may not be the real cause of our actions; "rationalizations" are the false but acceptable reasons we invent for our conduct when we do not know, or are ashamed of, the real reasons. Since we can never really know most of the unconscious mind, even after years of psychoanalysis, we are doomed to be irrational, or dubiously rational, most of the time. So Freud, intending to cure the irrationality of neurosis, seriously undermined the Aristotelian and Enlightenment ideal of the rational man. Freud asked whether civilization *could* be rational, if most of its reasonings were repressions, rationalizations, or sublimations? His study, *Civilization and its Discontents* (1930), claims that the renunciations that culture forces on men's sexual and aggressive instincts, resulting in feelings of guilt, are an intolerable burden, and the source of neurotic symptoms and tensions which threaten civilization itself. If any culture creates guilt, then do highly civilized ones create more guilt and unhappiness?

> Would not the diagnosis be justified that many systems of civilization—or epochs of it—possibly even the whole of humanity—have become "neurotic" under the pressure of the civilizing trends? (1930:103).

Freud avoided a final pronouncement, but he had seriously shaken the confidence of the age in civilization as progress, based on reason.

A third great anti-intellectual thinker is Marx, who was a rationalist, but whose "doctrine tended to undermine the rationalist belief in reason" (Popper, 1952, II:224). He held that ideas are not true social forces but merely epiphenomena in the stream of history. The real forces are material interests, covered by a smoke screen of ideology and mystification, as previously discussed in Chapter VIII. The fourth major anti-intellectual theory, that of Vilfredo Pareto was discussed in Chapter VIII. Pareto held that "deviations" (theories) do not count for much except as rationalizations of human actions—the real forces working in society are "residues" (sentiments, instincts, interests).

These four thinkers—Bergson, Freud, Marx, and Pareto—delivered a staggering blow to reason itself, as the source of the good life and doubted the possibility of using reason to improve civilization by conscious design and planning. They seemed to show that other forces such as unconscious motives and material interests, rather than ideals, rule men. All of them avoided using reason to explain or guide social change. Bergson, relied on evolution; Pareto chose equilibrium; Marx put his faith in a material conflict process (dialectic), as explained in Chapter 9.

Rationality was also apparently unable to supply satisfactory answers about the meaning of life and the ultimate scheme of things. Some scientists, like Jacques Monod and Harold C. Urey, disclaimed altogether the existence of any such answers. Although reason had already discredited religion and much of philosophy, it was now announcing that it had nothing to say about matters for which its predecessors had supplied comfort. Accompanying this sense of emptiness was the growing awareness that technology and bureaucracy were bringing about a "mechanistic dehumanization" of man rather than the good society (Matson, 1964:67), that had been clearly spelled out by Huxley (1932-1958).

Against such a background, it was no surprise to see developing in the 1940s and '50s a powerful intellectual movement which seemed in many ways the very opposite of liberal optimism about progress. It was called *existentialism,* and is associated with such thinkers as Jean-Paul Sartre, Martin Heidegger, and Soren Kierkegaard. This movement emphasized despair, anguish (Kierkegaard), forlornness (Heidegger), and "nausea" (Sartre), as the lot of man. It rejected progress ("We do not believe in progress. Progress is betterment. Man is always the same."— Sartre, 1947:52), and rejected all institutional programs, formulas, creeds, and rules—most of what Weber meant by rationalization. It asserted instead a radical freedom and subjectivity ("the complete arbitrariness and the complete freedom" of man's existence—Sartre, 1947:55), which when examined was found to reject the objective world of science and logic as the center of man's understanding:

> The world of the object is the world of the probable. You ought to recognize that every theory, be it scientific or philosophic, is probable. . . . If we granted that the world of the object, the world of the probable, is the only world, we should have no more than a world of probabilities, and, therefore . . . where does certainty come from? Our subjectivism allows for certainties. . . . We can find them only by placing ourselves on the grounds of subjectivity. We've never argued about the fact that man is constantly an object for man, but, reciprocally, to grasp the object as such, a subject is needed which is aware of itself as subject (SARTRE, 1947: 86-87).

Regarding progress in objective knowledge which does not lead to more awareness of self, Kierkegaard said:

> The more knowledge increases, the more it becomes a kind of inhuman knowing for the production of which man's self is squandered, pretty much as men were squandered for the building of the Pyramids . . . (1941:164).

Existentialists argued that inner certainty of freedom was prior to any probable generalizations about man drawn from past experience. Man was much freer than he had ever realized to change, to choose, and to despair.

Finally, among the currents of "intellectual anti-intellectualism" there appeared in the 1960s a new criticism of intellect which took the form of an attack on print, which after all is a vehicle of literacy. It came of all places from a university English department. For his analysis of the effects of media upon man, Marshall McLuhan was hailed as the "oracle of the electric age," with the New York *Herald Tribune* going so far as to call him "the most important thinker since Newton, Darwin, Freud, Einstein, and Pavlov." McLuhan's wide-ranging analysis investigated the "psychic and social consequences" of technology. He found many unexpected benefits in television, the "electric drama" which permitted man to live "mythically and in depth." But his analysis of print was much more gloomy: Its effect had been to confine human thought more and more to a series of alphabetical symbols on a white piece of paper. This had forced it to become linear, sequential, logical, restricted in many ways. For example:

> Uniformity reached . . . into areas of speech and writing, leading to a single tone and attitude to reader and subject throughout an entire composition. The "man of letters" was born. . . . Permeation of the colloquial language with literate uniform qualities has flattened out educated speech till it is a very reasonable acoustic facsimile of the uniform and continuous visual effects of typography (1964:162).

Other unexpected consequences of print included the homogenization of diverse regions, political unification, and the emergence of nationalism with increased aggression. But

> Perhaps the most significant of the gifts of typography to man is that of detachment and noninvolvement—the power to act without reacting. . . . The very word "disinterested," expressing the loftiest detachment and ethical integrity of typographic man, has in the past decade been increasingly used to mean: "He couldn't care less.". . . It is this kind of specialization by dissociation that has created Western power and efficiency. Without this dissociation of action from feeling and emotion people are hampered and hesitant. Print taught men to say, "Damn the torpedoes. Full steam ahead!" (157, 162).

So McLuhan seemed to have brought to light another weakness of reason: As reflected in the written and printed word it has been an unrecognized tyrant. Once such a restrictive medium could be replaced by newer electronic media permitting "all-at-onceness" of experience, things would be better again. Man could begin "again to structure the primordial feeling, the tribal emotions from which a few centuries of literacy divorced us."

Such conclusions help explain a turn to the mysticism of the East noticeable among intellectuals, such as Aldous Huxley, Christopher Isherwood, Gerald Heard, Alan Watts, and Walter Stace. This trend might be conveniently dated from Huxley's influential writings on Vedanta (1944), and the drug experience (1954). Such writers presaged the cultic and occultic boom of the '70s (Braden, 1970). Such a "turn to the East" signalled a rejection by intellectuals themselves of reason as the main way to happiness. Hinduism, Buddhism, and Taoism have in common denial of intellect as a way to wisdom, and rejection of materialistic striving as a way to happiness. Indeed, they reverse the picture of reason that had so captivated the Enlightenment: Nothing is so good but what thinking can spoil it, nothing is so bad but what thinking makes it worse; the mind is the prime source of misery. The way to wisdom is to relinquish logical thought, cultivate meditation, and to suspend the strivings of the ego; "freedom from the known" is the key to mystical insight (Krishnamurti, 1969). So North America in the 1960s welcomed a great influx of swamis and gurus teaching a message diametrically opposed to the faith of Benjamin Franklin and William James, indeed to that of Socrates.

As we have seen, serious misgivings had developed in the minds of intellectuals about the effectiveness of intellect—the main tool of progress—in living up to promises put forth in the eighteenth and nineteenth centuries. Intellectuals, at least, had few sugarplums dancing in their heads about either smooth progression from the present into a more perfect future, or a Utopian communal state after the proletarian revolution, as Marxists visualized. Honest and rigorous social thinkers could not avoid noticing the growing list of unsolved social problems. Formidable thinking by intellectuals themselves (such as Bergson, Freud, Marx, and Pareto) led to conclusions about the weakness of ideas in having much effect on such problems. "Rational" institutions, even science (in making weaponry, for example), seemed to have an insane logic. Some intellectuals were even ready to reverse the verdict about the general direction of change: It was not progress but decadence (Joad, 1948; Krutch, 1929; Sorokin, 1941). Arthur Koestler said:

> In the last, explosive stages of man's evolution, something has gone wrong. There is a flaw, some subtle engineering mistake built into our native equipment (1969).

Of course, such effete conclusions little affected the man on the street, who went to his office or work bench faithful to the idea of progress. But more was to come.

POLLUTION CRISIS

During the 1960s, another cloud gathered which added to the miasma of doubt. It was one which the common man could smell; it made his eyes smart and even stuck to his skin and clothing. Environmental pollution turned out to include not only air, but water, soil, plants, fish—almost everything. Certain notable events contributed to this growing awareness, such as Rachel Carson's *Silent Spring* (1962), which indicted DDT for killing birds and poisoning the environment, and the 1971 oil spill at Santa Barbara, California. People began to feel endangered by side-effects of progress—for example, by the estimated 100 million tons of oil products polluting the sea each year, as estimated by the National Academy of Sciences—to say nothing of nuclear stockpiles possessed by the United States and Russia sufficient to blast each person in the world with the equivalent of fifteen tons of TNT. No longer could the man on the street avoid seeing that Ogburn was right: the number one radical had been the automobile; or, to put it more broadly, the insensate thrust of technology with its unanticipated side-effects into human affairs. For the first time the average man realized that his environment was being destroyed.

Ramifications of the environmental crisis traveled in all directions at once, like cracks in a shatterproof window. A wave of community protest began against new airports and power plants. Citizens brought suit against industries polluting air and water. Audubon and other societies launched efforts to protect endangered species, from elephants to eagles. The international Union for the Conservation of Nature (IUCN) announced that 20,000 plant species were endangered—one in ten of all known—as a result of population explosion, technological development, poor land management, overgrazing, and overcollecting. Such thoughts of a shrinking green belt—on which, after all, all higher life depends—evoked justified apprehension. The administrator of the U.S. Environmental Protection Agency, William D. Ruckelshaus, warned:

> From now on mankind must discipline itself like the crew of a submarine, putting aside petty egoism to maintain its habitat (1971).

The world crisis was summed up by two important statements. One was by the prestigious Club of Rome, which included experts from many countries. Its study, *The Limits to Growth* (1972), prepared by a team of scientists led by M.I.T. professor Dennis Meadows, used a computer model developed by Jay Forrester to study projected curves of population, natural resources, food, and industrial output. They concluded that since population, technology, and industrial development were eating up scarce natural resources and increasing pollution, time was running out for the world—"all growth projections end in collapse." An equally influential and alarming report from Britain was the "Blueprint for Survival," written by thirty-three of the United Kingdom's most distinguished scientists, including Julian Huxley. It warned that unrestricted industrial and population expansion would lead to "the breakdown of society and of the life support systems on this planet—

possibly by the end of this century and certainly within the lifetime of our children" (*Time*, January 24, 1972:32, 37). To such theorists, the only solution to the world crisis was to reach an equilibrium by halting growth before disaster occurred; the "golden age" of expansion was over. As a result of the environmental crisis, industrial and population growth became twin villains, gobbling up resources and spewing pollution on the planet. Checks on population were necessary, of course; but now came the new and startling requirement to stop, or at least balance, industrial growth.

Against such a wave of public concern, it was understandable that there would be a reaction from economic interests, which began a counter-propaganda minimizing the dangers of pollution. Power companies argued that some pollution, whether from smoke or atomic energy, was part of the price of having enough electricity. The Atomic Energy Commission was found to have a conflict of interest, since it was supporting as clients the very industries it was supposedly regulating. Detroit auto-makers complained of impossible clean air standards, and asked for softened legislation.

The ultimate solution to these problems remained unclear in the early 1970s. It was clear however that never again in the public mind would economic growth have the unalloyed positive connotations that it had enjoyed in the years from McKinley to Eisenhower. "Growth" had become a dangerous, almost an ugly, word. Associations formed to oppose growth, with names like Zero Population Growth and Zero Economic Growth. It was radical, but no longer "insane" (as would once have been thought by North Americans) to oppose all growth in population, consumption, and GNP at least for leading countries. Bearing in mind that in the minds of most Western nations growth had been synonymous with progress and prosperity, we now have the interesting equation that progress equals prosperity equals growth equals pollution; therefore, progress equals pollution. The most radical conclusion yet was that if people did check consumption and economic development in the search for a better life style, the entire economic system would be in jeopardy. The vastly alarming fact was that the economic system so hinged on growth (even perhaps, on that infinite pollution, war) that to check such growth might mean the end of the whole profit system. Urging just that, a number of radical economists in the United States broke off from the American Economic Association to form a Union for Radical Political Economy. Expressing this view, a textbook on social problems starts off with the phrase, "capitalism stinks" (Christoffel et al, 1970). The environmental crisis was giving rise to a socialistic revolution.

Much of this revolution was occurring in a growing "counter-culture" (Roszak, 1969), most of whose premises were diametrically opposed to those of the material progress of the "straight" culture. For the counter-culture growth meant pollution, success meant participation in the "ratrace," profits were theft, respectability meant hypocrisy, status meant plastic values, peace by national security meant war and the "war-fare state" (Cook, 1962), and law and order meant repression of dissent and the right to live as one pleases. On the other hand, what the rest of the world called drug abuse and sexual promiscuity were to the counter-culture mind-expanding experiences, while socialistic and communistic schemes were simply alternate styles, more humane ways of living with one's fellow man. So a wave of change was underway, denying much of what the previous generation had called progress (Reich, 1970). The main task of the revolution was to wean men away from technocracy,

> subverting and seducing [it] by the force of innocence, generosity, and manifest happiness in a world where those qualities are cynically abandoned in favor of bad substitutes. To the end that there shall be more and more of our fellows who cease to live by the declared necessities of the technocracy; to refuse to settle for a mere after-hours outlet for the magical potentialities of their personalities; who become as if deaf and blind to the blandishments of career, affluence, the mania of consumption, power politics, technological progress ... (ROSZAK, 1969:266-67).

This rebellion signified a mass search for identity (Klapp, 1969).

Meanwhile, popular literature was full of articles and books asking what had happened to the "American dream"? To call all this a "generation gap" was to badly miss the point of the meaning-crisis that was affecting many over forty as well as under twenty. The counter-culture was no tiny minority group, as had been Bohemians, beatniks, and gay society of earlier years, nor was it a phalanx of teenagers storming the citadel of adulthood with electric guitars. Rather, it was a vast and uncounted population of disenchanted people, mostly in the middle class, in ages from eight to eighty, who, regardless of what tactics they adopted, shared the perception that material progress had failed.

CONCLUSION:
A NEW DIRECTION FOR PROGRESS

We have described in this chapter the rise and fall of a myth which made people comfortable for a long time, but which in the end proved to be an inadequate, if not destructive, model of reality. The other side of the coin of progress included social problems, dehumanization, and destruction of the environment—ultimately, perhaps man himself. The good genie of progress working through technology became a sorcerer's apprentice madly piling up troubles faster than man could sweep them away.

It would be a great mistake to suppose that the crisis of progress had occurred because men had failed to reach material objectives, such as equitable distribution of goods. Those were real shortcomings. But the failure of progress was due to two other causes: (1) Rationality—whether bureaucracy, mechanization, or market—had somehow dropped man out of the equation and become inhuman; and (2) Man was failing to take account of the larger implications of his actions—in seeking his own interest regardless of social costs he had brought on disasters like pollution. Both of these were faults of encoding. What the crisis of progress proved was that the encoding mechanisms of society—by analogy, the ship's radar screen, compass, and chart room— had failed to register an approaching iceberg until a disaster occurred. For example, modernism has often shown an uncritical willingness to accept anything new, while conventional wisdom like common business sense is often blind to any result beyond an increase in profit. Nor do the science and technology which manufacture bombs have to deal themselves with shrapnel. Indeed, some kind of public blindness is required to explain the following scene described by a visitor to America:

> Traditionally America has been the land of wide-open spaces— America the beautiful. There was the frontier myth of limitless space, and the city myth of beautiful modern architecture, with gleaming steel fingers pointing skywards, and homes of incomparable convenience and graciousness. Both myths are dying—indeed if they have not died already.
>
> Straight and ugly highways traverse the country, spreading gasoline pollution on the air and that equally noxious pollution of the spirit caused by hamburger stands, fried chicken houses, gas stations, motels, garish neon signs, blatant hoardings and all the other assorted eyesores that make the phrase "keep America beautiful" sound more like a plea than a command (BARNES, 1971).

It is such scenes that lead me to characterize progress as a stone idol with a blind eye.

As the result of the environmental crisis a great many people, not just a few intellectuals, had seen the idea of progress and its corollary of material "success" as an ill-serving myth. It had become plain to many that the crass ideals of material progress and success were not sufficient for the good life. Nor was it America only that was seeing through the myth. World polls showed that many people were unable to evoke the optimistic picture of the world implied by the progress ideology, and least optimistic were some of the most progressive countries! At the end of 1969, a Gallup poll of world opinion showed that Americans were by no means the world's leaders in optimism about progress. In percentage of positive answers to the question, "Do you think, for people like yourself, that the world in ten years' time will be a better place to live in than it is now?" the people of the more developed countries (including America) ranked below other, less developed, countries. Greece, Spain, Finland, and Colombia were the most optimistic, while Japan and Canada were the least optimistic, as indicated in Table 9.

Table 9   ANTICIPATED WORLD CONDITION
IN 10 YEARS

	Better %	Not So Good %	Same %	Don't Know %
Greece	71	7	9	13
Spain	60	6	17	17
Finland	54	19	24	3
Colombia	53	30	13	4
India	49	15	19	17
W. Germany	43	9	32	16
United States	39	27	29	5
Canada	35	33	26	6
Japan	30	31	23	16

(Gallup poll, December 4, 1969)

Within the United States both whites and blacks had become pessimistic about the plight of the cities. Whites, by a 4-to-1 margin, saw the cities growing worse, while among blacks the margin was 5-to-1 (Gallup Poll, November 4, 1971).

These figures seem to show that actual material conditions are not a good indicator of how people feel about progress. That is, sometimes the materially poorer populations have a more optimistic outlook than wealthier ones. Does this mean that those people on the lower rungs of the ladder of progress see more to gain and less to lose than those who have already risen a considerable way? Or is there more a complicated explanation of the relative depression of prosperous peoples? One complication comes from that imp in Pandora's box, rising expectations. That is, those who have already had much expect even more, and so are frustrated, while those who have little are made hopeful by small gains. It is thus quite possible that those with more affluence can be more frustrated than those with less. Thus we see that there is no reliable relationship between material progress and feelings of well-being among men. That is, one can be lonely in a split-level home, while all the wonders of technology—automobiles, snap-top cans, and color television —do not, despite the bedazzling claims of advertising, add up to a good life.

It was not to be expected that all classes, with their different levels of expectation, would see the shortcomings of progress equally. The disillusionment seems more an affliction of "haves" than of "have-nots." To see why this should be so, we may liken an open-class society to a department store, in which each floor advertises the wares of the other floors. In theory, all can buy on any floor, but in fact relatively few are able to afford the prices of the exclusive shops on the top floor. One would have a hard time convincing the man coming up the escalator for the first time that things were not really better up there. He would have to go up and see for himself. Only after much shopping might he reach satiation. So, to classes working up out of poverty, the disillusionment of the upper middle class and intelligentsia would seem inexplicably irritating. There is little use, then, in trying to explain to blue collar workers—and still less to those confined to the ghettos—that life in suburbia may have its own equally severe problems, though more along the order of human frustrations than of material deprivation.

Such were the perplexities of the concept of progress in North America, or in any affluent society. But one fact remained: There was a crisis of progress, in whatever terms it was seen, the old myth had fallen, and a new direction was needed.

The obsession with progress has thus produced a blind spot—in information theory terms, a defective filter—which has caused people to fail to recognize approaching troubles, and to act without sufficient reckoning of social costs. A progress-oriented society is not merely one which is open to change, but one which believes as an article of faith that progress occurs in a simple, automatic, perpetual, even destined way—that betterment is somehow guaranteed in the scheme of things, whether the guarantee is called reason, free enterprise, market, historical dialectic, or evolution. Such a modernistic society, overvaluing the new, leaves the gate open too long to too much (Chapter 1), and so suffers chronic information overload and pollution (Klapp, 1972: 263-302). It also encourages a reckless sense of freedom in what people may do to bring about progress, leading to many activities which are selfish, wasteful, exploitative or destructive, but which are all justified as progressive. The idea of progress also increases frustrations by inflating expectations, while at the same time paradoxically releasing forces likely to lead to frustration. In the meantime incoming signals of trouble are misread by the progress-filter in terms like profit. So there is a lag (and perhaps a vicious circle) in what should be done to make a good society.

The question remains, after "progress," what? We may hope from advances in the human sciences, from the criticisms of existentialists, and humanists, and from experiments of the counter-culture with alternate life styles, that all the good news is not yet in. One obvious remedy is to redefine progress, improve the filter, discarding crude measures like GNP in favor of others measuring true gain more accurately. In 1972, for example, Canadian Prime Minister Trudeau proposed that his country adopt "net human benefit" as a measure of progress, while the Belgian President of the European Communities, governing body of the Common Market, called for giving up GNP and introducing a radical five-year European economic plan to bring about a closed-circuit economy, in which waste was penalized, pollution phased out, the public sector improved, and a minimum standard of living guaranteed for everyone—gains in "utility" rather than "product" (*World*, July 4, 1972:49-50).

Also hoped for is a worldwide surge of humanism to make more visible and urgent the fair claims of all mankind regarding whatever "progress" there is. A related hope is to understand more clearly the systems with which man is dealing, perhaps abandoning the notion that simple inputs lead to simple outputs. Rather, we should assume that each improvement must be won by careful effort, at the cost of something else, and risk of something worse, from a nature which grudges each victory, and guarantees the outcome not at all. Such an effort seems to call for larger development of system theory, the idea that man can somehow make better use of the order within himself to make better order outside himself.

11

Order from Man

The mood of the early 1970s reflected a distinct feeling that things were awry in the world. Some spoke of a social malaise. Others spoke of loss of confidence—in progress, technology, in science itself, or in reason. The environmental crisis led to doomsday thinking, while the "law and order" panic led to the "police dog and padlock" syndrome. These crises are like the predicament of the Norse god Thor when, during a visit to the hall of the immortals, he was challenged to show his strength by lifting a cat. He was humiliated to find that after much effort, he could manage to get only one of the cat's paws off the floor. His host then said: "That was no cat you were lifting, Thor, but the whole world." So the problems of modern times seemed to be deeply imbedded not only in the social system but in man, who was finding himself to be both victim and culprit. The idea that not only the system but man himself might have to be revised led many to despair about the future. Barry Commoner in *The Closing Circle* (1971), wrote:

> One of the common responses to a recitation of the world's environ-
> mental ills is a deep pessimism, which is perhaps the natural
> aftermath to the shock of recognizing that the vaunted "progress"
> of modern civilization is only a thin cloak for global catastrophe.

Behind this sense of inevitable disaster was another crisis, a *failure
of common will*, that is, a feeling that one could not mobilize enough
people soon enough and consistently enough to bring about a general
improvement for the nation, let alone the world. For example, when
the Council on Environmental Quality in 1972 tried to curb damaging
clear-cutting of timber in the national forests, it was quickly defeated by
pressure groups from the lumber industry, who argued that wages and
construction, hence the economy, would suffer. So long-range general
good fell easy victim to short-run economic interest. Even if the man on
the street really did believe the warnings of ecologists, he was not willing
to jeopardize his own paycheck. Behind this lack of common will, this
failure on the part of the public at large to act together for the common
good, was the failure of larger systems to develop a feeling of group
identity (*Gemeinschaft*), as mentioned in Chapter 7. Added to that
was a feeling of alienation and powerlessness, expressed by public mistrust of media and leaders. It seemed that only a disaster severe enough
to generate a "halo effect" of fellowship in emergency might create the
common will that was needed.

We can analyze such a failure of common will in terms of models
already reviewed in this book. There was plainly a consensual problem,
resulting from decay of faith in traditional encoding (Chapter 2) combined with inability to generate a new consensus which would overcome
alienation, the feeling of being excluded and powerless to prevent
oligarchies from managing society according to their own interests.
Equally plainly, the sense of helplessness before technological forces
and power elites working at the international level for their own interest

was quite realistic. Twenty centuries had failed to produce one viable example of the Greek philosopher-king ideal (Chapter 4). Market (Chapter 8) had been proven unable by itself to adjust human affairs: It had no conscience, and was subject to degradations and disruptions showing that it was supplying neither much order nor equity in the world. Science also (Chapter 3), appeared to be generating more chaos than order in human affairs through uncontrolled technology and instruments of war. Nor was there much sign that struggle as envisioned by Marxists or social Darwinists (Chapter 9) was bringing increased order into the world: Class war did little but polarize conflict and, where successful, install new oligarchies at much cost; on the biological-ecological side, the system seemed more imbalanced than ever from overpopulation, destruction of natural habitats, and extinction of many species because of man's intrusions and abuse of technology. Finally, progress, instead of being an orderly development toward a better society (Chapter 9), had become a crass doctrine of technological development for profit-maximization and production of material goods which seemed to do as much damage as good to the quality of human life. So most of the models from the history of sociological theory, although purporting to explain some aspect of social order, seemed to be failing in the twentieth century, because they were too one-sided or too simple, or needed to be administered by wiser men. It remains to be discovered how market could be made to serve human needs sensitively and equitably, how common will could be developed, and how power could be distributed to best serve the common will and human needs. At the least, it seems plain that better models are needed, either a better combination of old ones, or quite new models of man and the world in which he lives.

Yet the gloom created by the failure of material progress and of common will could be quickly dispelled if there were another direction. Divine order may be an answer for some people. But for those who want man to be in charge of his own affairs, there is another solution which recognizes that once man starts to meddle he has to manage, but that to manage with popular consent, he needs a goal which will generate common will and enough knowledge of systems at all levels to assure that all inputs lead only to desired changes. Voices from the Third World, from ghettos, from almost everywhere, are asking for a humanized society to say nothing of better human beings—they need a picture that can rally men of all classes, races, or nations. To better understand the relatedness and harmony of all things, man needs to study all systems within which he lives: those he uses (mechanical, ecological and cultural) and those which contain and constrain him, which he must respect, and of which he will be a victim if he disregards, abuses or defies them. In short, true progress requires better information about what is human, and better ways for encoding such information into policy that will make a humanized system. So the 1960s and '70s saw a great resurgence of interest in two kinds of theory: *humanism*, the study of the potentialities and needs of mankind the world over; and *general systems theory*, a large-scale attempt to study the network of systems within which humans seek fulfillment—those he uses and those which constrain him, which he must respect. The only hope for true progress seemed to be to know better what men in general require, so that world consensus might be developed; and to understand how interactions—whether called power, market, consensus-making, natural selection, or class warfare—operate within systems.

Our task in this chapter will be to sketch the background, central ideas, and promise of humanism and general systems theory.

HUMANISM

Consider the following list of thinkers and see if it is possible to find a point of view common to all of them: Socrates, Goethe, Shakespeare, Balzac, Boccaccio, Rousseau, Montaigne, Rembrandt, Erasmus, Galileo, Leonardo, Petrarch, Aristotle, Epicurus, Cicero, Machiavelli,

Rabelais, Victor Hugo, J. S. Mill, Bertrand Russell, John Dewey, Thomas Mann, Albert Schweitzer, Santayana, Walt Whitman, Freud, Julian Huxley, Paul Goodman, Buckminster Fuller, Martin Buber, Carl Rogers, C. W. Mills, Erich Fromm, Karl Marx. It does not take long to arrive at humanism as the common denominator, since most of the more restrictive labels such as Christian, rationalist, democrat, will not do. After some challenges at rough edges, like Machiavelli and Marx, a vague image does emerge: These were men and women who asserted the fundamental value of being *human*, who glorified the human species in some way.

The counter-culture, with its bursts of protests against racism, sexism, and anything which seemed unfair, or dehumanized, might be viewed as an extension of humanism, further reflected in the search for fulfillment and authenticity, in "encountering" as an effort to rediscover humanness in an impersonal society, and in Utopian communal colonies of one kind or another.

The ancient Greeks provided the first full formulation of the idea that the good life in terms of happiness and fulfillment on this earth is possible for man because of his crowning glory, reason: "Man is the rational animal," said Aristotle; Plato made the first Utopia; Greek drama explored the range of human experience in tragedy and comedy. Epicurus (342-270 B.C.) taught that the good life consisted of pleasure, friendship, and cultural development, regulated by virtue and philosophy. Though limited to a somewhat aristocratic idea of perfection of the few, and the ethnocentric distinction of Greek versus barbarians and slaves, there is little question that they were humanists.

The fall of Rome ushered in a long period when, as we have seen in St. Augustine, Christian thought focused on the sinfulness of man and little on his happiness in this life. The Renaissance introduced the term "humanist," which was applied in the main to religious thinkers who expressed revulsion to dogma, hierocracy, and asceticism, and who affirmed the value of joy in life on earth. Erasmus (1466-1536), for example, was a Dutch Catholic priest who left the Augustinians to travel about Europe, make friends with Thomas More in England, study Greek in Italy, and express rationalistic views at variance both with the Roman Church and Protestant reformers. His best known essay, "In Praise of Folly," expressed his liberal attitude toward "sins":

> Can life be called life at all if you take away pleasure? ... Even the famous Stoics do not really scorn pleasure, but they studiously dissemble and attack it in public. ... What part of life is not sad, unpleasant, graceless, flat, and burdensome, unless you have plea-sure added to it, that is, a seasoning of folly? ... A people does not for long tolerate its prince ... a friend his friend ... except as they ... on occasion ... soothe themselves with sweetness of folly. ... For what is so foolish as to be satisfied with yourself? Or to admire yourself? Yet on the other hand, if you are displeased with your-self, what can you do that is pleasing or graceful or seemly? How necessary it is to ... appreciate your own value by a bit of self-applause, before you can be held in price by others.

Regarding churchmen, he said:

> It were better to pass over the theologians in silence. ... They are protected by a wall of scholastic definitions, arguments, corollaries. ... I do not see how anything could be more dismal than ... monks. ... When with asinine voices they bray out in church those psalms they have learned by heart, they are convinced that they are anointing God's ears with the blandest of oil. Some of them make a good profit from their dirtiness and mendicancy, collecting their food from door to door.

Thinking he may have gone too far, Erasmus concludes:

> If anything I have said shall seem too saucy or too glib, stop and think: 'tis Folly ... that has spoken. But of course you will also remember that Greek proverb, "Even a foolish man will often speak a word in season." ... And so farewell. ... Applaud ... live ... drink ... O most distinguished initiates of Folly! (DESIDERIUS ERASMUS, *The Praise of Folly*)

Thus humanism began to escape the confines of Christian asceticism. Indeed, it was strong stuff for a churchman to invite others to regard venial sins, and perhaps even the mortal one of pride, as part of the joy of life.

The Renaissance humanists turned away from Thomas Aquinas, to Greece and Rome for inspiration on how to live, rediscovering classics like Ovid's poetry and Lucian's *Satyricon*. They also wrote books like Boccaccio's *Decameron* which proclaimed the right of people to enjoy life here and now, even at some risk of penalty in the afterworld, and which emphasized more reliance on one's own intelligence and less on Providence. Rabelais' *Gargantua and Pantagruel* (1535) was a *tour de force* of humanistic ebullience: His description of life in a co-ed monastery still makes absorbing reading. The inscription over the main gate of the Abbey set forth the spirit of the place:

> Here enter not vile bigots, hypocrites. . . . Here enter you, and welcome from our hearts, all noble sparks, endowed with gallant parts. This is the glorious place, which bravely shall afford wherewith to entertain you all. . . . Here enter you all ladies of high birth, delicious, stately, charming, full of mirth. . . . Come joys enjoy.

The grounds contained a stately fountain of alabaster and buildings of marble filled with exotic art. All aspects and activities of life in the monastery were designed for pleasure:

> Before the . . . lodging of the ladies, that they might have their recreation . . . were placed the tiltyard, the barriers or lists for tournaments, the hippodrome or riding court, the theater or public playhouse, and natatory or place to swim in, with most admirable baths . . . and store of myrtle-water. By the river-side was the fair garden of pleasure . . . between the two other towers were the courts for the tennis and the baloon. Towards the tower . . . stood the orchard full of all fruit-trees . . . at the end of that was the great park, abounding with all sort of venison. Betwixt the . . . towers were the butts and marks for shooting with a snap-work gun, an

ordinary bow for common archery, or with a crossbow.... At the
going out of the halls, which belong to the ladies' lodgings, were
the perfumers and trimmers, through whose hands the gallants
passed when they were to visit the ladies.... All their life was spent
not in laws, statutes, or rules, but according to their own free will
and pleasure. They rose out of their beds when they thought good:
they did eat, drink, labor, sleep, when they had a mind to it ...
none did awake them, none did offer to constrain them to eat,
drink, nor to do any other thing.... In all their rule, and strictest
tie of their order, there was but this one clause to be observed,
DO WHAT THOU WILT (RABELAIS, 1535:CH. 54-57).

The gusto of Rabelais should not be misunderstood as an invitation to
license. It was an affirmation of a full life for man in opposition to the
life of self-denial idealized in the monasteries. The humanistic ideal was:

the happy, natural, and wholesome enjoyment of the goods of
human life in a refined civilization, and the wisdom and sanity of
balance, temperance, the golden mean.... Their ideal was "excellence," the complete and perfect functioning of all the potentialities of human nature; their maxim, "Be perfect"... do not miss a
single opportunity of well-rounded development in this rich world.
... The Italians revolted from the Christian ethic to a sheer delight
in the million forms of beauty, and cultivated every natural impulse
into its appropriate fine art.... They ceaselessly studied with
Leonardo ... the soul of things, seeking by every art and every
science to lay bare the Mona Lisa smile of life (RANDALL, 1940,
122, 125).

Machiavelli was for another kind of rounded development in his belief
than man should be politically restrained only by his lack of ability
(*virtu*), not by Christian morality. But, although he was one of the
pioneers in studying men as they are, he can hardly be credited with
celebrating man, unless one regards him as an inverted idealist (Brinton,
1953:103-4). Another strike against him as a humanist is that he was a
"supreme partiot" who made the State "an end in itself" (Randall,
1940:195).

The central theme of humanism is the affirmation, perfection, and celebration of man. For Americans, such an ideal is easiest to define as the opposite of Puritanism. The Puritan, with his distrust of pleasure, his sense of sin, and his emphasis on satisfaction in this life through hard work, is at the opposite pole from humanism. A humanistic priest, the Reverend Robert R. Boyle, S.J., attacked Puritan morality in these terms:

> All moralists . . . want to clear immorality from life. . . . They do not perceive, in their well meant zeal, that they are destroying the mirror which literature essentially is. . . . Any attitude which urges a human being to squint at reality is not Catholic. It is Puritan and damnable (BOYLE, 1959).

If Puritanism is a distortion of human life, then humanism is the balanced truth. It is primarily man-centered: Man is not to be measured by a suprahuman standard ("man is the measure of all things"—Protagoras); man is rightly central to his own concerns: to understand, find, and improve himself ("know thyself"—Socrates); man should promote his own happiness and well-being and a better life for all men ("I am not a citizen of France, I am a citizen of the world"—Victor Hugo); he should create a better life now for live men, not later for dead ones; and he should seek to rebuild the world and all culture on human terms—institutions and moral codes are made by and for man, to express his whole being.

Beyond this core, there are many kinds of humanism, not all necessarily reconcilable with one another. There was, for example, a split between the "two cultures" of humanistic and scientific studies (Snow, 1963), which showed technologists arrayed against artists, philosophers, and teachers of literature—with sociologists divided between them—all claiming to be humanists. An example of the debate between them is Joseph Wood Krutch's stubborn statement of the case for the human spirit versus B. F. Skinner and "objective science":

Undoubtedly there are good reasons for distinguishing the "objective" from the "subjective" phenomena ... but there is no justification whatsoever for calling only the one real. ... It requires a lot of resolute blindness to dismiss "mind" as a shadow, and a lot of faith in very fragmentary demonstrations, to explain human experience as well as human conduct without any recognition of consciousness and what consciousness means to imply (1954:123, 137-38).

But Skinner should hardly be excluded from the ranks of humanists, for he says: "We have not yet seen what man can make of man" (1971: 206).

There were Christian humanists, ranging from Roman Catholic monastics like Thomas Merton to Unitarians, many of whom while pronouncing themselves humanists had difficulty identifying themselves as Christians. Nor were Jews in a much better position: Though their ethical focus was on this world, their religion is basically God-centered, as illustrated in Ecclesiastes and the Book of Job, both of which insist that the pleasures of this life are mere vanity. The common ground of both Christian and Jewish humanists was an easy-going attitude toward the goods of this life, as opposed to stern judgements, punishment, original sin or self-imposed asceticism.

Existentialist humanists ranged from atheists like Sartre to devout believers like Kierkegaard, who held that no faith can be true as doctrine but only as experience deep within oneself. All existentialists agreed that man cannot be pre-defined by institutions, doctrines, or observance of his past performances; he is an open-ended set of possibilities—inherently free, choosing, changing. Such a radical emphasis on freedom led to Albert Camus' doctrine of revolt as a way of redeeming oneself, in an otherwise hopeless situation of stupefied inertia and oppression. Thomas Merton comments that Camus' doctrine of revolution was "a classic humanism" directly opposed to "the satanic nihilism of the great modern power structures" (1967).

274

Some versions of humanism stress socio-political action, such as socialist humanism. For example, Marx's favorite motto was, "nothing human is alien to me." Erich Fromm says:

> Marxism is humanism, and its aim is the full unfolding of man's potentialities. . . . Marx's concern was man, and his aim was man's liberation from the predomination of material interests, from the prison his own arrangements and deeds had built around him. . . . His aim was a society in which man *is* much, not in which he *has* or *uses* much. He wanted to liberate man from the chains of his material greed, so that he could become fully awake, alive, and sensitive. . . . He wanted to abolish extreme poverty, because it prevents man from becoming fully human; but he also wanted to prevent extreme wealth, in which the individual becomes the prisoner of his greed (1965:228-29, 237).

But, Fromm notes, socialist humanist faith has been somewhat dimmed by the Soviet and Chinese experiences:

> It is one of the historical ironies that the spirit of capitalism, the satisfaction of material greed, is conquering the communist and socialist countries which, with their planned economy, would have the means to curb it. . . . Socialism is in danger of deteriorating into a system which can accomplish the industrialization of poorer countries more quickly than capitalism, rather than of becoming a society in which the development of man, and not that of economic production, is the main goal. . . . Soviet communism, in accepting a crude version of Marx's "materialism," lost contact . . . with the humanist spiritual tradition of which Marx was one of the greatest representatives (237).

Humanist aims of social action went beyond the quarrel between capitalism and socialism to proposals for "one world," like those of the United World Federalists, illustrated in this statement by a Nobel Prize winning biologist, Dr. George Wald:

> I think we've reached a point of great decision, not just for our Nation, not only for all humanity, but for life upon the Earth.

> The thought that we're in competition with Russians or with Chinese is all a mistake, and trivial. Only mutual destruction lies that way. We are one species, with a world to win.... All men of all nations, colors and creeds. It has become one world, a world for all men. It is only such a world that now can offer us life and the chance to go on (1969).

Another group, the World Future Society studied the shape of things to come for all men. Buckminster Fuller proposed that a "desovereignized" colony of people who want to live as world citizens be built on Cyprus, under the protection of the United Nations. Another spokesman for the practical goals of humanism was the American Humanist Association, composed of "persons of good will, who appreciate the scientific viewpoint." They proposed to rally all men to work for goals like the reformation of religion, maintenance of civil liberties, mitigation of racial prejudice, advancement of planned parenthood, strengthening of the public schools, spread of adult education, separation of church and state, and even development of improved burial and cremation rituals. Though the focus of their work was practical, they believed that Julian Huxley was right when he said, "Some form of humanism will be the world's next great religion."

Another important form of humanism could be called bioevolutionary, which saw far-reaching future developments in man himself. Lecomte du Nouy, for example, believed evolution reflected but God's intent to develop a "finer and more perfect race," morally and spiritually as well as physically:

> Every man must tend to approach, within the limits of his ability, the most perfect human ideal, not only with the selfish aim of acquiring peace of the soul, internal happiness and immortality through integration in the divine task, but for the purpose of collaborating with this task and of preparing the advent of the superior race promised by evolution.... The Law is, and always has been, to struggle and ... the fight has lost nothing of its violence by being transposed from the material onto the spiritual plane; let

him remember that his own dignity, his nobility as a human being, must emerge from his efforts to liberate himself from his bondage ... (1947:164, 189).

Julian Huxley wrote in a similar vein that after a billion years of evolution, the universe was becoming conscious of itself through man's knowledge; it is as if man had been suddenly appointed managing director of the "biggest business of all, the business of evolution." "Transhumanism" was the name of the new belief that man could finally transcend himself:

> What the job really boils down to is this—the fullest realization of man's possibilities, whether by the individual, by the community, or by the species. ... Every man-jack of us begins as a mere speck of potentiality. ... This automatically unfolds into a truly miraculous range of organization: after birth ... the individual begins to realize his mental possibilities. ... The end-result can be satisfactory or very much the reverse: in particular, the personality may grievously fail in attaining any real wholeness. One thing is certain, that the well-developed, well-integrated personality is the highest product of evolution, the fullest realization we know of in the universe (1957:13-17).

But man will not use merely the methods of science to attain a better life; his main goal is:

> comprehensive wholeness: the cultivation of inner harmony and peace. ... This has been the aim of the saints, the sages, and the mystics. ... Our rather meager knowledge of mysticism and yoga makes it clear that some regions of human potentiality remain virtually unexplored, or at least unavailable to mankind as a whole ... (299-301).

The distinguished anthropologist, Teilhard de Chardin, saw an even more remarkable evolution, an "integration of the Social with the Biological," in a wholeness-of-mankind which he called the "noosphere":

In contrast to the "simple" animals, who may well be world-ranging, but never succeed in organizing themselves into a biological unity over all the continents, man has unceasingly ... gradually woven above the old biosphere a continuous layer of thought all round the earth: the *Noosphere*.... *True* intelligence ... tends to make the species possessing it coextensive with the earth (1965:224-25).... The Noosphere begins ... to be woven: a Noosphere still loose, of course, but one in which we already recognize the strong envelope of thought in which we exist today: that of a humanity finally joined together at all its edges—and traversed by a network of links which ... more and more literally present, in the immensity of their organism, the image of a nervous system (233).... Humanity as a whole is continuing to cerebralise itself collectively.... Will not the individual man, with the help of all his fellows, succeed in one day perfecting his own nervous system? (254).... Certain collective actions, still unrealizable ... have every chance of becoming both natural and beautiful for our descendants. At a considerably higher "psychic temperature" than ours ... we have no idea of what each man, united with all other man (without deforming, but in order to transform himself) will become *capable of doing* nor ... can we suspect what, at these high altitudes, *he will begin to see.* Now, if this is really the case, what crisis of consciousness (too dazzling for us to be able to "place") are we not justified in supposing the Noosphere will reach when ... there will ... be ... a focus *finally in sight* of evolutionary convergence ... a single passion, that is to say a single "mysticism"? (267).... How can we fail to be struck by the revealing growth around us of a strong mystical current, actually nourished by the conviction that the universe, viewed in its complete workings, is *ultimately lovable and loving?* (273).

The "Omega Point" thus envisioned by Teilhard is not, of course, an organic unity but, as a biologist points out,

a cultural concept, a world in which the *minds of men* have attained a common language of scientific humanism, just as long ago the *genes of men* were encompassed in a common gene pool, as a single species. Just as the genes form "a membrane that stretches over all the earth," so the minds of men ... will form a continuous network of communication around the world. Teilhard's Omega Point is thus the birth of a new God or Great Being in the form of a world culture ... (POTTER, 1971:34-35).

In Teilhard's own words, "compressive socialisation" will not so much be a threat to our individuality as

> a higher state of collective reflection.... At the term of the "expanding" phase of socialisation that has just come to a close, we had believed that we were to attain the limit of our own selves in a gesture of isolation, in other words through individuation. From now on ... it is becoming clear that ... the ultimate center of each one of us is not to be found at the term of an isolated, divergent, trajectory: rather ... the point of confluence of a human multitude, freely gathered in tension, in reflection and in one common mind, upon itself (1966:114-115).

A more mundane position of humanism consists of fairly down-to-earth propositions like the following:

- Man is one species; races and other biological and social subdivisions are relatively unimportant.

- If progress exists, it is to be measured by improvement in the life of *all* mankind.

- Killing one another for national or ideological reasons is not justified.

- A world order representing all mankind should be created as soon as possible.

- Certain weapons and technologies should be prohibited if for no other reason than because they threaten the future of man on this earth.

- Every culture and style of life that does not destroy human rights should be preserved.

- Customs, taboos, beliefs, and institutions which cramp the development of human potential should be reformed or abandoned.

- Social systems which restrict free activity of writers, artists, thinkers, and scientists are suspect.

- The standards which govern man should come from man himself and be cut to his measure.

- Concern for the well-being of man in this world should not be obscured by concern for the next.

- Much work is dehumanizing and should be changed to make it more satisfactory to the worker even at some loss of "efficiency" or profit.

- Many modern cities are unfit for human habitation.

- Many of the activities of the "counter-culture" today are an important part of experimentation to find a better life style for man.

In view of all these fine ideals, it may seem surprising that anyone could oppose, let alone condemn, such a wholesome doctrine. Yet humanism has been bitterly opposed from the time of its inception. Many theologians of various faiths object to a man-centered religion. Some Protestants speak of a modern "idolatry" which has substituted man for God as the center of faith. Billy Graham, for example, defines humanism as:

the philosophy which has lost its perspective and deifies man, while at the same time humanizing God. The Apostle Paul . . . says in the epistle to the Romans: "Who changed the truth of God into a lie, and worshiped and served the creature rather than the creator." We all know that God has endowed men with marvelous capabilities but . . . when mankind becomes proud and sees himself as the master of his own destiny . . . he has lost his perspective and trusts in himself and his fellow man rather than in God the sovereign and omnipotent creator. Such a humanistic concept runs directly contrary to the teachings of the Bible and, where carried to its logical conclusions, leads men into all kinds of folly (1956).

A Catholic, Giacomo Cardinal Lercaro, holds that humanism is as much a modern blight as atheism:

> The development of humanism—understood as a shifting of history's and life's center from God to man—has become a part of man's mentality, and has grown through the centuries to the point that besides atheism there has grown up an indifference to God. ... Man feels sufficient unto himself. In this atmosphere God is relegated to the place of a "poor relation" (1957).

Catholic Bishop Paul J. Hallinan adds:

> The greatest challenge to Christianity today is a popular, bland, respectable faith termed secular humanism. It is often called "The American Way of Life." It is not Godless, but it keeps God in His place—the pulpit. It equates the Christian moral code with such terms as decency, brotherhood, the Golden Rule. It is the orthodoxy of the nonbeliever, but it is a ready refuge for the half-believer too.... It simply says: "Take up your credit card and follow me" (1961).

A secular source, the advisory committee to the California State Board of Education (1969), denounced humanism as the cause of "moral decay" in American society, mentioning its expressions in the United Nations, the U.S. Supreme Court, the film industry, group therapy, sensitivity training, modern educational practices, Margaret Mead, and John Dewey—as well as communism. The antidote was return to "religious views of our founding fathers and the bases of morality understood by our founding fathers." The committee had apparently forgotten that Benjamin Franklin and Thomas Jefferson were creditable humanists.

To understand bitter opposition to humanism, one must go beyond religious objections to its social action program. So long as one thinks merely of individual cultivation, one may have a bland Epicurean or esthetic doctrine. But once one focuses on creating a system which will fulfill *all* men, the result is a social program that could hardly be more radical. Its goal, at that point includes transforming by humane, non-violent, non-coercive methods almost every institution that represses or alienates man. The goals of change are so sweeping, however, that many people become alarmed by them.

A particularly alarming aspect of humanism is, for many people, its tendency to sweep away venerable ideas which it regards as super-stitions. Vigorously rejected, for example, are religious ideas like original sin (or even sin itself), Satan, hell, and the Last Judgment, for humanism holds that the consequences of actions are their own reward or punish-ment. Humanism also rejects moral teachings about chastity, sex, and birth control which would interfere with human happiness. The essen-tial argument is for a *reasonable*, not an authoritarian, morality, as summed up by Santayana:

> It would undermine Jewish morality to doubt that the Ten Com-mandments were written by the finger of God. For then there would be no harm in breaking the Sabbath....Everyone would also commit adultery when tempted, if not deterred by prudence or by some contrary private allegiance. For a man on rational grounds may resist a weak temptation; but resistance becomes irrational when the temptation is stronger than the love of all other things, including life itself. The function of religious com-mands is precisely to load the dice, to load them with mystical authority and disproportionate fears, so that no temptation should overcome the force of the official precepts....Undoubtedly, when any social convention is relaxed, there is a flutter of loose living... yet the decay of a religion, or of any marked social discipline, far from undermining the general principle of morality, sets that principle free and permits human morality to become rational and normal (1950).

"Loading the dice" sums up the humanist charge against traditional moralities and systems: Too rickety to stand by themselves, they must be propped up by artificial terrors. Humanism, obviously, abolishes such notions as it would a belief in witches. In this spirit, another humanist, Max Eastman, attacks St. Paul for his teachings about virginity and chastity, which he claims distorted Christianity into a "sin against life":

> No other epigone in history, I suspect, has done mankind the damage St. Paul did with his strident demand for the suppression of conviviality and natural passion (1953).

So we see that humanism becomes an extremely uncomfortable doctrine when it confronts notions like hell, original sin, aceticism, or "duty" to anything that will not add to human well-being.

The second radical element in humanism is its opposition to institutions which dehumanize man or make the world an unfit place for all men to live in, including economic exploitation, racism, environmental pollution, and war. Events like Hiroshima—even the testing of H-bombs—are an outrage against man, a threat to the future of all men and their children. Outraged humanists speak of the Vietnam War and its defoliation program as "earth rape," in which over 5,000,000 acres were defoliated, and 1,000 peasants and 13,000 head of livestock killed by herbicides (Sunrise, December 16, 1970). The "women's liberation" movement is, of course, a vanguard of humanism, fighting the dehumanized roles of women as either household slaves or sex objects. The entire counter-culture is also in many ways a radical humanistic movement.

A third radical element in humanism is its opposition to power structures per se, because of their tendency to put absolute goals, values, and ideologies above man. Many great humanists have been such rebels —Gandhi, Thoreau, Camus, Victor Hugo (in his defense of Dreyfus)— standing on principle as individuals against what they regarded as an abuse of power.

> No free man can allow himself passively to accept and identify with any one of these power structures in an unqualified way. . . . In every department of life the cart is before the horse, ends are

sacrificed to means, man is alienated and destroyed in order to serve what is supposed to serve him. The state is theoretically for man, money is theoretically to help him live more easily, arms are supposed to protect him, and so on. But in fact man now lives and works in order to assemble and to stockpile the weapons that will destroy him, in an effort to serve a power structure which he worships as an end in itself and which makes his life more and more meaningless and absurd. Instead of using money to make life reasonable, man makes life unbearable by living for money (MERTON, 1967).

Power is not inherently anti-human; it is so only because special interests or ideologies make it serve distorted ends. Even technology can be humanistic if made to benefit the world. In fact, Buckminster Fuller says that it is ideologies and leadership, not technology, which must be changed:

Take the technological tools of industrialization away from the United States, Russia, France, China, England, West Germany, Japan, and Italy, and leave them all their respective ideologies and, within six months, two billion world humans would die of starvation. Contrawise, take away from those eight sovereign states all their political ideologies and political leaders, and leave them their industrial tools and human operators and habitual daily production and distribution systems, and no more will starve than are starving now. . . . Energy-wealth advantages will be so vast as to tend swiftly to cancel out ideological differences. . . . Revolution by design and invention is the only revolution tolerable to all men . . . (1967).

The simple fact is that humanism transcends most current local loyalties, from tribe and gang to class, nation, religion, and ideology. Hence it must necessarily in some sense be disloyal to them—"My country right or wrong" has no meaning to a humanist.

284

A fourth revolutionary element of humanism is its belief that there is a higher source of knowledge in man—call it intuition, conscience, grace—which cannot be derived from mere logic (intellect), and which is superior in authority to reason. From such a gift, man is both free and moral (Luther). This higher source (which Bergson called intuition, and Heidegger meditative versus calculative thinking), allows man to remain both free and moral, if he will but consult and obey it. With it he may guide his own course, and no power structure or bureaucrat has the authority to oppose him.

Humanism, is thus a very radical doctrine calling for reconstruction of society and for the reform of inhuman institutions. It has generated, and doubtless will continue to generate, endless idealistic rebellion for the good of man.

A world good for man and man good for one world is in the last analysis a world system for man. To many people, even to discuss system theory in conjunction with humanism may seem like chaining a bear to a peacock. Yet the padlock which fastens this chain is the fact that no good life for very large numbers of humans will be possible without a well-running system. The reason is simple: Values like "happiness," "freedom," "justice," are attained for whole societies only through a net of relationships in which other values are also attained in varying degrees by oneself and others. Reduce social scale to one hundred people living on an island a mile in diameter, and it is plain enough that values attained by one will depend on relationships with all. With a world population of two billion it is no less true, but by no means so obvious, that the same reciprocity holds. Some values are mutually exclusive: One cannot have more freedom without less order in the same sector, or the stimulation of battle without less cooperation and friendship with the same people; privilege for one becomes surplus-value to another. Hence a good life, however defined, is an optimum balance of various values obtained by various members of a system. Without realization through a system, humanism, like liberty, would be merely a word.

THE PROMISE OF
GENERAL SYSTEMS THEORY

There was a time when sociology would have risen rather grandly to announce that it was going to solve the general problem of how to create a world to meet human needs. Sociology was after all "general" social science. Now we find that an even more general theory is needed. The ecological crisis especially has made man aware of the many vital links between all earth life, of the relatedness of all things by systems of one kind or another, the "closing circle" referred to by Commoner (1971). General systems theory would explore every kind of relationship necessary for man to understand if he is to control his destiny, instead of being locked into a cultural system and at the mercy of his environment and the destructive consequences of his own ineptness. In general systems theory, nothing is free, not even the air, not even freedom itself.

Nothing can be presumed to be outside some system registering its consequences and costs. In broadest terms, *system* is merely a term for durable relatedness among things. The largest conceivable system would be something like Aquinas' eternal law; or in secular terms, the universe in all time. Such a stupendous totality, of course, is beyond our direct concern here. But everywhere man experiences systems on a similar scale. We have come finally to the uncomfortable realization that the world is a system which could be damaged, if not controlled, by man.

Systems are *holistic*, that is, each part must be seen in the context of its relation to the whole. Whether traffic congestion in a city, or a thought in one's mind, nothing happens "by itself." System, therefore, means that simple "If A, then B" predictions are unrealistic, if not impossible. If effects flow all ways (A, B, C ... X), what sense does it make to say "A" causes "B"? A sociologist puts it this way:

> There could be no useful way of employing "cause" in understanding a system, or any things we want to know about a system, that

involve the interaction among its parts. Should these interactions be spread along a time scale so that some precede others, only in the sense of time precedence can we assign "causal" significance to the earlier appearing interactions. But if *all* we can make of causality is time precedence, then why not talk about time sequence and drop the notion of causality? ... Since all variables in the system interact lawfully with at least some others, the values on any single variable cannot be viewed as either the cause of values for other variables or the product of their causalty (DUBIN, 1971).

The only adequate statement of causality would be a two-way flow chart of all interdependencies. This is the reason for Forrester's (1969, 1971) claim that only observation (or computer simulations) of complex outcomes, not intuition, can predict the effects of policies on systems. It is the abundance of feedback loops which defeats the attempt to separate parts or causes, and treat them as though they were independent of one another. Emergence of quite unexpected properties in new levels or states of systems would be especially baffling to the old "if A then B'" thinking.

This change in thinking called *general systems theory* (GST) not only presented a new view of causality, but broke down the separateness of specialized sciences. The process began in 1948, when technologists and mathematicians found common terms by which to communicate with biologists, psychologists, and social scientists, thus reversing the trend toward separate specialization which had been taking place since Comte. Two major breakthroughs contributed to this reversal: *cybernetics* (Wiener, 1948), and *information theory* (Shannon and Weaver, 1949). Cybernetics showed how the life-likeness of living and social, as well as mechanical, systems depended on feedback, thus establishing common ground between physics and biology, and ultimately sociology. Information theory developed from using information as the coordinating factor of systems of all kinds, from electronic circuitry to proteins to social symbols. This was achieved by adopting Shannon's postulate that information is the *negative reciprocal* of entropy (commonly defined as disorder); that is, information is that input which increases the order, as distinguished from merely the energy or matter, of a system. So information came to be called *negative entropy*. Life itself is organized by information—all living things survive and grow by processing information. It is the business of life to defeat entropy by encoding information at a rate to offset entropy at least temporarily. Information theory as a new conceptual tool led to startling developments in molecular biology, such as analyzing and synthesizing protein structures, "reading" DNA and RNA codes and analyzing the interactions of "chemical messengers" (Quastler, 1964).

Although the first open system formulations had been made in social contract theories of government by consent and by J. S. Mill's free market of ideas, it was not until the 1960s (for example, Cadwallader, 1959; Buckley, 1967; Monane, 1967) that sociologists began to seriously consider revamping their concepts of social organization, structure, and function in terms of general systems theory. The major hindrance was the concept inherited from Spencer of society as an equilibrium. To make use of information theory, it was necessary to shift to an open system concept of society. By processing ever new inputs of information, an open system is not only adaptive but capable of moving on into new balances, like the re-grouping of men on a battlefield, or the poise of a surfer on a wave. The feedbacks of society

> constitute a complex adaptive system—not simply an equilibrium or homeostatic system—operating as an ongoing process or transaction which is continually generating, maintaining, or altering meanings and patterns of behavior (BUCKLEY, 1967:124).

In other words, open systems are morphogenic, able to grow and create new structures. All coordination, from a sponge colony to a sovereign state, requires a flow of information (Ashby, 1969). So the separate social sciences began to share a common body of theory that could be turned to various applications, and that permitted a physicist and a social scientist, for example, to talk usefully about entropy. This synthesis for sociology was much helped by theorists like J. G. Miller in behavioral science, Karl W. Deutsch in political science, and Kenneth Boulding in economics.

Let us look at a few of the basic concepts of GST which are creating a common language among the physical and behavioral sciences, enabling them to work together in attacking world-human problems which they could hardly expect to defeat separately.

Levels of System

GST distinguishes various levels of system, from the simplest to the most complex and relatively rare. Boulding (1956), for example, distinguishes nine levels: (1) static structure; (2) simple dynamic system, like a clock; (3) cybernetic or self-adjusting system, like a thermostat; (4) self-maintaining open system, as in organisms which take in various kinds of food and information; (5) genetic-societal system, as in the division of labor between cells in a plant to form a cell-society with "blueprinted" growth; (6) the animal system, characterized by mobility, enormous information intake, goal-seeking and self-awareness; (7) the human system, at which there is self-consciousness and symbolic language; (8) social systems; and (9) transcendental systems of which we have as yet little knowledge. Elsewhere, in another writing, Boulding (1970:16-17) describes the "sociosphere," including the "infosphere" as the total encoding and exchange of information in society, including ethical systems and culture.

We suggest a simpler classification of five levels of system, going from broader and simpler to more complex and exclusive, as in a series of concentric circles. Moving from outer to inner circles, they are: (1) physical systems, dealt with by the sciences so named; (2) ecological systems, consisting of that portion of the physical world which constitutes an environment for organisms and the relations occurring therein; (3) the organismic sphere; (4) social groups of organisms; and (5) social-symbolic systems, which are coordinated by information stored in symbols. In this scheme information exchange by signals becomes more important as one moves from larger to smaller spheres, while bio-molecular codes and mere matter-energy exchange predominate as one moves from the inner to the outer circles.

What we call human society, of course, contains many sub-levels, but sociologists focus on social-symbolic systems (groups), based on *networks* of communication, in which members participate and hold positions, and from which cohesiveness, coordination, and other group properties come.

> Groups are not held together by physical forces . . . as are lower-level systems . . . rather, they depend primarily upon messages, information flows over the group channel and net, to increase or decrease their cohesiveness. . . . Whether the group remains close in space depends on what is required to accomplish its purposes and goals. . . . Three astronauts . . . remain coordinated . . . because of the radio and television transmission . . . and . . . their previous programming. . . . Social insects . . . act in coordination . . . by exchange of pheromones, chemical signals . . . [or] other modes of information . . . such [as] . . . the "language" conveyed by the flight of bees (MILLER, 1971:376).

Studying larger groups, sociologists find themselves tracing communication nets of whole institutions (for example, Barton and Anderson, 1961), while economists and political scientists, of course, deal with nets and flows much larger (Deutsch, 1953).

Information versus Entropy

According to GST, the effort of all higher systems is to use information to counteract entropy. Matter and energy exchange is also always involved, but this exchange is a separate process from the reception and transmission of information. That is, physical movement of people, raw material, and energy through societies is distinguished from communication of information.

> Communications, while being processed, are often shifted from one matter-energy state to another, from one sort of marker to another. If the form or pattern of the signal remains relatively constant during these changes, the information is not lost. For instance...a chest X-ray...to pulses in an electrical current ...stored in the core memory of a computer.... Matter-energy and information always flow together. Information is always borne on a marker. Conversely there is no regular movement in a system unless there is a difference in potential between two points, which is negative entropy or information. Which aspect of the transmission is most important depends upon how it is handled by the receiver. If the receiver responds primarily to the material or energic aspect, it is a matter-energy transmission; if the response is primarily to the information, it is an information transmission. For example, the banana eaten by a monkey...has its informational aspect...but its use to the monkey is chiefly to increase the energy available to him.... The energetic character of the signal light that tells him to depress the lever which will give him a banana is less important than the...patterned organization which conveys information to him (MILLER, 1971:280-81).

Information has different rules of behavior from matter-energy. For example, it is more expensive to increase the energy than the information of a signal, or it costs little more for one hundred than for one to receive it. It is especially important to note that increased use of information always means less entropy, whereas more matter-energy introduced into a situation can easily lead to more entropy, as, for example, a fire-hose sprayed into a crowd. This is the meaning of Boulding's (1970:44) statement that by information the world is being "organized into structures of increasing improbability." The "package" in which information comes to us from other people is a message physically embodied in a signal of some kind, which we can only decode by some investment of information and energy. In broader terms, any input which increases the order of a system is called information. Higher systems have the ability to find and use (encode) information to decrease their own entropy ("life feeds on negative entropy"), by gaining more information than they lose in energy degradation, according to the Second Law of Thermodynamics (Schrodinger, 1945; Brillouin, 1949, 1950; Raymond, 1950). This does not mean that life has no use for disorder. On the contrary, Potter (1971:65, 83-101) holds that life does not banish entropy but that a balance of order and disorder, built-in disorderliness, is necessary for learning, adaptation and evolution.

Nevertheless, severe loss of information, or gain in entropy, leads in higher systems to *anomie*, normlessness, or meaninglessness, because social-symbolic systems build order by storing information in codes which, if undecipherable or unacceptable to the system's members, leads to loss of coordination and survival ability.

Since the sociologist is primarily concerned with the symbolic level in studying the ordering and disordering of systems, he asks, for example: How is information encoded into symbols for memory and signaling? How is information decoded from signals and memory into action, goals, and creativity? How do group properties such as coordination, integration, cohesion, collective identity, morale, differentiation, emerge from which kinds of information exchange? What kinds of nets and feedback loops are the basis of social "structures"? When are steady-states needed, and when are they entropic for social systems? What kinds of information flow establish meaning for social systems? What kinds of symbolic transactions distinguish power from consensus, market, or evolutionary systems?

Equilibrium Revisited

Higher systems are characterized by coordination through symbolic interaction and by their ability to maintain homeostasis ("the ability of living beings to maintain their own constancy"—Cannon, 1939). That is, higher systems can maintain steady states through a range of variations by regulating themselves according to feedback (as in models described by Bertalanffy, 1962), of which a thermostat is a simple illustration. So, at the social level, an umpire might be regarded as a "thermostat" for a ball game. In any case, a homeostatic system must have a decider which receives information about its own performance, relates it to state "A" through memory, and executes a new output to rectify the situation. Such responses are obviously required at many points in higher systems.

Nevertheless, many open system theorists felt an aversion to the concept of equilibrium, perhaps as a reaction against Herbert Spencer. To some it became a sign of "conservatism" to talk about homeostasis in social systems. This view, however, was rudely shaken by events like the ecological crisis, which showed that nature had more of a liking for equilibrium than they may have supposed. Indeed, the truth must be faced that man within his limited world has to find an equilibrium or perish. Once the world is seen as a "spaceship earth," a balance must be found among population, capital investment, natural resources, quality of life, and pollution—sooner by design, or later by disaster (Forrester, 1971). Here a turnabout in the political meaning of equilibrium occurred, for, while focus on steady states now may seem conservative, a focus on those to come later are by no means so. The means for achieving this eventual equilibrium could hardly be more radical in their implications for change in present institutions: How can we, for example, reconcile a static-state world economy with capitalism's need for expansion?

Another kind of balance was reemphasized by information theory: Symbols need equilibrium. It is true not only of legend and tradition but of all symbols, that they are devices for encoding information about one thing into something else (a marker) that can be used in signals. Symbols store information in memory and culture in an inherently stabilizing manner —they transform new information into familiar terms. All symbols must be supported by feedback which reinforces old meaning, even in encoding new information. For example, in speaking a language one must hear and use the words with old meanings as well as learning to use them with new; language would be destroyed if people changed the meanings too rapidly, i.e., there was an imbalance between redundancy and new information.

Symbolic Interaction

Another turnabout in thinking is needed in the tendency to think of "system theory" as somehow mechanical. A polemic by Duncan (1968), chides system theorists, such as Talcott Parsons, for discussing symbolic action in language "heavily steeped in mechanical imagery," and for thinking poorly about communication because they relied too much on models derived from the physical sciences, which make it "all but impossible for the sociologist to deal with meaning."

> Sociologists of the behavioral persuasion ... must, if they are consistent, do away with consciousness, intention, and meaning, in their research models. In place of "harmony," "order," "integration," we hear of "process," 'equilibrium," "homeostasis," and "gearing." Order and disorder in human relationships are caused not by individuals enacting roles, but by "processes" which "occur" in "patterns" or "systems" (DUNCAN, 1968:5, 14).

So the question is raised as to whether information theory must operate with "push-pull" concepts of influence and communication, or whether it can handle the subtler aspects of transactions, of constructing and interpreting definitions of situations, stressed by symbolic interactionism (Blumer, 1969)? If a role-relationship is thought of as merely a kind of throughput for information mechanically transmitted, such a concept of communication would fail to do justice to symbolic interaction.

But system theory does not need to be mechanical in this way. In fact, there is no contradiction between a feedback model and G. H. Mead's theory of constructing perceptual objects, including one's self, pragmatically from the responses of others; indeed, the models are quite harmonious (Shibutani, 1968). Likewise, Hulett (1966) has worked out a detailed information-flow model, with feedback loops, of the social act and role-taking. Symbolic interaction is not therefore so ineffable that it cannot usefully be analyzed as information flow with concepts of GST. Duncan's case against the "push-pull" concept of interaction does not refute information theory, but merely calls attention to the subtlety of the information transactions to be observed while studying interaction. What GST does is help avoid exclusive focus on the information of micro-systems, as though that were all there was.

Nor is there any necessity to treat information transactions as coercive. A very interesting study (Hampden-Turner, 1970) depicts psychosocial development, for persons and groups in the form of a helix spiralling upwards and downwards, depending upon whether feedback loops favor anomie and social distance or growth through openings, bridging distance, and self-confirmation. Moving up or down such a spiral would correspond to what GST would call losing or gaining entropy.

Perhaps the most interesting point is that freedom or creativity, come out of the loss of entropy in higher systems—not necessarily order in a constraining sense but in the sense of the creation of new patterns by which to do new things. (The ambiguity of entropy in regard to creativity and disorder in art is explored by Arnheim, 1971.)

Meaning and Social Entropy

Meaning is the highest kind of ordering, the perception of wholeness of information and awareness of all relations. It might be defined as information about one's relation to an entire state of affairs. For humans, an important part of meaning is identity, one's meaning to oneself and others, maintained by a continuous flow into memory of information about one's own situation, past performance, and social recognition. In this sense, higher systems such as corporations or nations can develop and maintain identities in terms of the meaning to members of what "we" have been doing. In other words, groups as well as individuals can have identities (Klapp, 1972). It follows that only systems with identity can be autonomous, that is, act for themselves, decide on the basis of who they are or were, what to do and to be. Collectivities, just as individuals, enjoy growing and cultivating a proud and honorable identity which they will defend if shamed. It follows, also, that the more meaning a system has to members, the greater will be the potential for societal self-guidance through technology and cybernetics (Breed, 1971:4) and system design (Boguslaw, 1965).

On the other hand, loss of meaning in a higher system is increased entropy, whether expressed as disorder in personal identity or loss of a sense of social identity. Symptoms of such entropy include the closing of ranks against the stranger (Chapter 1), nostalgia, emphasis on ethnic identity, and turning to cults which provide a greater sense of harmony than can be gotten from society at large. Social indicators such as cohesiveness, morale, and alienation, will reflect such trends. With respect to the individual, indicators of social entropy include cognitive dissonance (Festinger, 1957) and frustrations in achieving "self-actualization" (Maslow, 1962) or identity (Erikson, 1963, 1968; Klapp, 1969).

A key contribution which information theory can make here is to see increasing entropy as a disorder of information-processing within the system. For example, people may not be getting the information they need, or are getting too much "bad news" they do not need, which perhaps is spreading contagiously. In other words, information is a general accounting term for what goes on in systems, while entropy indicates what is going wrong, how the system is failing to handle information properly. Such an accounting might tell us that much of what we have been doing in the name of "progress" has actually increased entropy.

Those who wish to study the means for creating a better society will need to look into such communication imbalances as: information-overload from the media, especially of "bad news," versus encouraging and reinforcing; the problem of the lack of relational (meaningful) information versus that received piecemeal; lack of information nourishing individual or group identity (Klapp, 1969, 1972); and decay of oral networks supplying personal feedback and status-related information, leading to the condition of "massness," where the individual feels lost because "nobody listens," the ego "screams" to get attention; malfunctions of non-discursive language, perhaps because its cues are inconsistent with discursive language (for example, one's words might express friendship while one's gestures betray lack of trust); too high a ratio of information input to output, leading to passivity and frustration (boredom from lectures, for example); lack of significant ritual and ceremony to offset technical information; or the problem of banality, a malaise of symbols which have become boring, restrictive and defeating to the imagination. In such terms, "information pollution" is just as meaningful as its environmental parallel.

Further study of such problems may give us answers to questions such as: What kinds of education will reduce entropy from information overload? What is the optimal human scale for maximum meaning (minimum entropy) of place or social organization? When do style change and faddism make for more, and when for less, entropy in a social order? Which kinds of deviance are entropic, and which lead to freedom through higher patterns? Does the counter-culture indicate a disintegration of social order or is it a path to a new Utopia?

One of the larger problems that general system theory may solve is to make better tradeoffs of information against entropy. As yet information may still be used to oppress by power as well as liberate through education, to displace rather than enrich human values (Chapter 3); or to pollute in the name of "progress." What are the kinds of information, transcendental and mystical as well as material and rational, in what mix, and how transacted in a social system, that will finally give man a good society?

The idea that what we have longed for in freedom is really a higher kind of pattern attained through some system is challenging rather than depressing, in my judgment. Perhaps at higher levels the apparent opposition between freedom and order will disappear. Indeed, that may well have been what Plato had in mind. For surely Machiavelli was wrong in defining a good order as the freedom of the few derived from power over the many. The contract and consensus theorists were groping for a better sense of freedom and order in their notion of a voluntary ordering reached through consent, in which natural freedom was relinquished for the higher good of civil liberty. Market theorists, too, were fascinated by the order and equilibrium resulting from the free exchanges of many. So, too, the conflict theorists tried to trade struggle for higher order, whether by natural selection or by class synthesis. Humanism has stated the claim for a higher order than man has yet known, while demonstrating that "progress" as crass economic or national aims is as often against man as for him.

Sociology can help redefine progress by delineating more clearly the kinds of social systems that deliver optimization of values by voluntary choice, perhaps by voting, market, or other consensus-making, with a minimum of constraint in a Machiavellian sense. Thus optimization means the best bargain one can obtain among the variables of a system—basically a reapplication of Aristotle's golden mean.* Is there really any other kind of freedom for a society than this?

During the 1970s there were promising signs that developments in sociological systems theory would supersede relatively static structural-functional and equilibrium models as predicted, for example, by Buckley (1967), leading to a better understanding of what is possible within

---

*The new twist is that system behavior may be counterintuitive (Forrester, 1969: 110): all of Aristotle's logic or wisdom may be unable to deduce what the optimum is or how to reach it.

social systems. This would hinge, of course, on application of cybernetic ideas more widely, on both smaller and larger scales; for example, J. G. Miller (1971, 1972); Boguslaw, 1965; Katz and Kahn, 1966; Monane, 1967; Buckley, 1967. The ideal of a "self-guiding" society was hailed, based on new possibilities of cybernetic communication, "second-order organizations of first-order organizations that do the work" (Breed, 1971:4):

> The active society writes a dynamic social contract, not a Lockean one, fixed for all time. It is open to amendment, revision, and reformulation, as new forces and options appear. The changing forces are the previously passive and underprivileged groups ... the spread of consciousness, the expansion of options, and the greater vision in more persons, and—most generally—a decline in the emphasis on material wealth in favor of increased symbolization in society (1971:9).

On the individual level, such cybernetic modeling would include the social self, as suggested by Shibutani (1968), Hulett (1966), and Sims (1971), to fill in some of what George H. Mead (1934) said. Such modeling would, of course, take in the loops of interpersonal and intrapersonal interaction. For sociologists, of course, such progress hinged on better analysis of the nets constituting collectivities and organizations. Nets need to be carefully analyzed with respect to flow and content of messages and feedback closure, thus translating gross notions, whether of function or of feedback, into kinds and mixes of messages and symbols.

Two good field studies illustrate the kinds of social net-systems that need to be traced and filled in. McCleery (1961) with Barton and Anderson (1961) charted the flow of communication in a prison. They found, for example, that the more successful was control by authoritarian measures, the greater was the order, but the less was the participation of prisoners in treatment activities, and the stronger became the power of an inmate elite in alliance with custodial officers, buying illegal privileges in exchange for cooperation. The price of success by authoritarian methods was thus defeat in other ways, including loss of general participation in treatment activities and resentment of the "arbitrariness" of the power structure. A more unexpected (counterintuitive: Forrester, 1969, 1971) finding was that when liberal reforms were introduced into the prison, the immediate price was a great increase in disorder, because the new programs did not for some time create primary group controls to replace the old coalitions of the elite structure which had held disorder in check (Barton and Anderson, 1961, 408-409, 415). Feedback flow charts, depicting such interaction help us, then, to see more clearly what happens when an institution functions, or fails to function.

Another example of the cybernetic approach to describing social net-systems analyzed the exchange of messages which bring about cooperation in reciprocal labor systems among peasants in Latin America. These systems of exchange of help, work, money, goods, and personal favors are linked almost entirely by intercommunication of information —that is, a net. Two types of systems are identified: "exchange labor groups" of about ten peasants who help each other regularly, in much the same way that North American farmers once turned out to help each other reap or build a barn; and "festive labor groups," in which a wealthier landowner acts as host to a large number of workers, rewarding them with a fiesta, the lavishness of which also confers prestige and future good will to the landowner. Reinforcing, aversive, discriminative, and contingent stimuli encourage participation in both the festive and exchange labor groups by providing workers with information about present and future rewards. Lattices show the flow of information maintaining both kinds of systems. For example, in the festive type:

> If less work is completed than the host feels is customary, this information leads to action such as providing a smaller quantity of liquor for the fiesta. The smaller amount, in turn, provides guests with information concerning their work and indicates displeasure of the host. . . . The host watches the workers and, upon completion of the labor, pays or feasts them. . . . Even when dis-

satisfied with the performance of his guests, [he] cannot indicate his displeasure directly, such as by overt criticism. . . . Noise may take the form of orders and directions being lost or misunderstood, ritualized responses of the host concerning his evaluation of the workers' performance, or workers' inadequate conception of what constitutes a "fair return" for their labor (KUNKEL, 1970:189-195 using data from ERASMUS, 1956).

Patiently tracing such flows of information from person to person, by verbal, kinesic, or contextual communication seems to describe the very stuff of social function and tell us what is meant by the application to systems of such general terms as "power," "fairness," or "freedom."

One hope—perhaps we should say requirement—of information theory is that it should bridge the gap between stimulus and symbol, that is, between behavioristic (S-R) and symbolic interactionist viewpoints, the latter of which stresses that meaning is brought to stimuli by constructive interpretation, and not merely derived from them as triggers to action. Behaviorism, of course, has long eschewed inquiry into the "internal state," or subjective realm of "mind," whereas symbolic interactionism, following Cooley's famous distinction between physical and social knowledge (1930), requires subjective understanding of meaning in order to say what the information of behavior is. As it happens, however, the concept of information is acceptable to many scholars in both these schools, and may provide a common ground if not a unifying theory for these two viewpoints. After all, even machines respond to information. What kinds of information are needed to respond to a flag or a poem? Symbolic interactionism (also perhaps ethnomethodology) has sometimes assumed a rather precious stance as dealing with ineffable, changing, perhaps unique meanings, which cannot be translated into the crass language of behaviorism. But we may hope that better treatment of information, including a better account of meaning as information about one's relation to a system (for difficulties of such translation, see, for example, Rapoport, 1956; Osgood, 1957; E. Becker, 1962), will enable behaviorists and symbolic interactionists to join the same circle. It would seem that if meaning were fully accounted for in terms of kinds of information, the major difference between S-R behaviorism and symbolic interactionism would be resolved.

If the problem of systemic meaning were solved by specifying the kinds of messages which carry meaning and the forms of information it takes, and if there were better accounts of such network flows as we have illustrated above, sociology would be in a position to replace the current vague notion of function and the equally vague notion of positive or negative feedback with an account of entropy loss or gain in nets. If this speculation seems vague, it is unavoidably so, for we are as yet hardly in a position to spell it out.

CONCLUSION

We have explored some of the main models of social order that have been developed in the history of Western social thought. Briefly, they are ideas of the social order implied by encoding and institutionalizing: rationality, scientific knowledge, divine law, power, consensus, market, class struggle, natural selection, progress, humanism, or general systems theory.

While no model is a picture of Reality, all good ones help in understanding what social order is or could be. The Greek model of rationality was an effort to order society by wisdom, a high kind of intellectual virtue found only among the few. Hence it tended to establish a benevolent despotism, rather than a democracy, even though the few with wisdom might vote democratically. Since government would filter down through subordinates from an all-wise leadership at the top, bureaucracy seems a reasonable outcome of their model. Positivism puts scientists, not philosophers, at the top, preferring to be guided by experimental evidence rather than wisdom. It favors an elite of experts whose technical knowledge and control raise serious questions about democracy, as well as posing the puzzle of how "value-free" information can provide ethical and other values to society. The notion of a divine order translated into institutions led to a tension which generated various accommodations such as hierocracy (theocracy) sectarianism, monasticism, or denominationalism with the church separated from the state. On the other hand, sheer power models, from Machiavelli on, led to oligarchy, disguised or open, without benefit of supernatural justification but often using religious ideology to dominate believers (as Marx claimed). The consensus model, stressing social order by voluntary acceptance of values and consent—not compliance—favored the idea of democracy as maximum popular participation in decision, *Gemeinschaft*, whether in small societies or as depicted in Utopias. The model of market is compatible with consensus, applying wherever goods and information are offered, sought, and exchanged competitively. Its feedback serves as a "pricing" mechanism to allocate goods and information and establish values beyond what consensus could achieve by agreements or power by commands. Market works well, however, only when relatively free from power concentration (monopoly), but even then is subject to fluctuations and degradations which both reason and conscience deplore. Conflict provides two major models of how society can be ordered by struggle. One is natural selection of variations leading to bit-by-bit evolution of new forms. This model, however, may be harsh, and what evolves may not be a rational order, however viable. Also, to some people, especially reformers and revolutionaries, its progress seems too slow. Unfortunately, dialectical conflict, in which people are split between two apparently irreconcilable alternatives, seems worse when it polarizes relations, divides classes or factions into intransigent positions, and creates states of war where costs to both sides exceed payoffs. "Progress," too, as indiscriminate modernism, has been a costly model for mankind, although it is hoped that deeper humanistic and system study can correct its mistakes.

Each of these great models possesses explanatory beauty and far-reaching implications. By their metaphoric power, they can be extended endlessly into theory and into beliefs by which men live. Yet this very power also allows them to be carried too far, to produce a picture of reality too good to be true, or a real order too cruel to be borne. Total reason would not be sweet reasonableness. It is even conceivable that too much humanism could be inhuman. But such models help us to analyze real social systems, and to think systematically along one line or to try and fit several models together. They are great because, whatever else is necessary to an adequate understanding of society, these ideas must be included.

In any given system it is desirable to search for a balance or "mix" of models such as power, consensus, market, and natural selection. Probably the mix, rather than prevalence or absence of any one, distinguishes between good, bad, or indifferent societies. Separating models for study should not obscure the fact that in reality such systems interwork in various ways. However they mix, they are not congruent, for sometimes one or another is salient. If one traces a consensus system, one may run into a market system, or a power system, or a dialectical conflict. Also, one system may be a facade for another. The mix of subsystems in any society—from capitalism to socialism, from communalism to frontier laissez-faire, from democracy to fascism, from urbanism to tribalism—needs to be studied. We might, for example, study the Swiss balance of order and economic independence: How do dollars flow so easily while everything is ordered so neatly? How do they manage to enjoy a high sense of both social order and freedom? Somehow, the Swiss wandered close to Plato, but without resorting to his idea of a benevolent dictator.

Our hopeful view of general system theory does not imply that it supersedes any of the great models of the past. Rather, they should and will be incorporated into more comprehensive system theory. General system theory is simply that which embraces the best in all preceding system theories. To describe the ways in which such models (power, consensus, conflict, etc.) are to be combined to create good social systems is beyond our scope here. Indeed, such a design might be no less than the solution of the major problem of the twentieth century —how men can live together contentedly in one world.

When and if this is done, we may perhaps regain some of the hope of Comte—that progress in a scientific sense can occur. We should for the time being, at least, resist the pessimism of some sociologists (for example, Etzioni, 1972), that people cannot be changed much. Of course people do not change much, as long as the systems or disorders within which they exist remain the same. But the horizon is much more open if one searches for better ways to improve those systems. Let us continue to hope.

Bibliography

Ackoff, Russell L. 1957-58. Toward a Behavioral Theory of Communication. *Management Science*, 4:218-34.

Andrews, Charles M., ed. *Famous Utopias*. New York: Tudor.

Angell, Robert Cooley. 1958. *Free Society and Moral Crisis*. Ann Arbor: University of Michigan Press.

Appelbaum, Richard P. 1970. *Theories of Social Change*. Chicago: Markham.

Ardrey, Robert. 1970. *The Social Contract*. New York: Atheneum.

Arendt, Hannah. 1963. *Eichmann in Jerusalem: A Report on the Banality of Evil.* New York: Viking.

Aristotle. 1911. *The Ethics of Aristotle*. New York: E. P. Dutton. Translated by D. P. Chase.

——————— 1912. A Treatise on Government. New York: E. P. Dutton. Translated by William Ellis.

Arnheim, Rudolph. 1971. *Entropy in Art, An Essay on Disorder and Order*. Berkeley: University of California Press.

Arnold, Thurman W. 1937. *The Folklore of Capitalism*. New Haven: Yale University Press.

——————— 1935. *The Symbols of Government*. New Haven: Yale University Press.

Ashby, W. Ross. 1969. *Information Flows within Coordinated Systems*. Biological Computer Laboratory, Publication #203. Urbana, Illinois: Univeristy of Illinois.

Augustine, Saint. 1931. *The City of God*, New York: E. P. Dutton.

Ayer, Alfred Jules. 1936. *Language, Truth and Logic*. London: V. Gollancz.

Back, Kurt W. 1971. Biological Models of Social Change. *American Sociological Review*, 36:660-67.

Bacon, Francis. 1960. *Novum Organon.* 1620. In *The New Organon and Related Writings,* ed. F. H. Anderson. Indianapolis: Bobbs-Merrill.

——————— 1968. *The New Atlantis.* (1627) In *Ideal Commonwealths,* ed. Henry Morley. Port Washington, N.Y.: Kennikat Press.

Bagehot, Walter. 1872. *Physics and Politics.* New York: Appleton-Century.

Bainton, Roland H. 1955. *Here I Stand, A Life of Martin Luther.* New York: Mentor Books. Originally published 1950.

Bales, R. F. 1950. *Interaction Process Analysis.* Cambridge, Mass.: Addison-Wesley.

Barnes, Clive. 1971. Money Out of the Dead Land. *The Times Saturday Review,* London: 2 January 1971.

Barton, Allen, and Anderson, Bo. 1961. "Change in an Organizational System: Formalization of a Qualitative Study." In *Complex Organizations,* ed. Amitai Etzioni, New York: Holt, Rinehart and Winston. pp. 400-18.

Bauer, R. A., and Gleicher, D. B. 1953. Word-of-Mouth Communications in the Soviet Union. *Public Opinion Quarterly* 17:297-310.

Becker, Ernest. 1962. *The Birth and Death of Human Meaning: A Perspective in Psychiatry and Anthropology.* New York: Free Press.

Bell, Daniel. 1961. *The End of Ideology, On the Exhaustion of Political Ideas in the Fifties.* New York: Collier Books.

Bellah, Robert N. 1970. *Beyond Belief, Essays on Religion in a Post-Traditional World.* New York: Harper and Row.

Bellamy, Edward. 1926. *Looking Backward 2000-1887.* Boston and New York: Houghton Mifflin. Originally published 1887.

Benedict, Ruth. 1934. *Patterns of Culture.* Boston: Houghton Mifflin.

Bennis, Warren G., and Slater, Philip E. 1968. *The Temporary Society.* New York: Harper and Row.

Berger, Peter L. 1963. *An Invitation to Sociology.* Garden City, N.Y.: Doubleday.

——————— 1968. *A Rumor of Angels: Modern Society and the Rediscovery of the Supernatural.* New York: Doubleday.

Berger, Peter L., and Luckmann, Thomas. 1963. Sociology of Religion and Sociology of Knowledge. *Sociology and Social Research* XLVII (July).

——————— 1966. *The Social Construction of Reality: A Treatise in the Sociology of Knowledge.* New York: Doubleday.

Bergson, Henri. 1944. *Creative Evolution.* New York: Random House, Modern Library. Originally published 1911.

Berle, Adolph A., and Means, Gardiner C. 1932. *The Modern Corporation and Private Power.* New York: Macmillan.

Bernays, Edward L. 1928. *Propaganda.* New York: Horace Liveright.

Berne, Eric. 1964. *Games People Play*. New York: Grove Press.

Bertalanffy, Ludwig von. 1962. General System Theory—A Critical Review. In Buckley, ed. 1968, pp. 11-30.

Blanshard, Paul. 1951. *Communism, Democracy and Catholic Power*. Boston: Beacon Press.

Blau, Peter M. 1955. *The Dynamics of Bureaucracy*. Chicago: University of Chicago Press.

——————— 1956. *Bureaucracy in Modern Society*. New York: Random House.

——————— 1967. *Exchange and Power in Social Life*. New York: John Wiley.

Blumer, Herbert. 1969. *Symbolic Interactionism, Perspective and Method*. Englewood Cliffs, N. J.: Prentice-Hall.

Boguslaw, Robert. 1965. *The New Utopians, A Study of System Design and Social Change*. Englewood Cliffs, N. J.: Prentice-Hall.

Boorstin, Daniel J. 1962. *The Image, or What Happened to the American Dream?* New York: Atheneum.

Borkenau, Franz. 1969. The New Morality and the New Theology. In *Sociology and Religion, A Book of Readings*, ed. Norman Birnbaum and Gertrud Lenzer, Englewood Cliffs, N. J.: Prentice-Hall.

Bottomore, T. B. 1956. *Karl Marx, Selected Writings in Sociology and Social Philosophy*. New York: McGraw-Hill.

——————— 1964. *Karl Marx, Early Writings*. New York: McGraw-Hill.

Boulding, Kenneth E. 1956. General Systems Theory—The Skeleton of Science. *Management Science* 2:197-208.

——————— 1970a. *Economics as a Science*. New York: McGraw-Hill.

——————— 1970b. *A Primer on Social Dynamics, History as Dialectics and Development*. New York: Free Press.

Boyle, Robert R. 1959. Quoted U.P.I., San Diego Union, 13 December 1959.

Braden, William. 1970. *The Age of Aquarius, Technology and the Cultural Revolution*. Chicago: Quadrangle Books.

Breed, Warren. 1971. *The Self-Guiding Society*. New York: Free Press.

Brillouin, L. 1949. Life, Thermodynamics, and Cybernetics. In Buckley, ed. 1968, pp. 147-56.

——————— 1950. Thermodynamics and Information Theory. In Buckley, ed., 1968, pp. 161-5.

Brinton, Crane. 1953. *The Shaping of the Modern Mind*. New York: Mentor Books.

Buber, Martin. 1950. *I and Thou*. Edinburgh: T. & T. Clark. Translated by R. G. Smith.

Buckley, Walter. 1967. *Sociology and Modern Systems Theory*. Englewood Cliffs, N. J.: Prentice-Hall.

Buckley, Walter, ed. 1968. *Modern Systems Research for the Behavioral Scientist*. Chicago: Aldine Publishing.

Burke, Edmund. 1910. *Reflections on the Revolution in France and Reflections on the French Revolution and Other Essays*. New York: E. P. Dutton. Originally published 1790.

Burke, Kenneth. 1937. *Attitudes Toward History*. New York: The New Republic.

Bury, J. B. 1955. *The Idea of Progress, an Inquiry into its Growth and Origin*. New York: MacMillan, Dover ed. Originally published 1921.

Butterfield, H. 1956. *The Statecraft of Machiavelli*. New York: Macmillan.

Cadwaller, Mervyn L. 1959. The Cybernetic Analysis of Change in Complex Organizations. *American Journal of Sociology* 64:154-7. New York: Macmillan.

Callaghan, Daniel, ed. 1966. *The Secular City Debate*. New York: Macmillan.

Campbell, Donald T. 1965. Variation and Selective Retention in Socio-Cultural Evolution. In Blanksten, and R. Mack, *Social Change in Developing Areas*, ed. H. R. Barringer, G. I. Blanksten, and R. Mack, pp. 19-49. Cambridge, Mass.: Schenkman.

Camus, Albert. 1956. *The Fall*. New York: Vintage, Random House.

Cannon, Walter B. 1939. Self-Regulation of the Body. In Buckley, ed., 1968, pp. 256-58.

Carson, Rachel. 1962. *Silent Spring*. Boston: Houghton Mifflin.

Chapman, A. H. 1968. *Put Offs and Come Ons: Psychological Maneuvers and Stratagems*. New York: G. P. Putnam's Sons.

Chase, Stuart. 1962. *American Credos*. New York: Harper and Brothers.

Christie, Richard; Geis, Florence, et al. 1970. *Studies in Machiavellianism*. New York: Academic Press.

Christoffel, Tom, Finkelhor, David, and Gilbarg, Dan. 1970. *Up Against the American Myth*. New York: Holt, Rinehart & Winston.

Cicero. 1913. *De officiis* (offices). New York: Macmillan.

Cleaver, Eldridge. 1968. Interview. *Playboy*, December 1968.

Clinard, Marshall. 1952. *The Black Market*. New York: Rinehart.

Coch, L., and French, J. R. P., Jr. 1948. Overcoming Resistance to Change. *Human Relations* 1:512-532.

Colby, Benjamin N. 1958. Behavioral Redundancy. *Behavioral Science* 3:317-22.

Commoner, Barry. 1971. *The Closing Circle: Nature, Man and Technology*. New York: A. A. Knopf.

Condorcet, Jean Antoine. *Outline of an Historical Picture of the Human Mind.* Originally published 1795.

Cook, F. J. 1962. *The Warfare State.* New York: Macmillan.

Cooley, Charles H. 1902. *Human Nature and the Social Order.* New York: Charles Scribner's Sons.

_____ 1930. Roots of Social Knowledge. In *Sociological Theory and Social Research.* New York: Henry Holt.

Cooley, John K. 1972. Arms Merchants. *Christian Science Monitor.* 23 June 1972.

Coser, Lewis A. 1956. *Functions of Social Conflict.* Glencoe, Ill. Free Press.

Cox, Harvey. 1966. *The Secular City, Secularization and Urbanization in Theological Perspective.* Rev. ed. New York: Macmillan.

Crick, Sir Francis. 1966. Article in *Saturday Review,* 3 September 1966, p. 55.

Dahl, Robert A. 1956. *A Preface to Democratic Theory.* Chicago: University of Chicago Press.

Dahrendorf, Ralf. 1959. *Class and Class Conflict.* Stanford, Cal.: Stanford University Press.

_____ 1968. *Essays in the Theory of Society.* Stanford, Cal.: Stanford University Press.

Darwin, Charles. 1859. *The Origin of Species.* London.

Deutsch, Karl W. 1953. *Nationalism and Social Communication, an Inquiry into the Foundations of Nationality.* Cambridge, Mass.: M. I. T. Press.

Dewey, John. 1916. *Democracy and Education.* New York: Macmillan.

_____ 1930. *Individualism, Old and New.* New York: Minton, Balch.

_____ 1934. *Art as Experience.* New York: Minton, Balch.

_____ 1938. *Logic, The Theory of Inquiry.* New York: Henry Holt.

Dodds, E. R. 1969. *The Greeks and the Irrational.* Berkeley, Cal.: University of California Press.

Drew, Roy M. 1966. Blindness to Good Design, Quoted in San Diego *Union,* 8 January 1966.

Dubin, Robert. 1971. Causality and Social Systems Analysis. Paper read at joint meeting of American Sociological Association and the Society for General Systems Research at Denver, Colo.

Duncan, Hugh D. 1968. *Symbols in Society.* New York: Oxford University Press.

du Nouy, Lecomte. 1947. *Human Destiny.* New York: Longman's Green.

Durkheim, Emile. 1915. *The Elementary Forms of Religious Life.* New York: Macmillan.

_____1938. *The Rules of Sociological Method.* Chicago: University of Chicago Press. Originally published 1895.

Durkheim, Emile. 1947. *The Division of Labor in Society.* Glencoe, Ill.: Free Press. Originally published 1893.

——— 1951. *Suicide.* New York: Free Press.

Eastman, Max. 1953. The Cardinal Virtues. *The American Scholar,* Winter, 1953-54.

——— 1961. What Plato Says to Us. *Readers Digest,* September 1961, pp. 140-144.

Elliott, Mabel A., and Merrill, Francis E. 1934. *Social Disorganization.* New York: Harper and Brothers.

Ellis, Desmond P. 1971. The Hobbesian Problem of Order. *American Sociological Review* 36:692-703.

Ellul, Jacques. 1965. *The Technological Society.* New York: A. A. Knopf.

Erasmus, Charles J. 1956. Culture Structure and Process: the Occurrence and Disappearance of Reciprocal Farm Labor. *Southwestern Journal of Anthropology* 12:444-469.

Erasmus, Desiderius. 1941. *In Praise of Folly.* Princeton, N. J.: Princeton University Press. Translated by Hoyt H. Hudson.

Erikson, Erik H. 1963. *Childhood and Society.* New York: W. W. Norton.

——— 1968. *Identity, Youth and Crisis.* New York: W. W. Norton.

Etzioni, Amitai. 1972. Human Beings Are Not So Easy to Change After All. *Saturday Review,* 3 June 1972, pp. 45-47.

Festinger, Leon. 1957. *A Theory of Cognitive Dissonance.* Evanston, Ill.: Row, Peterson.

Festinger, L., Schachter, S., and Back, K. 1950. *Social Pressures in Informal Groups.* New York: Harper.

Filler, Louis. 1961. *Crusaders for American Liberalism.* Yellow Springs, Ohio: The Antioch Press.

Firth, Raymond. 1965. *Primitive Polynesian Economy.* London: Routledge and Kegan Paul. Originally published 1939.

Fogel, Lawrence J., Ownes, Alvin J., and Walsh, M. J. 1965. Artificial Intelligence Through a Simulation of Evolution. In *Biophysics and Cybernetic Systems,* ed. Myles Maxfield, Arthur Callaghan and Lawrence J. Fogel, pp. 131-55. Washington, D. C.: Spartan Books.

Forrester, Jay. 1969. *Urban Dynamics.* Cambridge, Mass.: The M.I.T. Press.

——— 1971. *World Dynamics.* Cambridge, Mass.: Wright-Allen Press.

Freud, Sigmund. 1938a. *Basic Writings of Sigmund Freud.* New York: Modern Library. Translated by A. A. Brill.

——— 1938b. *A General Introduction to Psychoanalysis.* New York: Garden City Publ.

_____ 1949. *The Future of an Illusion*. New York: Liveright.

_____ 1958. *Civilization and Its Discontents*. Garden City, N. Y.: Doubleday. Originally published 1930.

Fromm, Erich. 1941. *Escape From Freedom*. New York: Rinehart.

_____ 1955. *The Sane Society*. New York: Rinehart.

_____ 1965. *Socialist Humanism, An International Symposium*. Garden City, N. Y.: Doubleday.

Fuller, Buckminster. 1967. Report on the "Geosocial Revolution." *Saturday Review*, 16 September, 1967, p. 31.

Galbraith, John Kenneth. 1958. *The Affluent Society*. Boston: Houghton Mifflin.

_____ 1967. *The New Industrial State*. Boston: Houghton Mifflin.

Gamson, William A. 1968. *Power and Discontent*. Homewood, Ill.: Dorsey Press.

Gardner, John W. 1970. *The Recovery of Confidence*. New York: Norton.

Gerard, R. W. 1957. Units and Concepts of Biology. *Science* 125:429-33.

Gerard, R. W., Kluckhohn, C., and Rapoport, A. 1956. Biological and Cultural Evolution. *Behavioral Science* 1:6-43.

Gerth, Hans, and Mills, C. W. 1958. *From Max Weber, Essays in Sociology*. New York: Oxford University Press.

Giddings, Franklin H. 1896. *Principles of Sociology*. New York: Macmillan.

Glaser, Barney G., and Strauss, A. L. 1965. *Awareness of Dying*. Chicago: Aldine.

Gluckman, Max. 1955. *Custom and Conflict in Africa*. Glencoe, Ill.: Free Press.

Goffman, Erving. 1952. Cooling the Mark Out. *Psychiatry* 15:451-63.

_____ 1959. The Moral Career of the Mental Patient. *Psychiatry* 22:123-142.

_____ 1969. *Strategic Interaction*. Philadelphia: University of Pennsylvania Press.

Goldhamer, Herbert, and Shils, Edward. 1939. Types of Power and Status. *American Journal Sociology* XLV:171-182.

Goode, William J. 1960. A Theory of Role Strain. *American Sociological Review* 25:483-96.

Goodman, Paul, and Percival. 1960. *Communitas*. New York: Random House, Vintage Books. Originally published 1947.

Goodwin, Glenn A. 1971. On Transcending the Absurd: An Inquiry in the Sociology of Meaning. *American Journal of Sociology* 76:831-46.

Gouldner, Alvin W. 1969. *The Hellenic World, A Sociological Analysis*. New York: Harper and Row.

Graham, Billy. 1956. Humanism Runs Contrary to the Bible. *Chicago Tribune* (New York News Syndicate).

Graham, Billy. 1960. Mystery Veils Predestination. San Diego *Union*, 14 December 1960. Copyright by Chicago *Tribune* (New York News Syndicate).

Gross, Edward. 1956. Symbiosis and Consensus as Integrative Factors in Small Groups. *American Sociological Review* 21:174-179.

Gross, Neal, Mason, Ward S., and McEachern, Alexander W. 1958. *Explorations in Role Analysis: Studies of the School Superintendency Role.* New York: John Wiley.

Gumplowicz, Ludwig. 1899. *The Outlines of Sociology.* Philadelphia: American Academy of Political and Social Science. Translated by F. W. Moore.

—————— 1928. *Der Rassenkampf.* Innsbruck: Wagner, 1928. Originally published 1883.

Guterman, Stanley S. 1970. *The Machiavellians. A Social Psychological Study of Moral Character and Organizational Milieu.* Lincoln, Neb.: University of Nebraska Press.

Hajda, Jan. 1971. Social System Integration. Paper read at annual meeting of American Sociological Association, 30 August-2 Sept. 1971, at Denver, Colo.

Hall, Clarence W. 1971. Must Our Churches Finance Revolution? *Readers Digest,* October 1971, pp. 95-100.

Hallinan, Paul J. 1961. Voices. *Life,* 15 September, 1961.

Hamilton, Edith. 1942. *The Greek Way to Western Civilization.* New York: W. W. Norton.

Hampton-Turner, Charles. 1970. *Radical Man, the Process of Psycho-Social Development.* Cambridge, Mass.: Schenkman.

Hauser, Philip M. 1969. The Chaotic Society—Product of the Morphological Revolution. *American Sociological Review* 34 (January).

Hechinger, Grace and Fred M. 1962. *Teenage Tyranny.* Greenwich, Conn.: Fawcett.

Heilbroner, Robert L. 1953. *The Worldly Philosophers: the lives, times and ideas of the great economic thinkers.* New York: Simon and Schuster.

Henry, Jules. 1964. *Culture Against Man.* New York: Random House.

Herskovits, Melville J. 1952. *Economic Anthropology, the Economic Life of Primitive Peoples.* New York: W. W. Norton.

Hobbhouse, Leonard, Wheeler, and Ginsberg, Morris. 1915. *Material Culture and Social Institutions of the Simpler Peoples.*

Hoffman, Arthur S., ed. 1968. *International Communication and the New Diplomacy.* Bloomington: Indiana University Press.

Hofstadter, Richard. 1955. *The Age of Reform.* New York: Random House.

—————— 1959. *Social Darwinism in American Thought,* Rev. ed. New York: Geo. Braziller.

Homans, George C. 1950. *The Human Group.* New York: Harcourt, Brace.

_____ 1958. Social Behavior as Exchange. *American Journal of Sociology* 63:597-606.

Horton, John. 1966. Order and Conflict Theories of Social Problems. *American Journal of Sociology* May, 1966:701-713.

Hosken, Fran P. 1971. Katmandu: Paradise Lost. *Christian Science Monitor,* 31 July 1971.

Hulett, J. Edward. 1966. A Symbolic Interactionist Model of Human Communication. *AV Communication Review* 14:5-33.

Hume, David. 1957. *An Enquiry Concerning Human Understanding.* Oxford: The Clarendon Press. Originally published 1748.

Hunter, Floyd. 1953. *Community Power Structure.* Chapel Hill: University of North Carolina Press.

Huxley, Aldous. 1932. *Brave New World.* Garden City, N. Y.: Doubleday, Doran.

_____ 1944. *The Perennial Philosophy.* New York: Harper & Bros.

_____ 1954. *Doors of Perception.* New York: Harpers.

_____ 1958. *Brave New World Revisited.* New York: Harper and Row.

Huxley, Julian. 1957. *New Bottles for New Wine.* New York: Harper.

Inkeles, Alex, and Bauer, Raymond A. 1966. Keeping Up With the News. In *Reader in Public Opinion and Communication,* ed. B. Berelson and M. Janowitz, pp. 569-70.

Joad, C. E. M. 1948. *Decadence; A Philosophical Inquiry.* New York: Philosophical Library.

_____ 1950. *A Critique of Logical Positivism.* Chicago: University of Chicago Press.

Jones, W. T. 1947. *Masters of Political Thought, Vol. II.* Boston: Houghton Mifflin.

Kafka, Franz. 1954. *The Castle.* New York: A. A. Knopf.

Kahler, Erich. 1957. *The Tower and the Abyss.* New York: George Braziller.

Kanter, Rosabeth Moss. 1968. Commitment and Social Organization: A Study of Commitment Mechanisms in Utopian Communities. *American Sociological Review* 33:499-517.

Katz, Daniel, and Kahn, Robert L. 1966. *The Social Psychology of Organizations.* New York: John Wiley & Sons.

Keller, Albert G. 1915. *Societal Evolution.* New York: Macmillan.

Kierkegaard, Soren. 1955. *Fear and Trembling; and The Sickness Unto Death.* Garden City, N. Y.: Doubleday, 1955. Translated by Walter Lowrie. Originally published 1941.

Klapp, Orrin E. 1954. The Clever Hero. *Journal of American Folklore* 67:21-34.

——————— 1964. *Symbolic Leaders, Public Dramas and Public Men.* Chicago: Aldine.

——————— 1969. *Collective Search for Identity.* New York: Holt, Rinehart and Winston.

——————— 1972. *Currents of Unrest, an Introduction to Collective Behavior.* New York: Holt, Rinehart and Winston.

Koestler, Arthur. 1969. Quoted by William Springer, Why Pessimism. *Christian Science Monitor,* 2 December 1971.

Krishnamurti, J. 1969. *Freedom from the Known.* New York: Harper and Row.

Kroeber, Alfred L. 1917. The Superorganic. *American Anthropologist,* 1917.

Kropotkin, Peter. 1902. *Mutual Aid: A Factor in Evolution.* New York: Doubleday, Page.

Krutch, Joseph Wood. 1929. *The Modern Temper.* New York: Harcourt, Brace.

——————— 1954. *The Measure of Man; on Human Values, Survival and the Modern Temper.* Indianapolis: Bobbs-Merrill.

Kuhn, Manford H., and McPartland, Thomas C. 1954. An Empirical Investigation of Self-Attitudes. *American Sociological Review* 19:68-76.

Kunkel, John H. 1970. *Society and Economic Growth, A Behavioral Perspective of Social Change.* New York: Oxford University Press.

Laing, R. D. 1967. *The Politics of Experience.* New York: Ballantine Books.

Lasswell, Harold D. 1936. *Politics; Who Gets What, When and How.* New York: McGraw-Hill.

LeBon, Gustave. 1960. *The Crowd, A Study of the Popular Mind.* New York: Viking Press. Originally published 1895.

Lenin, V. I. 1918. *State and Revolution.* New York: International Publishers.

Levy-Bruhl, Lucien. 1927. *How Natives Think.* London: George Allen and Unwin.

Lilienfeld, Paul de. 1896. *La Pathologie Sociale.* Paris: Alcan.

Lindesmith, Alfred R., and Strauss, Anselm L. 1968. *Social Psychology.* New York: Holt, Rinehart and Winston.

Linton, Ralph. 1936. *The Study of Man.* New York: Appleton-Century.

Lippman, Walter. 1955. *The Public Philosophy.* Boston: Little, Brown.

Lipset, Seymour M. 1962. *Michels' Theory of Political Parties.* Berkeley, Cal.: Institute of Industrial Relations, Reprint #185, University of California.

——————— 1972. Marx is in the Eye of the Beholder. *Saturday Review,* 3 June 1972, p. 53.

Locke, John. 1924. *Of Civil Government, Two Treatises.* New York: E. P. Dutton, Everyman's Library.

Loomis, Charles P., ed. and tr. 1940. *Fundamental Concepts of Sociology by Ferdinand Toennies*. New York: American Book.

Lundberg, George A. 1939. *Foundations of Sociology*. New York: Macmillan.

_____ 1961. *Can Science Save Us?* Rev. ed. New York: Longmans, Green.

Lyman, Stanford M., and Scott, Marvin B. 1970. *A Sociology of the Absurd*. New York: Appleton-Century-Crofts.

Lynd, Staughton. 1969. *Intellectual Origins of American Radicalism*. New York: Vintage Books.

Machiavelli, Niccolo. 1940. *The Prince and Discourses*. New York: Modern Library.

_____ 1970. *The History of Florence, and Other Selections*. New York: Twayne Publishers. Edited by M. P. Gilmore.

Malinowski, Bronislaw. 1931. Culture. *Encyclopedia of Social Sciences* VI:621-645.

Malthus, Thomas R. 1914. *An Essay on Population*. New York: E. P. Dutton, Everyman's Library. Originally published 1789.

Mannheim, Karl. 1936. *Ideology and Utopia*. New York: Harcourt, Brace.

Maritain, Jacques. 1951. *Man and the State*. Chicago: University of Chicago Press.

Marx, Karl. 1906. *Das Kapital*. New York: The Modern Library. Originally published 1867.

Mark, Karl, and Engels, Friedrich. 1848. *Communist Manifesto*.

Maslow, Abraham. 1962. *Toward a Psychology of Being*. New York: D. Van Nostrand.

Matson, Floyd W. 1964. *The Broken Image*. Garden City, N. Y.: Doubleday.

Matson, Floyd W., and Montagu, Ashley, eds. 1967. *The Human Dialogue; perspectives on communication*. New York: Free Press.

Mauss, Marcel. 1954. *The Gift; forms and functions of exchange in archaic societies*. Glencoe, Ill.: Free Press.

Mayo, Elton. 1933. *The Human Problems of an Industrial Civilization*. Boston: Harvard University and Macmillan.

McCleery, Richard H. 1961. Policy Change in Prison Management. In *Complex Organizations*, ed. Amitai Etzioni, pp. 376-400. New York: Holt, Rinehart and Winston.

McDougall, William. 1921. *An Introduction to Social Psychology*. Boston: J. W. Luce.

McKinnon, Harold R. 1953. The Higher Law. *The Gadfly* Vol. 4, February-March.

McLuhan, Marshall. 1964. *Understanding Media: The Extensions of Man*. New York: McGraw-Hill.

Mead, George H. 1934. *Mind, Self and Society*. Chicago: University of Chicago Press.

Mead, Margaret. 1964. Some Cultural Approaches to Communication Problems. In *The Communication of Ideas*, ed. Lyman Bryson, pp. 9-26. New York: Cooper Square Publishers.

Merriam, Charles E. 1945. *Systematic Politics*. Chicago: University of Chicago Press.

Merton, Robert K. 1968. *Social Theory and Social Structure*. New York: Free Press.

Merton, Thomas. 1949. *The Waters of Silce*. New York: Harcourt, Brace.

——————— 1967. Can We Survive Nihilism? *Saturday Review*, 15 April 1967, pp. 16-19.

Michels, Robert. 1949. *Political Parties, A Sociological Study of the Oligarchical Tendencies of Modern Democracy*. Glencoe, Ill.: Free Press. Translated by Eden and Cedar Paul. Originally published 1915.

Michener, James. A. 1965. *The Source, A Novel*. New York: Random House.

Mill, John Stuart. 1859. *On Liberty*.

——————— 1861. *Representative Government*.

Miller, James G. 1965. Living Systems. *Behavioral Science* 10:193-237, 337-411.

——————— 1971. Living Systems: The Group. *Behavioral Science* 16:277-398.

Mills, C. Wright. 1951. *Whitecollar, The American Middle Classes*. New York: Oxford University Press.

——————— 1956. *The Power Elite*. New York: Oxford University Press.

Monane, Joseph H. 1967. *A Sociology of Human Systems*. New York: Appleton-Century-Crofts.

Monsen, R. Joseph. 1963. *Modern American Capitalism: Ideologies and Issues*. Boston: Houghton Mifflin.

Mosca, Gaetano. 1939. *The Ruling Class*. New York: McGraw-Hill. Originally published 1884.

Mumford, Lewis. 1970. *The Myth of the Machine; The Pentagon of Power*. New York: Harcourt, Brace, Jovanovich.

Niebuhr, H. Richard. 1957. *Social Sources of Denominationalism*. New York: Living Age Books. Originally published 1929.

Nietzsche, Friedrich. 1918. *Genealogy of Morals*. New York: Boni and Liveright. Translated by H. B. Samuel. Originally published 1887.

——————— 1885. *Thus Spake Zarathustra*. New York: Modern Library.

Nisbet, Robert A. 1953. *The Quest for Community*. New York: Oxford University Press.

Ogburn, William Fielding. 1946. *Machines and Tomorrow's World*. New York: Public Affairs Committee.

——————— 1950. *Social Change*. New York: Viking. Originally published 1922.

Ortega y Gasset, Jose. 1932. *The Revolt of the Masses.* New York: W. W. Norton.

Orwell, George. 1949. *1984.* New York: Harcourt, Brace.

Osgood, Charles E. 1957. A Behavioristic Analysis of Perception and Language as Cognitive Phenomena. In Buckley, ed., 1968, pp. 186-203.

Pareto, Vilfredo. 1935. *The Mind and Society.* New York: Harcourt, Brace, Jovanovich.

Park, Robert E. 1927. Human Nature and Collective Behavior. *American Journal of Sociology* 32:733-741.

Park, Robert E., and Burgess, Ernest W. 1924. *Introduction to the Science of Sociology.* Chicago: University of Chicago Press.

Parsons, Talcott. 1951. *The Social System.* Glencoe, Ill.: Free Press.

——————— 1964. *Social Structure and Personality.* New York: Free Press of Glencoe.

——————— 1966. *Societies, Evolutionary and Comparative Perspectives.* Englewood Cliffs, N. J.: Prentice-Hall.

Parsons, Talcott, and Shils, Edward A. 1951. *Toward a General Theory of Action.* New York: Harper and Row. Originally published 1951.

Plato. *The Works of Plato.* New York: Tudor. Translated by B. Jowett.

Poincaré, Henri. 1948. *Dernières Pensées.* In *Modern American Society,* ed. K. Davis, Bredemeier, and Levy. New York: Rinehart.

Polanyi, Karl. 1944. *The Great Transformation.* New York: Farrar and Rinehart..

Popper, Karl R. 1952. *The Open Society and Its Enemies.* London: Routledge and Kegan Paul.

Potter, Van Rensselaer. 1971. *Bioethics, Bridge to the Future.* Englewood Cliffs, N. J.: Prentice-Hall.

Quastler, Henry. 1964. *The Emergence of Biological Organization.* New Haven: Yale University Press.

Rabelais, Francois. 1929. *Gargantua and Pantagruel,* Vol. I. New York: E. P. Dutton. Originally published 1535.

Radcliffe-Brown, A. R. 1935. On the Concept of Function in Social Science. *American Anthropologist* New Series, 37.

Randall, John Herman. 1940. *The Making of the Modern Mind.* Boston: Houghton Mifflin.

Rapoport, Anatol. 1956. The Promise and Pitfalls of Information Theory. *Behavioral Science* 1:303-309.

——————— 1970. *N-Person Game Theory; Concepts and Applications.* Ann Arbor: University of Michigan Press.

Ratzenhofer, Gustav. 1898. *Soziologische Erkenntnis.* Leipzig.

Raymond, Richard C. 1950. Communication, Entropy and Life. In Buckley, ed., 1968, pp. 157-60.

Redfield, Robert. 1947. The Folk Society. *American Journal of Sociology* LII:293-308.

Reich, Charles A. 1970. *The Greening of America.* New York: Random House.

Riesman, David, with Nathan Glazer and Reuel Denney. 1950. *The Lonely Crowd.* New Haven: Yale University Press.

Rimmer, Robert H. 1966. *The Harrad Experiment.* New York: Bantam Books.

Roethlisberger, Fritz J. 1941. *Management and Morale.* Cambridge: Harvard University Press.

Rogers, Carl R. 1961. *On Becoming a Person.* Boston: Houghton Mifflin.

Röpke, Wilhelm. 1950. *The Social Crisis of Our Time.* Chicago: University of Chicago Press. Translated by A. and P. Jacobsohn. Originally published 1942.

Rose, Arnold M. 1967. *The Power Structure, Political Process in American Society.* New York: Oxford University Press.

Ross, Edward Allsworth. 1929. *Social Psychology.* New York: Macmillan. Originally published 1908.

Ross, Irwin. 1959. *The Image Merchants; the Fabulous World of Public Relations.* Garden City, N. Y.: Doubleday.

Rostow, Walt Whitman. 1960. *The Stages of Economic Growth, a Non-Communist Manifesto.* Cambridge, England: University Press.

Roszak, Theodore. 1969. *The Making of a Counter Culture; reflections on the technocratic society and its youthful opposition.* New York: Doubleday.

Rousseau, Jean Jacques. 1910. *Discourse Upon the Origin and the Foundation of the Inequality among Mankind In French and English Philosophers.* New York: P.F. Collier, the Harvard Classics.

——————— 1935. *The Social Contract.* New York: E. P. Dutton, Everyman's Library.

Rubinoff, Lionel. 1968. *The Pornography of Power.* Chicago: Quadrangle.

Ruckelshaus, William D. 1971. Quoted in *Christian Science Monitor,* 19 January 1972.

Russell, Bertrand. 1938. *Power, A New Social Analysis.* New York: W. W. Norton.

——————— 1945. *A History of Western Philosophy.* New York: Simon and Schuster.

——————— 1951. *The Conquest of Happiness.* New York: Signet Books. Originally published 1930.

Rytina, Joan H., and Loomis, Charles P. 1970. Marxist Dialectic and Pragmatism: Power as Knowledge. *American Sociological Review* 35:308-18.

Salomon, Albert. 1955. *The Tyranny of Progress; reflections on the Origins of Sociology.* New York: Noonday Press.

Samuelson, Paul A. 1970. *Economics.* New York: McGraw-Hill.

Santayana, George. 1950. Morality and Religion. *Atlantic,* November 1950, pp. 61-63.

Sartre, Jean Paul. 1947. *Existentialism.* New York: Philosophical Library. Translated by Bernard Frechtman.

Scheff, Thomas J. 1967. Toward a Sociological Model of Consensus. *American Sociological Review* 32:32-46

Schlesinger, Arthur, Jr. 1962. The One Against the Many. *Saturday Review,* 14 July 1962, p. 9.

Schneider, Louis. 1971. "Dialectic in Sociology." *American Sociological Review* 36: 667-78.

——————, ed. 1967. *The Scottish Moralists on Human Nature and Society.* Chicago: University of Chicago Press.

Schrag, Peter. 1971. What's Happened to the Brain Business? *Saturday Review,* 7 August 1971, p. 12.

Schrodinger, Erwin. 1945. "Order, Disorder and Entropy." In Buckley, ed., 1968, pp. 143-6.

Shannon, Claude E., and Weaver, Warren. 1949. *The Mathematical Theory of Communication.* Urbana: University of Illinois Press.

Shapley, Harlow. 1970. On Being a Scientist. *Intellectual Digest,* November 1971, p. 53.

Sheen, Fulton J. 1950. Good Always Self-Preserving While Evil Vanquishes Itself. San Diego *Union,* 25 June 1950. Copyright 1950 by the George Matthew Adams Service.

Sherif, Muzafer and Carolyn W. 1964. *Reference Groups, Exploration into Conformity and Deviation of Adolescents.* New York: Harper and Row.

Shibutani, Tamotsu. 1968. A Cybernetic Approach to Motivation. In Buckley, ed., 1968, pp. 330-36.

——————— 1966. *Improvised News, A Sociological Study of Rumor.* Indianapolis: Bobbs-Merrill.

Simmel, Georg. 1950. *The Society of Georg Simmel.* Glencoe, Ill.: Free Press. Translated and edited by Kurt H. Wolff.

Simmons, J. L., and Winograd, Barry. 1968. *It's Happening.* Marc-Laird Publications.

Sims, Dennis C. 1971. *Self-Image and Social Change, Toward an Integrated Theory of Cybernetic Behavior.* Stanford, Cal.: Stanford University Press.

Skinner, B. F. 1948. *Walden Two.* New York: Macmillan.

Skinner, B. F. 1966. Quoted by Jonathan Root, Harvard's Skinner: Prophet of Utopia. In *Voice of the Faculties*, newsletter of the Association of California State College Professors, September 1966.

——————— 1972. *Beyond Freedom and Dignity*. New York: Doubleday.

Small, Albion W., and Vincent, George E. 1894. *An Introduction to the Science of Society*. New York: American Book Co.

Smith, Adam. 1971. *Theory of Moral Sentiments*. New York: Garland. Originally published 1759.

——————— *The Wealth of Nations*. New York: The Modern Library.

Smith, Dr. Fred. 1965. The Greatest Experiment. *Decision*, March 1965, p. 10.

Snow, Charles Percy. 1963. *The Two Cultures: and a Second Look*. Cambridge: University Press.

Sorel, Georges. 1969. *The Illusion of Progress*. Berkeley: University of California Press. Translated by J. and C. Stanley. Originally published 1908.

Sorokin, Pitirim A. 1950. *Altrustic Love, a Study of American "Good Neighbors" and Christian Saints*. Boston: Beacon Press.

——————— 1957. *The Crisis of Our Age*. New York: E. P. Dutton. Originally published 1941.

Spencer, Herbert. 1880. *First Principles*. New York: Clarke, Given and Hooper.

——————— 1914. *Man Versus the State; and Social Statics*. New York: Appleton-Century.

——————— 1914. *Principles of Sociology*. New York: Appleton-Century. Originally published 1897.

——————— 1946. Illustrations of Universal Progress. In *Introduction to Contemporary Civilization in the West*. Vol. II. New York: Columbia University Press. Originally published 1857.

Spengler, Oswald. 1926. *The Decline of the West*. New York: A. A. Knopf. Originally published 1918.

Stace, W. T. 1952. *Religion and the Modern Mind*. Philadelphia: J. B. Lippincott.

Stinchcombe, Arthur L. 1968. *Constructing Social Theories*. New York: Harcourt, Brace & World.

Strauss, Leo. 1958. *Thoughts on Machiavelli*. Glencoe, Ill.: Free Press.

Sumner, W. G. 1906. *Folkways*. New York: Ginn.

Sutherland, Edwin H. 1949. *Whitecollar Crime*. New York: Dryden Press.

Suzuki, D. T. 1962. *Mysticism: Christian and Buddhist, the Eastern and Western Way*. New York: Collier Books.

Tarde, Gabriel. 1903. *The Laws of Imitation*. New York: Holt.

Tawney, Richard Henry. 1954. *Religion and the Rise of Capitalism*. New York: New American Library.

Teilhard de Chardin, Pierre. 1964. *The Future of Man*. New York: Harper and Row.

——————— 1965. *The Appearance of Man*. New York: Harper and Row.

——————— 1966. *Man's Place in Nature, The Human Zoological Group*. New York: Harper and Row.

Thomas, W. I., ed. 1902. *Source Book for Social Origins*. Boston: R. G. Badger.

Thurnwald, Richard. 1932. *Economics in Primitive Communities*. London: Oxford University Press.

Tiryakian, Edward A. 1962. *Sociologism and Existentialism*. Englewood Cliffs, N. J.: Prentice-Hall.

Tocqueville, Alexis de. 1966. *Democracy in America*. New York: Harper and Row. Translated by George Lawrence.

Toffler, Alvin. 1970. *Future Shock*. New York: Random House.

Toennies, Ferdinand. 1887. *Gemeinschaft und Gesellschaft*.

Toynbee, Arnold J. 1947. *A Study of History*. New York: Oxford University Press.

Troeltsch, Ernst. 1931. *The Social Teaching of the Christian Churches*. New York: Macmillan.

Trotsky, Leon, ed. 1939. *The Living Thoughts of Karl Marx*. New York: Longman's, Green.

Trotter, W. 1917. *Instincts of the Herd in Peace and War*. New York: Macmillan.

Turk, Herman. 1963. Social Cohesion Through Variant Values. *American Sociological Review* 28:28-37.

Urey, Harold C. 1952. Quoted in *Time*, 24 November 1952, p. 94.

Vaihinger, H. 1925. *The Philosophy of 'As if'*. New York: Harcourt, Brace.

Veblen, Thorstein. 1899. *Theory of the Leisure Class*. New York: Macmillan.

——————— 1904. *The Theory of Business Enterprise*. New York: Charles Scribners and Sons.

Wagner, Donald O., ed. 1947. *Social Reformers*. New York: Macmillan.

Wald, George. 1969. It Has Become One World. *The Federalist*, April 1969, pp. 4-8.

Waley, Arthur. 1934. *The Way and Its Power*. London: George Allen and Unwin.

Wallace, Anthony C. 1956. Revitalization Movements. *American Anthropologist* 58:264-81.

Waller, Willard. 1937. The Rating and Dating Complex. *American Sociological Review*, October 1937:727-735.

Walzer, Michael. 1966. *The Revolution of the Saints: A Study in the Origin of Radical Politics*. London: Weidenfeld and Nicolson.

Ward, Lester F. 1883. *Dynamic Sociology*. New York: Appleton.

——————— 1906. *Applied Sociology*. Boston: Ginn.

Warriner, Charles K. 1956. Groups Are Real: A Reaffirmation. *American Sociological Review*, October 1956:549-554.

Weber, Max. 1930. *The Protestant Ethic and the Spirit of Capitalism*. New York: Charles Scribner's Sons. Translated by Talcott Parsons.

——————— 1947. *Theory of Social and Economic Organization*. Glencoe, Ill.: Free Press. Translated by A. M. Henderson and Talcott Parsons. Originally published 1922.

——————— 1964. *The Sociology of Religion*. Boston: Beacon Press, 1964. Translated by Ephraim Fischoff. Originally published 1922.

——————— 1969. Church and State. Also: State and Hierocracy. In *Sociology and Religion, a Book of Readings*, ed. Norman Birnbaum and Gertrud Lenzer, pp. 318-32. Englewood Cliffs, N. J.: Prentice-Hall.

Wheelis, Allen. 1958. *The Quest for Identity*. New York: W. W. Norton.

White, Leslie A. 1959. *The Evolution of Culture*. New York: McGraw-Hill Book.

Whyte, William H., Jr. 1956. *The Organization Man*. New York: Simon and Schuster.

Wiener, Norbert. 1954. *The Human Use of Human Beings, Cybernetics and Society*. New York: Houghton Mifflin.

——————— 1961. *Cybernetics, or Control and Communication in the Animal and the Machine*. 2nd ed. New York: M.I.T. Press.

Wirth, Louis. 1948. Consensus and Mass Communications. *American Sociological Review* 13:1-15.

Wrong, Dennis R. 1961. The Oversocialized Conception of Man in Modern Sociology. *American Sociological Review* XXVI:183-193.

Yntema, Theodore O. 1969. The Changing Profile of World Communism. *Saturday Review*, 14 June 1969, pp. 15-18.

Zeitlin, Irving M. 1968. *Ideology and the Development of Sociological Theory*. Englewood Cliffs, N. J.: Prentice-Hall.

Zhukov, E. M. 1961. Concepts of Progress in World History. *Soviet Review*, October 1961, pp. 40-52.

Index

Machiavelli, Niccolo, 105-14
Machiavelli: doctrine, 106-14; humanism and, 129, 272
Machiavellian: model of order, 126-29; personality, 124-26; situations, 120-26
Machiavellianism: entropy and, 128, 159; freedom and, 128, 129; trust and, 124, 128
Majorities. *See* Democracy
Malinowski, Bronislaw, 222-23
Malthus, Thomas H., 208
Manipulated society, 44
Manipulation: role, 122-26; and power, 115n
Manipulators, 124-26
Mannheim, Karl, 18, 23, 168
Maritain, Jacques, 93-94
Market; black, 187; black, information, 185; consensus vs., 163; definition, 162-63; degradations, 185-91; exchange vs., 174; feedback, 181; filtering mechanism, 187-88, 191; of ideas, free, 176-81; information system, 181-85; invisible hand of, 163-70, 179; justice and, 185-86, 191; order from, 161-92; personality, 70, 175-76; power vs., 163, 182-83; primitive, 170-72; vs. rationality, plan, 182-83; sociological aspects, 170-76
Martyr, consensus test, 158
Marx, Karl, 23, 199, 204-6, 217-18, 250, 275; vs. Adam Smith, 197-99; power theory, 117
Marxism: critics, 204-7; contributions to sociology, 207-8
Maslow, Abraham, 296
Mason, Ward S., 152
Mass society, 151
Matson, Floyd W., 44, 152, 251
Mauss, Marcel, 171
Mayo, Elton, 242
McCleery, Richard H., 299
McDougall, William, 144
McEachern, Alexander, 152
McLuhan, Marshall, 151, 252-54

McPartland, Thomas, 152
Mead, George H., 9, 148-50, 299
Mead, Margaret, 189
Meadows, Dennis, 256
Meaning: defined, 295; entropy, social and, 295-98; systemic, 301-2
Meaninglessness. *See* Alienation, Absurdity
Means, Gardner, 169
Meditation, 101
Merriam, Charles, 118
Merrill, Frances, 241
Merton, Robert K., 122, 133, 152, 223
Merton, Thomas, 89, 274, 285
Metaphysics. *See* Positivism
Michels, Robert, 116-17
Mill, John Stuart, 16, 176-81, 237-38
Miller, James G., 7, 153, 156, 181, 190, 225, 228, 290, 291, 299
Mills, C. Wright, 70, 118, 175
Model: systemic, Greek, 71-74; selection, natural, 228-32; pragmatic, 24-26; 43, 304
Models: cultural patterns, 25; fiction in, 25; roles, social, 25; scientific, 24-26, 43; social, reviewed, 302-3; types, ideal, 25; types, social, 25
Monasticism, 85, 88-89
Modernism, 240, 263
Monane, Joseph, 288, 299
Monopoly, information, 178-79
Monsen, R. Joseph, 169
Montagu, Ashley, 152
Moody, Dwight L., 89
Morale, 148
Morphogenesis, 225, 288
Mosca, Gaetano, 115
Mumford, Lewis, 242, 247
Mysticism, 79; humanism and, 277; westerners turn to, 254
Mystification, 133, 134, 203, 250
Mythology, 20

Nader, Ralph, 186
Networks, communication. *See* communication

Niebuhr, H. Richard, 89
Nietzsche, Friedrich, 117, 217
Noosphere, 278
Nouy, Lecomte du, 276

Ogburn, William F., 223-24- 242
Objective knowledge, rejection, 252
Oligarchy, iron law, 116
Omega point, 278
Opening and closing, 13-16, 155
Operant psychology. See Behaviorism
Operational definitions, 39-40
Optimism, scientific progress, 235
Optimization as progress, 298
Oral network, 171-72
Order: levels, three, 10; otherworldly, 75-103
Order, Social: from above, 75-103; from consensus, 131-59; encoded, x, 10-13; freedom vs., 298; in ideas, 17-26; from man, 265-305; from reason, 51-74; sources problem, 1; from struggle, 193-232; from power, 105-29; from progress, 233-64; from science, 27-49; symbolic, 13
Organismic analogy, 213, 218-19, 221
Organization of differences, 148
Ortega y Gasset, Jose, 68
Oscillations, social, 204
Osgood, Charles, 301
Other, generalized, 148
Otherworldliness, 76-103
Oversocialized man, 152

Parasitic strategy, 127-28
Pareto, Vilfredo, 115, 250-51
Park, Robert E., 89, 145, 147-48
Parsons, Talcott, 69, 222, 224-25
Pathology, social, 218
Paul, Saint, 84-85
Perfectibility, human, 235-36
Philosopher-kings, 64-65
Philosophers, 30
Philosophy. See Encoding
Pilgrim path, 85-90
Plan-rational orientation, 182-83

Plato, 16; criticism, Popper, 66-67; The Republic, 62-66; totalitarianism, 66-67
Pluralistic society, 15
Poincare, Henri, 41-42
Polanyi, Karl, 167
Pollution crisis, 255-58
Popper, Karl R., 66-67, 180, 204, 250
Positive philosophy, Comte, 31-35
Positivism, 27-49; critique, 43-47; hume, 33; and ideology, 37; logical, 42; and metaphysics, 36-37; modern, 38-43; and morality, 35, 47; program of, 35-38; and religion, 35; and social action, 46; and socialism, 36-37
Potter, Van Resselaer, 5, 12, 196, 232, 279, 292
Power: cunning and, foxes, 108; information theory, 112-13; justice vs., 55-58, 112; secrecy and, 112-13, 123, 125-28. See Gyges
Power models, 105-29; conflict element, 114
Power theorists: consensus theorists vs., 114, 119, 151, 157-58; modern, 114-20
Pragmatic modeling, 24-26, 43
Predestination, doctrine, 97
Prelogical mind, 237
Primary group, 144
Prince, The, Machiavelli, 107
Profit-motive, 165
Progress, 13, 157, 209-12, 233-64; crisis, 240-59; definition, 239; entropy and, 296; happiness and, 239, 240-41; ideology of, 234-41; information theory, 234; law of three stages, 32; Marxism, 238; new direction, 259-64; optimism-pessimism, 261-62; optimization as, 298; problems, social and, 241-42; redundancy vs., 157
Proletariat, 199, 202-3
Protestantism, 95-99 and strain, 98
Punishment, religious, 81-82
Prudence, justice and, 107-8

Self: looking glass, 144; G. H. Mead, 148-49
Self-interest, business, 164
Separation, sociology and biology, 2-8, 13, 228
Shannon, Claud, 3, 287
Shapley, Harlow, 232
Sheen, Fulton J., 91-92
Sherif, Carolyn, 152
Sherif, Muzafer, 152
Shibutami, Tamotsu, 153, 229, 295, 299
Shils, Edward, 115n, 222
Signals, 9
Signs, natural, 9
Sims, Dennis, 299
Simmel, Georg, 128
Sin, 81-82, 84-88, 98
Skinner, B. F., 44, 274
Slater, Phillip, 15
Small, Albion W., 221
Smart operator, 126
Smith, Adam, 144, 163-67, 180; vs. Marx, 197-99
Smith, Fred, 45
Snow, C. P., 273
Socially constructed reality, 18
Social thought. *See* Encoding
Sociocracy, 219
Sociology: and biology, 2-8, 13, 228; Comte, 29, 34; Spencer, 34; value-free, 41-2, 47
Socrates: as teacher, 54-8 mission of, 58
Solidarity: mechanical, 147; organic, 147
Sorel, George, 238
Sorokin, Pitirim, 89, 133, 242, 255
Spencer, Herbert, 209-15, 238
Spengler, Oswald, 219
Stace, Walter, 33
State and church, separation of, 94-95
State, limited, 136
Stinchcombe, Arthur, 225
Strain, systemic, 223-24
Strauss, Anselm L., 122, 150
Strauss, Leo, 107, 110

Struggle: for existence, 214-18; order through, 193-232
Success ethic, 109
Suffering, 81-2
Summum bonum, 60-2
Sumner, William Graham, 31, 109, 219
Superorganic, 3, 34, 220
Surplus value, 200-1
Survival of the fittest, 208-9, 214-18, 227
Sutherland, Edwin, 127
Suzuki, D. T., 81-82
Syllogism, 60
Symbolic interaction, 147-50, 152, 301-2; and system theory, 294-95
Symbols, 9, 147-50
System: levels, 289-90
System, social: balance or "mix" of models for, 304-5; closed, 11, 72; freedom in, 298; open, 11, 15, 72, 288; reciprocal labor, 300-1
System theory, general, 228, 264, 268-85; humanism and, 285; in sociology, 288-89

Tao, 80
Tarde, Gabriel, 144
Tawney, Richard H., 168
Teilhard de Chardin, 232, 277-79
Telesis, social, 34, 219
Theocracy. *See* Hierocracy
Theology. *See* Encoding
Theories. *See* Models
Theory, information. *See* Information theory
Thomas Aquinas, Saint, 90-95
Thomas, William I., 243
Thomism. *See* Thomas Aquinas
Thracymachus, sophist, 55-58
Thurnwald, Richard, 172
Tiryakian, Edward, 152
Tocqueville, Alexis de, 67
Toennies, Ferdinand, 69-70, 144-45
Toffler, Alvin, 15, 73, 133, 244
Tolstoy, Leo, 27

333